Bibliothèque de
LITTÉRATURE GÉNÉRALE ET COMPARÉE
dirigée par Jean Bessière
154

SHAKESPEARE'S
POSSIBLE WORLDS

DÉCOUVREZ TOUS LES TITRES DE LA COLLECTION
ET
DES ÉDITIONS HONORÉ CHAMPION
SUR NOTRE SITE

www.honorechampion.com

Cindy CHOPOIDALO

SHAKESPEARE'S POSSIBLE WORLDS

PARIS
HONORÉ CHAMPION ÉDITEUR
2018

www.honorechampion.com

Diffusion hors France: Éditions Slatkine, Genève
www.slatkine.com

ISBN: 978-2-7453-4876-0   ISSN: 1262-2850
e-ISBN: 978-2-7453-4877-7

For my family

Though this be madness, yet there is method in't.

(*Hamlet* II.ii. 205-206)

Table of Contents

FOREWORD

By Jonathan Hart

Cindy Chopoidalo has written an important study of adaptation and, more specifically, of that aspect of Shakespeare and his reception. As she argues in *Shakespeare's Possible Worlds*, writers adapted Shakespeare's plays early on. Moreover, Shakespeare adapted from many sources classical and modern. Since the Restoration, writers have used Shakespeare's texts to make their own.

In this book, Chopoidalo discusses adaptations of works in connection with their original sources. Moreover, she examines these texts in relation to performance and printing history and to the worlds of authors and readers. Chopoidalo argues in a convincing fashion that these links permit an exploration of the relations of textual worlds to the actual worlds in which those texts are produced and received as well as to the intertextual ties between the worlds of the original work and its adaptation.

To focus the study, Chopoidalo chooses to discuss *Hamlet* as adaptation and source. This is a wise move as *Hamlet* has inspired interpretations and adaptations across time and space. Chopoidalo contends that these adaptations deserve attention for two main reasons. First, they constitute transformations of Shakespeare's original text. Second, they are distinct literary works. An adaptation itself, Shakespeare's *Hamlet* has been adapted over and over in various genres and media.

One of Chopoidalo's significant contributions is to place Shakespeare as adaptor and adapted in a comparative western European context. In addition to analyzing Shakespeare's *Hamlet* as an adaptation of its historical and literary source texts, Chopoidalo discusses English, French, and Spanish texts that employ *Hamlet* as their source. Her book explores Saxo Grammaticus's *Historiae Danicae*, Belleforest's *Histoires Tragiques,* and Kyd's *The Spanish Tragedy*. She also raises the issue that from the Restoration up to the end of the nineteenth century, most of Shakespeare's plays on stage in Britain and elsewhere were adaptations of the original texts, such as Nahum Tate's 1681 version of *King Lear* and Jean-François Ducis's French translation and adaptation of *Hamlet* (1769) as a neoclassical play. Ducis based his work on Pierre-Antoine de la Place's prose translation in *Le Théâtre Anglais* (1745).

By exploring versions of *Hamlet* in languages other than English, from Ducis's version to Robert Gurik's political satire *Hamlet, Prince du Québec* (1968) and from Leandro Fernández de Moratín's prose-dramatic Spanish translation of 1798 to Marcos Mayer's prose-narrative retelling in *Shakespeare Para Todos* (1997), Chopoidalo compares how writers in different times, places, and languages have reworked Shakespeare's original text. Furthermore, she examines the ways the fictional worlds of these versions of *Hamlet* represent the literary, social, and political concerns of their societies. Another key point that Chopoidalo makes is that translation, like adaptation, depends upon the translator's desire to make the text either culturally, socially and/or historically accessible to the target audience. Moreover, she argues that the act of translation can be a way to conform to or resist dominant ideologies.

Chopoidalo also uses theory that is not in the mainstream of Shakespearean studies, and this approach is fresh and suggestive. More particularly, I mean that she draws on the theories of possible worlds and fictional worlds. In a helpful fashion, Chopoidalo discusses the origins of possibility theory in Duns Scotus, William of Ockham, John Wallis, and St. Thomas Aquinas, but reminds us that possible-worlds theory as it is now known (modal logic and fictional-worlds theory) has its roots in the mid-seventeenth and early eighteenth centuries, most especially in René Descartes's *Principles of Philosophy* (1644) and Gottfried Wilhelm von Leibniz's *Theodicy* (1710). Descartes and Leibniz had an influence on later theorists: in this context, Chopoidalo discusses Saul Kripke's work on modal logic and naming during the 1960s and 1970s and David Lewis's counterpart theory and his discussion of the plurality of worlds in the 1970s and 1980s. Moreover, Chopoidalo argues that twentieth-century theories of plurality and intertextuality in literature, ranging from Bakhtinian heteroglossia to possible-world and fictional-world theories, have created more appreciation for literary adaptations. She finds Lubomír Doležel's and Douglas Lanier's taxonomies of adaptations particularly helpful in her study of *Hamlet*.

In short, *Shakespeare's Possible Worlds* provides an overview of possible-worlds and fictional-worlds theories and their use in the study of adaptations. Further, Chopoidalo's study discusses the source texts of *Hamlet* and the use Shakespeare made of them in his play. Her book compares four translations in French and Spanish as well as texts that present counterparts of the plot and characters of *Hamlet*. This is a significant achievement with implications beyond its ostensible topic. Rather than go on, I would like to point the reader to the book that lies ahead, one that itself deserves careful study.

Acknowledgments

First of all, to my family, for all their love and support, even during the most difficult times.

To Jonathan L. Hart: thank you for helping me develop a love for all things Shakespearean. I hope someday I will be as much of an inspiration to my own students as you have been to me.

To Uri Margolin, who first introduced me to possible-worlds theory and suggested the idea for this book.

To Irene Sywenky, Massimo Verdicchio, Gary Kelly, David Gay, Troni Grande, Claudine Potvin, Julian Martin, Andrei Zlatescu, Sarah Jefferies, Kris Conner, and the anonymous reviewers: thank you for your kind words and helpful questions and comments on earlier versions of this work.

To Brahma and Nandini Chaudhuri for providing me with experience in the academic environment.

To Khalida Tanvir Syed, my co-author on the article "Teaching *Hamlet* in 21st-Century Pakistan and Canada," *English Quarterly* vol. 43, no. 1-2, 2012, pp. 53-61. Thanks also to Karen Magro, editor of *English Quarterly,* for permission to reprint some of the material from that article here.

To my colleagues and students at the University of Alberta and Lakeland College: thank you for the experience teaching *Hamlet* and other works, some of which are discussed in these pages.

To the University of Alberta Library for assistance in obtaining some of my source texts.

To the organizers and attendees of the conferences at which portions of this work were originally presented. Special thanks to the Canadian Comparative Literature Association and Editors Canada.

To the directors, actors, designers, and organizers of the various productions of *Hamlet* and related plays I attended during the writing of this book.

In memory of Milan V. Dimic, John Orrell, and Terry Butler.

And to everyone else who contributed to the making of this book: many thanks.

Cindy CHUPUIDALO
Edmonton, Alberta, Canada
June 2017

INTRODUCTION

The processes of adaptation, whether in creating a play from a narrative source text, preparing a play text for performance, translating a text from one language to another, altering a text from one culture to fit better with another culture's literary conventions, or creating a new text as a reply to an earlier one, permeate virtually every aspect of the study of Shakespeare's plays and their reception by audiences and readers from the time of their first performances to the present day. However, critical analysis of, and responses to, the various ways in which Shakespeare's works have been adapted for contemporary audiences and readers, as well as how these works were themselves adapted from existing materials, have historically been mixed.

Thanks in part to the concepts of literary originality and genius that originated in the Romantic period and are still very much with us today, a prevailing tendency among many discussions of adaptations, especially of Shakespearean adaptations, has been to view *adaptations* as *adulterations*, as something 'less' than the original, for as Susan Bassnett notes, "In the case of Shakespeare... there is a strong belief that his works should not be tampered with" (57) but should be revered as works of 'high art' that exist above and beyond the specific needs of the audience/readership. Especially in the academic environment, adaptations have traditionally been dismissed in favour of originals, and especially so in the case of literary texts which have inspired non-print adaptations. A typical example of this sort of "literary fundamentalism" (Weber 53) is demonstrated in Alan Sinfield's observation of a British O-level English examination which insists that students refer to "the books [they] have read, NOT to any radio, television, musical, or film version of them" (qtd. in Hulbert et al. 14), even though the majority of students are probably just as, if not more, familiar with the adaptations as with the text itself.

Yet, as studies such as Barbara A. Murray's *Restoration Shakespeare* and Douglas Lanier's *Shakespeare and Modern Popular Culture* have pointed out, such views tend to overlook the fact that, from the Restoration up to the later nineteenth century, most of the 'Shakespearean' plays that were actually performed on stage in Britain and elsewhere were in fact adaptations of the original texts, whether merely cut for decorum and/or time constraints or reworked to fit post-seventeenth-century dramatic conventions. Two of the more famous, or infamous, examples of this process of reworking include Nahum Tate's 1681 version of *King Lear* with a happy ending (B.A. Murray 153-66) and Jean-François Ducis's 1769 translation/adaptation of *Hamlet* as a French Neoclassical play (Heylen 29-43; McMahon 15-18). The desire on the part of literary purists to preserve a 'pristine' original text also overlooks the often thorny history of Shakespeare's texts themselves (see e.g. Bullough VII. 3-5; Lanier 26-30), with the existence of the so-called 'good' and 'bad' quarto texts published, respectively, from the author's manuscripts and/or prompt copies, or from memorial reconstruction, as well as of the First Folio of 1623, compiled by members of Shakespeare's acting company after the playwright's death. These print texts may themselves be considered adaptations of the original play text, not only because of the discrepancies resulting from the existence of several parallel versions of the same text, but also because of the very different attitudes toward publishing between Shakespeare's society and the societies that came afterward. In the absence of copyright laws and considering the relative novelty of print in Renaissance culture, "for Shakespeare publication... took the form of stage performance, not print" (Lanier 24).

Furthermore, the 'degenerative' view of an adaptation in comparison to its original becomes highly problematic when one remembers that Shakespeare himself, like most playwrights of his time, was an adaptor of existing historical and literary material (cf. Fischlin and Fortier 1). On confronting the brilliance of a text such as *Hamlet*, it is easy to forget that the original story, first recorded "by the Dane Saxo Grammaticus at the end of the twelfth century" (Bullough VII. 5) and probably known long before it was first written down, was essentially what Lars Walker describes in his novel *Blood and Judgment* as "a Clever Jack fairy tale... [which] even on its own terms... doesn't hold together" (10). Daniel Fischlin and Mark Fortier, on the other hand, identify another commonly-cited objection to the study of adaptations, one that comes from the opposite pole: "In as much as it echoes natural adaptation and a residual myth of progress, the word *adaptation* implies that adaptations are better than originals, which is no more tenable as a general principle than its opposite would be" (3). In either case, be it the degenerative view or the pseudo-Darwinian evolutionary view, the relationship between an 'original' and an 'adaptation' is thus figured as a zero-sum game, with one necessarily 'better' or 'worse' than the other. The result of such a binary opposition is that neither work can be fairly judged upon its own merits and/or shortcomings.

Twentieth-century theories of the plurality and intertextuality of literature, ranging from Bakhtinian heteroglossia to possible/fictional-world theory[1] (Doležel, *Heterocosmica* 199-226; Hart 320-21), have created a more favourable environment for the appreciation of literary adaptations. Rather than simply dismissing adaptations with negative judgment calls such as the so-called 'watering down,' 'dumbing down,' or 'ripping off' of their originals (see e.g. Burt 1-28), or assessing the merit of an adaptation solely on its 'fidelity' or presumed lack thereof to the original (cf. Fischlin and Fortier 4), readers and scholars are more able and more willing to appreciate how each work of literature draws upon what has come before it and points ahead to what may come after it, and how writers of adaptations use earlier and well-known texts as raw materials for the creation of a new and distinct literary work.

As Lubomír Doležel states in *Heterocosmica*, "rewrites of classic works pursue the same goal by literature's own means: they confront the canonical protoworld by creating a new, alternative fictional world" (206). Examining adaptations of literary works in relation to their 'original' source texts, to their performance/printing history, to each other, and to the world(s) of authors and readers allows us to explore the relationships of textual worlds to the actual worlds in which those texts are produced and read/seen/listened to, and the intertextual relationships between the worlds of the original work and an adaptation of that work into a new text.

By examining each new text as the embodiment of a new fictional world, albeit one that draws upon other, previously 'existing' fictional worlds for its basis, we can more fully appreciate adaptations of classic texts such as *Hamlet* as viable literary works in their own right, as their authors' transformations of the plays – as Shakespeare transformed his own source texts – into new, fresh, and original interpretations of familiar stories that draw as much attention to their authors' skill in reshaping the material for their readers as to Shakespeare's skill in retelling stories familiar to his original audience.

Furthermore, the ways in which the world of the adaptation differs from that of the source text depend in large part on the author's purpose in adapting that text, which itself depends upon the author's initial reading and interpretation (or misinterpretation) of the source text. The relationship between the fictional worlds of the original and the adaptation may range

---

[1] The most prominent applications of possible/fictional-worlds theory in Renaissance and Shakespearean studies can be found in the works of Thomas Pavel; however, I have chosen Lubomír Doležel's *Heterocosmica* as my primary theoretical source because it is a detailed and comprehensive introduction to possible/fictional-worlds theory.

from a straightforward retelling of the original work in a different literary genre – for example, a Shakespearean play retold as a modern English prose narrative – to a radical transformation, often a reversal, of the original work, where the adaptation is meant as a "polemical antiworld" (Doležel, *Heterocosmica* 207) to challenge the literary and/or sociopolitical worldviews of the original. The former case is generally meant for much the same purpose as a translation from one language to another: to make the original more accessible to readers who are less familiar with the language/genre/style of the original text. The purposes of the latter case, however, may range from satire to shift of emphasis (for example, basing the new text on a minor character in the original) to complete rejection of the base text and/or its worldview, in which case the author perhaps hopes his/her new text may not only *dis*place but *re*place the original, rather than merely complementing it. As Doležel's use of the word "polemical" indicates, this last type of adaptation often has a specific sociopolitical purpose at its foundation, interrogating some element of the culture that produced the source text and using that text as its means of doing so. It is this type of adaptation that is often the most privileged among postmodern[2] literary critics, many of whom favour those in which "readers debated with Shakespeare rather than celebrated or interpreted him, when they questioned what they saw as the plays' assumptions and offered alternative possibilities" (Rozett 4). Indeed, Martha Tuck Rozett's description of such adaptations as "talking back to Shakespeare," with its connotation of impertinence or disrespect of authority, implies a dismissive attitude toward more reverent and 'traditional' retellings whose worlds and worldviews differ minimally from those of the source text – in effect, swinging the pendulum from 'literary fundamentalism' to its opposite extreme, 'literary iconoclasm.' Fictional-world theory, however, allows for the appreciation of "celebratory as well as contestatory engagement... [and] conservative as well as radical harnessing of the Shakespearean intertexts" (Sanders 2), without necessarily imposing these sorts of value judgments either on the new texts and their worlds, or on the source text and its world.

The purpose of this study is to examine worlds created through the adaptation of the text of *Hamlet*, both Shakespeare's creation of his fictional world from those of his sources, and other writers' use of his text to create

---

[2] The term "postmodern" generally refers to works that are meant to question and/or re-examine dominant literary, social, and historical perspectives, while simultaneously remaining products of these perspectives. According to Linda Hutcheon, "postmodern culture uses and abuses the conventions of discourse... culture is challenged from within: challenged or questioned or contested, but not imploded" (xiii).

new and diverse fictional worlds of their own which nonetheless share common origins and elements. Using possible/fictional-worlds theory as its framework, this book will explore the intertextual relationships between Shakespeare's *Hamlet,* its source texts, and various adaptations and/or translations in English, French, and Spanish, and the relationships between those texts and the worlds of the authors who produce them and the readers/spectators who enjoy them. These adaptations take numerous forms in various literary genres – poetry, historical novel, mystery, popular fantasy, short story, drama, and juvenile fiction – demonstrating the breadth and diversity of Shakespearean adaptations and the ways in which each reader, writer, genre, and work draw upon the world of *Hamlet* to create worlds of their own. An important element of the intertextuality of the worlds of the original and adaptation to take into consideration is the counterpart relationship, which Roderick M. Chisholm defines as one in which "among the possible worlds... there are those in which you play the role that I play in this one and... I play the role that you play" (83). In terms of literary intertextualities, this relationship encompasses the connections, similarities, and differences between an established character in an original text and his/her reappearance in an adaptation of that original.

I have chosen to examine *Hamlet* and a representative sample of its adaptations in this investigation for two reasons. First, as Shakespeare's best-known and most written-about text, indeed one of the world's most studied texts, *Hamlet* has inspired countless interpretations and adaptations by artists and writers the world over. Second, these adaptations are worthy of study in their own right, both as transformations of Shakespeare's original text(s) and as distinct literary works themselves. Previous studies of Shakespeare's use of his sources, such as Geoffrey Bullough's *Narrative and Dramatic Sources of Shakespeare,* and of other writers' use of Shakespeare's works for either translation or adaptation, such as Ruby Cohn's *Modern Shakespeare Offshoots,* have tended to focus on adaptations and translations primarily in terms of their 'fidelity to' and/or 'departure from' the source texts. To discuss these two examples further, Bullough's study examines the source texts of the plays, such as Saxo Grammaticus's *Historiae Danicae* to *Hamlet* (VII. 5-9), in large part as the building blocks from which Shakespeare constructed his plays, noting the alterations and 'improvements' he made to the previous versions. Cohn, on the other hand, examines works based on Shakespeare's plays in much the opposite manner to Bullough, concerning herself predominantly with the aesthetic differences between the Shakespearean original and the adaptations, and giving the highest marks primarily to those that stay closest to the source text, or those which most successfully use extended allusions to Shakespeare rather than to adaptations per se (106-231).

Other studies, such as Martha Tuck Rozett's *Talking Back to Shakespeare*, Douglas Lanier's *Shakespeare and Modern Popular Culture*, Robert Shaughnessy's *The Cambridge Companion to Shakespeare and Popular Culture*, and Jennifer Hulbert and her co-authors' *Shakespeare and Youth Culture*, treat Shakespearean adaptations more as a cultural phenomenon than as a literary/dramatic/artistic exercise, placing more emphasis on the actual worlds of the adaptor and intended audience than on the fictional worlds of the texts themselves.

The present investigation will build upon what these and other previous studies have done and discuss works that have been published since the earlier studies first appeared, but the most significant way in which my work differs from previous efforts in this field is my use of possible/fictional-world theory. According to Lubomír Doležel, possible/fictional-world theory is an ideal lens through which to examine intertextuality and adaptation because:

> Fiction thrives on the contingency of worlds, emphatically asserted by the idea of possible worlds: every world and every entity in the world could be or could have been different from what it is... every fictional world, however canonical, however authoritative, however habitualized, can be changed, can be displaced by an alternative world. The complexity of the rewrite's meaning and its challenge to semantic interpretation is due precisely to the fact that it refers not only to its own fictional world but also, in various ways and degrees, to its source, the protoworld. (*Heterocosmica* 222)

Doležel's statement refers specifically to revisionist texts or polemical rewrites, fictional worlds whose authors place them in opposition to some aspect of the world of the original text. This sort of rewriting may be done for serious reasons, as in Douglas Brode's *Sweet Prince,* which investigates Elizabethan gender roles by imagining Hamlet as a woman raised as a man, or for humorous ones, such as the nineteenth-century burlesque performances which satirized Victorian society and both Elizabethan and Victorian dramatic conventions in equal measure (Schoch 1-30).[3] However, new and distinct fictional worlds also come into being even when the adaptor attempts to be as 'faithful' as possible to the world of the original, for each new fictional work/world creates a counterpart to the previous works/worlds. For example, Jean-François Ducis's widely influential translation/adaptation of *Hamlet* not merely into French, but into the French Neoclassical dramatic style, envisions a fictional world in which Shakespeare was a Neoclassicist at the same time

---

[3] This is not, of course, to say that seriousness and humour are polar opposites, as both elements may be, and often are, present in the same text.

that it envisions one in which the characters speak in French. Similarly, adaptations of *Hamlet* into works of juvenile fiction, ranging from Charles and Mary Lamb's *Tales from Shakespeare* in prose to Marcia Williams's comic-strip retellings of the same title,[4] attempt to recreate Shakespeare's fictional world in ways that are more accessible to younger readers less accustomed to his style and language, yet cannot help but blend something of the adaptors' views of the play, its worlds, and the authors' own worlds into their treatments, from the gentle yet conservative moralizing of the Lambs (cf. Lanier 35-36) to the delightfully subversive multilayering of Williams.

The process of translation, much like that of adaptation, depends upon the translator's desire to make the text either culturally or sociohistorically accessible to the target audience, and the act of translation itself can be a means of either conformity or resistance to dominant ideologies (Heylen 16-21). In translating a text into another language, the translator is also often faced with a choice between prosody and meaning in attempting to reproduce as much of the 'original' text as the inherent differences between the source language and the target language will allow. Although a detailed discussion of Shakespearean dramaturgy is beyond the scope of this investigation, it is important to recognize that staging a performance of a play also involves adaptation on three levels: the literary, the auditory, and the visual, which, when working together, serve to create/recreate the fictional world of the text in ways that the printed text, the dialogue and/or music, or the visual performance, alone do not (Alter 114). The interdependence of word and image is also important in the production of illustrations, which can be considered yet another form of adaptation.

Although I have chosen *Hamlet* as a specific example, this work will contribute to the study and appreciation of literary adaptations in general. As is evident in everything from casual discussion of, for example, a film based on a favourite book, to a more complex academic discussion of one writer's influence on others after him/her, it is easy for an admirer of a specific literary work to judge adaptations of that work based on "the... theology of Fidelity-To-The-Original" (Folkart 333) – or more precisely, to that reader's particular mental image of the text's world. It is equally easy for a postmodern reader to judge adaptations of a literary work based on how transgressive those adaptations are to the original – in this case, to that reader's perception of which elements of the text's world need to be challenged (cf. Folkart 333-35).

---

[4] At least in the North American editions; the British editions are entitled *Mr. William Shakespeare's Plays* and *Bravo, Mr. William Shakespeare*.

Despite his extensive and insightful analysis of the process of adaptation and the worlds that process creates, even Lubomír Doležel's statement at the end of *Heterocosmica*, "The game [of transworld adaptation] is no longer exciting, and it is time to invent a new one" (226), seems somewhat dismissive of the prevalence of transworld narratives and adaptations both 'faithful' and 'polemical' in relation to their originals. Through the use of possible/fictional-worlds theory in relation to intertextuality, translation, and adaptation, I hope to demonstrate that the creation of a new fictional world from the materials of an older one does not necessarily weaken or even displace the earlier text but rather enhances it, challenging readers to familiarize themselves with both the prototext and the derived text to appreciate more fully how each acts upon, and is acted upon by, the other in a cross-temporal and/or cross-cultural intertextual discourse. Just as Shakespeare kept earlier stories from mythology, folklore, and history alive for his audiences by re-enacting them on the stage, authors of Shakespearean adaptations keep his works alive for their contemporary audiences by retelling them in new and exciting forms. Though the sheer number of *Hamlet* adaptations prevents me from discussing every such work, I will, in the following pages, explore some representative examples of these forms. First, however, the study begins with an overview of the historical development of possible/fictional-worlds theory, from its beginnings in philosophy to its applications as a literary theory in general, as well as a discussion of various types of adaptations.

CHAPTER ONE

POSSIBLE WORLDS AND FICTIONAL WORLDS

> There are more things in heaven and earth, Horatio,
> Than are dreamt of in your philosophy.
>
> (*Hamlet* I.v. 166-67)

As the epigraphs to this chapter and the next both indicate,[5] possible worlds and/or fictional worlds are a recurring theme in Shakespeare's *Hamlet*. This is seen from the beginning of the play with the appearance of the Ghost representing the possibility of worlds beyond the here and now. Hamlet's use of a play to "catch the conscience of the king" (*Hamlet* II.ii. 605) and his conversations with the actors are vivid demonstrations of the effect of fictional worlds on the actual world and vice versa, and of the power of fictional worlds to become temporarily 'real' in the mind of the reader/spectator. Hamlet's celebrated soliloquies are themselves expressions of possibility and possible worlds, both in the sense of alternative pasts and/or presents (e.g. *Hamlet* I.ii. 129-59; III.i. 55-87) and in the sense of the simultaneous divisions and continuities between 'fiction' and 'reality,' most eloquently expressed in Hamlet's "O, what a rogue and peasant slave am I!" speech (*Hamlet* II.ii. 550-605). It is for these reasons that possible-world theory is an ideal way into the worlds of *Hamlet*, its source texts, and its derived texts.[6]

Philosophers and literary scholars have both used the possible-world model to account for the properties of fictional worlds and vice versa; but what exactly is the difference, if any, between a possible world and a fictional world? As Jonathan Hart states, "Possible world theory is the modal logical delineation of relations. Fictional world theory is the analysis of how fictional texts are read" (321). Both of these aspects are important in examining how

---

[5] Quotations of Shakespeare are taken from *The Riverside Shakespeare*, 1st edition, except where indicated.

[6] Portions of this chapter have previously been published in Chopoidalo and Syed, "Teaching *Hamlet* in 21st-Century Pakistan and Canada."

the interactions between authors, texts, readers, and worlds (actual and fictional) contribute to the creation and endurance of the fictional world(s) embodied in a literary work.

The Atomists

What we now know as possible-worlds theory ultimately descends from the works of Leucippus and Democritus, pioneers of the Greek theory of atomism. This theory posits that "Though the earth is at the centre of our world,[7] that world is merely one of an infinite number of worlds which come into and go out of existence in endless sequence throughout a universe infinite in space and time" (C.C.W. Taylor 197). These infinite worlds, furthermore, may be similar to, or vastly different from, our world though existing in the same universe, such that "all alternative possibilities are in fact actualized in... various subworlds embraced within one infinite superworld" (Rescher, *On Leibniz* 11). In other words, according to the atomist theory, each possible state of affairs not only *can* exist but *does* exist, if not in the actual world, then elsewhere in the infinite set of all possible worlds including the actual world, which we identify as the universe. It is this definition of the universe as a single yet infinite set of worlds that differentiates atomism from later formulations of possible-worlds theory which not only propose multiple worlds within one universe, but multiple universes each containing many worlds, as ways of categorizing "the different ways things might have been" (Loux 30) in comparison to the ways things actually are. On the other hand, the atomist theory is the earliest known expression of the idea that "*every* way a world could be is a way that some world *is*" (D. Lewis, *Plurality* 2; emphasis in original), which over the millennia has proved fertile ground for both philosophers and writers of literature.

Descartes, Leibniz, and Early Fictional-World Theories

While early versions of possibility theory have been found "in the work of such figures as Duns Scotus, William of Ockham, [and] John Wallis" (Copeland 99) as well as St. Thomas Aquinas (Rescher, *Imagining Irreality* 118-19), the possible-worlds theory that is best known today as the root of both modern-day modal logic and fictional-worlds theory was developed in

---

[7] This statement can be read either as referring to the geocentric cosmology of the ancient Greeks, or as referring to the 'world' of human experience, in which "the earth is at the centre of our world" because it is where we live.

the mid-seventeenth and early eighteenth centuries. In his 1644 masterwork *Principles of Philosophy,* René Descartes elaborated upon the atomist model of one universe containing infinitely many worlds, although he disagreed with the atomists' belief in "parts of matter which are by their own nature indivisible" (48). His concept of possible worlds stemmed from his opposition to the atomist concept of indivisible units of matter, and was a logical extension of that opposition to the other pole. If, contrary to the opinion of the atomists, matter can be infinitely divided into smaller units, it can also be infinitely extended, and thus:

> From this it can also be easily inferred that the matter of the heaven does not differ from that of the earth; and that even if there were countless worlds in all, it would be impossible for them not to all be of one and the same kind of matter. And therefore there cannot be several worlds, but only one. (Descartes 49-50)

Descartes's theory, therefore, does not accept the "plurality of worlds" (49) of later possible-worlds theorists, but does allow for different worlds within the same universe embodying different possibilities. Although everything in the universe is composed of the same essential substance, that substance is itself infinitely variable:

> it must change continually, until it finally forms a world exactly similar to this one (although perhaps with more difficulty from some suppositions than from others). Because, given that these laws cause matter to assume successively all the forms it is capable of assuming, if we consider these causes in order, we shall finally be able to reach the form which is at present that of this world. (Descartes 107-08)

The wording of Descartes's statement on the infinite mutability of matter, however, does not suggest a theory of possibility per se, but rather a theory of evolutionary progress and variety. The words "continually," "finally," and "successively" imply not so much that every way a world could be is how some world is, as that every way a world could be is how some world was, is, or will be at some point in time.

Descartes's ideas of possibility, variety, and change over time did influence the most significant development of possibility theory as we know it today. This development is exemplified in the writings of Gottfried Wilhelm von Leibniz, who explored the concept through "a large number of notes... written over a long period of time and apparently not intended for publication" (Mates 507). Leibniz's theory of possibility incorporates elements of logic, metaphysics, and theodicy – a term he introduced in his 1710 book of the same title – in its assertion that, although every aspect of the actual world is one of an infinite number of alternative possibilities, the actual world, the world in which we live, "must indeed be better than every other possible universe" (*Theodicy* 378) because it is the world that God chose to create. Furthermore, in contrast to the theories of the atomists and Descartes, Leibniz's theory states that the *actual* world is the only one that truly exists. All other *possible* worlds are just that: unactualized "nonexistent possibilities [which] 'exist' – or rather *subsist* – ... only in conception with the mind (or, more specifically, imagination)... of God" (Rescher, *On Leibniz* 3; emphasis in original) as well as in the imaginations of philosophers or writers of fiction.

Leibniz meant his theory as a justification of why, if Christian theology holds that God is infinitely wise and infinitely good, evil and suffering exist in the world, even in the 'best of all possible worlds.'[8] However, his theory goes beyond the Augustinian view "that God permitted evil in order to derive from it... a greater good" (*Theodicy* 378) in positing a more complex reason for the world being the way it is, one that does much to explain the appeal of possible-worlds theory to literary study as well as to philosophy and theology. As Nicholas Rescher notes, "The... most perfect possible world is that which exhibits the greatest variety of its contents... consonant with the greatest simplicity of its laws" (*On Leibniz* 27). That is, for Leibniz, an ideal world is one that achieves a balance between order and variety without descending into monotony on the one side or chaos on the other, and which is not static – in other words, is not 'perfect' at the outset – but moves infinitely toward greater degrees of perfection. Thus, it may be said that, according to Leibniz, God chooses not so much the 'best possible *world*' but the 'best possible *outcome*' as the deciding factor for the existence of this world as opposed to other possible worlds.

Leibniz's theory of the creation of the actual world from an infinity of possibilities, all of which are in some way conceptually inferior to the actual world, has its analogy in the writing process: in creating a fictional world, a writer considers various possibilities for the design of the fictional world/work and optimally chooses those elements that will make the fictional world most effective for its author and readers. The analogy between the creation of the actual world and that of a fictional world diverges in two aspects, however. For a writer or reader of fiction, the 'goodness' or 'rightness' of a fictional world is usually determined primarily from an

---

[8] The theological and optimistic aspects of Leibniz's possible-worlds theory have themselves had a significant influence in fiction aside from fictional-worlds theory in general; they are probably best known to present-day readers from Voltaire's satirical treatment of them in *Candide*.

aesthetic rather than an epistemological or ontological perspective; and, unlike God, a writer can create only representations of entities and not those entities themselves – as we will see later, this latter point holds true in both literal and metaphorical readings of possible-worlds theory.

Indeed, Leibniz himself recognized the parallels between God's creating the actual world and writers' creating fictional worlds. Although he believed that possible worlds do not share the same space-time or ontological status as the actual world, making "trans-world causality... [and] trans-world travel" (D. Lewis, *Plurality* 80), as well as the atomist and Cartesian models of many possible worlds in one overarching universe, impossible, he did believe that fictional entities occupy their own world-spaces, distinct from that of the actual world, as he explains in his 1689 essay "On Freedom":

> Nor can we really deny that many stories, especially those called novels, are thought to be possible, though they might find no place in this universal series God selected – unless one imagined that in such an expanse of space and time there are certain poetical regions, where you can see King Arthur of Great Britain, Amadis of Gaul, and the illustrious Dietrich von Bern of the German stories, all wandering through the world. This seems not too far from the view of [Descartes], who... affirms that matter successively takes on all the forms of which it is capable..., something hardly defensible. For it would obliterate all beauty from the universe and all choice among things, not to speak of other considerations by which the contrary can be proved. (94-95; cf. Descartes 108)

Even though Leibniz recognized that literary worlds constitute a class of possible worlds, he used literary examples more "for explaining the logical category of possibility" (Doležel, *OP* 40) than for conceptualizing fictionality. The earliest theorists to adapt Leibniz's models to the study of literature were two Swiss poeticians, Johann Jakob Bodmer and Johann Jakob Breitinger,[9] who in their writings of, respectively, 1728 and 1740, attempted to combine Leibnizian possible-worlds theory with Aristotelian mimesis theory to expand the traditional view of the relationship between literature and the actual world. In Breitinger's seminal fictional-worlds theory, "the artist is equipotent to nature: he is capable, by the power of his imagination, of converting possibles into fictional existents... [and] imaginary worlds enter the universe of existing worlds, side-by-side with the world of reality" (Doležel, *OP* 42). Breitinger's theory allows for the presence in a fictional world of analogues to real-world entities that are given "the status of fictionally existent

---

[9] Bodmer's and Breitinger's theories have not yet, as far as I am aware, been translated into English. As the original German texts were unavailable to me, I follow Doležel's summary in *Occidental Poetics* (hereafter cited as *OP*).

possible" (Doležel, *OP* 43), while Bodmer's more traditionally Leibnizian concept of fictional possibility postulates that "poetry *discovers* rather than creates the imaginary universe" (Doležel, *OP* 51; emphasis in original).

However, Bodmer's and Breitinger's adaptations of Leibnizian possibility theory to literary models proved to be ahead of their time: in general, literary theories of the eighteenth through early twentieth centuries continued to adhere either to the Aristotelian idea of literature as a reflection of reality or to the Romantic concept of literature as the embodiment of the writer's original genius. It was left to theorists in the latter half of the twentieth century to develop the possible-worlds model into a more viable method of analyzing the relations between actual and fictional worlds, by moving away from – though not entirely abandoning – "the mimetic relations between the worlds of literature and an actual world" (Ronen 18) as well as the Romantic emphasis on the writer's unique talent, and recognizing the ways in which literary discourse creates and defines its own worlds.

Kripke: Modal Logic and Naming

Though Leibnizian possible-worlds theory had a relatively limited impact on literary criticism until the twentieth century, it did leave a lasting impression on modal logic and semantics, especially in regards to questions of identity and truth value. Modal logic, the formal study and explanation of how things *could be* in comparison and contrast to how things *are* (see Norris 232), uses the Leibnizian definition of a possible world as "a set of mutually compossible complete individual concepts" (Mates 511). Furthermore, while each possible world may be vastly different from or extremely similar to other possible worlds, all possible worlds must by definition follow the two basic laws of logic: the Law of Non-Contradiction, which holds that in any one possible world, a statement and its negation cannot both be true, and the Law of the Excluded Middle, which holds that every statement in any one possible world must be either true or false. Modal logicians also make use of Leibniz's differentiation between necessary and contingent truths, the distinction being "that something is possible [i.e. a contingent truth] if it is so in at least one possible world and something is necessary if it is so in all possible worlds" (Girle 3; cf. Leibniz, *Theodicy* 143-49).

These models of possibility and truth value were significant influences on twentieth-century theories of semantics, most notably those proposed by Saul Kripke in his 1963 essay "Semantic Considerations on Modal Logic,"[10]

---

[10] Hereafter cited as "SC."

one of the earliest uses of possible-world models in modal logic; and in his 1972 book *Naming and Necessity*. Kripke's essay proposes a system of quantified modal logic – that is, a modal logic relating to a certain definite set of entities – using the following model structure:

> An ordered triple (G, K, R) where K is a set, R is a reflexive relation on K, and G [is included in] K.... K is the set of all 'possible worlds;' G is the 'real world.' If H_1 and H_2 are two worlds, H_1 R H_2 means intuitively that... H_2 is 'possible relative to' H_1; i.e. that every proposition *true* in H_2 is *possible* in H_1. ("SC" 804)

Each possible world in this model is further associated with "a domain of individuals...that exist in that world" ("SC" 805), and these domains need not be the same in all possible worlds. Some possible worlds may contain individuals that are not found in the actual world; and the actual world may contain individuals that are not found in other possible worlds. Kripke's view of possible worlds departs from the traditional Leibnizian view, but approaches the prototypical fictional-world theories of Bodmer and Breitinger, in one significant respect: where Leibnizian possibility theory holds that possible worlds subsist in the mind of God, to be 'discovered' by the philosopher/writer's imagination, in Kripke's theory, "Possible worlds are stipulated, not discovered" (*Naming* 44). In other words, a possible world has no 'existence' of any kind unless and until a writer or logician gives us a description and/or set of properties to be associated with that world.

The acknowledgment that different possible worlds may have different domains of individuals not found in the actual world, or vice versa, is Kripke's first step toward bridging the gap between logical philosophy and literary theory, as it allows us to conceptualize "new individuals, like Pegasus" ("SC" 805) or other fictional/mythical entities, as inhabitants of a possible world even if they are not inhabitants of the actual world. Kripke further, and more explicitly, uses fictional entities as examples for determining the truth value of statements about possible worlds when he asks, "are we to assign a truth-value to the substitution instance 'Sherlock Holmes is bald'? Holmes does not exist, but in other states of affairs, he would have existed" ("SC" 805). However, in his later work, *Naming and Necessity,* he admits that the existence in the actual world of an individual who has all the properties usually associated with a fictional entity may be purely coincidental and does not necessarily prove that entity's actual existence (*Naming* 156-58; cf. Crittenden 70-74). Kripke's example stands in contrast to earlier theories of the meaning and truth value of names, such as Bertrand Russell's famous argument that statements with no referents in the actual world, such as "The present king of France is bald" (155) – of which Kripke's argument is a partial restatement – "are denoting phrases which do

not denote anything" (Russell 156) and thus cannot be said to have any
inherent truth value. Kripke, however, posits that "a statement containing free
variables has a truth-value in each world for every assignment to its free
variables" ("SC" 806); that is, a statement about an entity that does not exist
in the actual world is true or false only for the possible world(s) in which
that entity does exist. Thus, Kripkean modal logic recognizes a difference
between 'truth *of* fiction' and 'truth *in* fiction' (cf. Proudfoot 9-15); the
former refers to the truth value of a fictional statement relative to the actual
world, and the latter to the truth value of a fictional statement relative to the
world embodied in the fictional work.

Kripke's discussion of the truth value of statements about possible and
fictional entities demonstrates how, in literature and literary study as well as
in logic and philosophy, we discuss "nonexistent entities" (Doležel,
Heterocosmica 1) as though they were real people, places, or things. If we
adhere to classical 'one-world' logics that deal only with the actual world,
'fiction' would be the opposite of reality, virtually synonymous with
'falsehood' or 'error' or 'impossibility'; as Bertrand Russell summarizes,
"only the thoughts, feelings, etc. in Shakespeare and his readers are real, and
there is not, additional to them, an objective Hamlet" (qtd. in Doležel,
Heterocosmica 2). However, the practice of reading fiction, by general
readers and literary scholars alike, demonstrates that to equate 'fiction' with
'falsehood' is itself a fallacy, even though such comparisons are indeed often
made in popular usage. The fact that we are able to speak of fictional entities
as though they do exist shows that "The stories told among men [*sic*] have
a reality of their own.... more than other fictional characters but less than real
people" (Walker 96-97). This is a primary reason why possible-worlds
semantics has proven attractive to literary scholars: although the entities that
make up a work of literature do not exist in the actual world, they do exist
in the possible world embodied in the literary text and in the minds of
authors and readers. Taking Kripke's views on domains and names of
possible individuals into consideration, we can thus summarize the
ontological status of a possible/fictional entity as Doležel does:

> While Hamlet is not a man to be found in the actual world, he is an
> individualized possible person inhabiting an alternative world: the fictional world
> of Shakespeare's play. The name *Hamlet* is neither empty nor self-referential; it
> refers to an individual of a fictional world. (*Heterocosmica* 16)

Kripke's later work on identity and designators in *Naming and Necessity*
brings another element of possible-world formation into consideration: the
relation of necessary and contingent truths to the naming and definition of
entities in any world. Just as "a possible world is given by the descriptive

conditions we associate with it" (*Naming* 44), each individual entity is associated with, and identified by, a name and a set of properties. Names and descriptions of properties are, strictly speaking, not interchangeable, although they often are in everyday discourse. For example, we can use the name "Hamlet" and the property "Prince of Denmark" to identify the same fictional entity; similarly, we can use the name "William Shakespeare" and the property "the author of *Hamlet*" to identify the same actual-world entity. Kripke identifies the distinction between names and sets of properties by analogy to that between necessary and contingent truths: "Let's call something a *rigid designator* if in every possible world it designates the same object, a *nonrigid* or *accidental designator* if that is not the case" (*Naming* 48; emphasis in original). Names, according to this definition, are rigid designators that, once assigned to a specific entity, have the same fixed referent in every possible world; sets of properties are nonrigid designators which may vary between counterparts of the same entity in different possible worlds (see *Naming* 48-70).

This distinction between rigid and nonrigid designators is particularly useful in cases of determining transworld identity or even identity over time, because by viewing names as rigid designators and sets of properties as nonrigid designators, we are able to modify our thinking about an entity should some property traditionally associated with that entity prove false for him/her/it, either in another possible world or as the result of new evidence discovered in the actual world. To return to the examples of name/property pairing mentioned above, and to follow an example cited by Christopher Norris, a strict descriptivist account of identity would have to conclude, "should it prove to be the case that... somebody else wrote the plays... standardly attributed to Shakespeare... [that] 'Shakespeare wasn't Shakespeare'" (232). A Kripkean view of identity, on the other hand, would conclude that, even if he were not in fact the author of *Hamlet,* he would still be the same individual identified by the name "William Shakespeare." Examples such as this demonstrate that, following Kripke's name/properties differentiation, transworld identity depends more on which entity in one possible world is known by the same name as a counterpart in another possible world than it does on the properties shared by those counterparts, in contrast to the counterpart theory of David Lewis[11] in which "counterparts closely resemble [each other] in content and context in important respects" ("CT" 112; cf. Kripke, *Naming* 76-77) yet may not always share the same name.

---

[11] In "Counterpart Theory and Quantified Modal Logic," hereafter cited as "CT".

Lewis: Truth and Fiction, Counterpart Theory, and Modal Realism

Lewis proposed his counterpart theory as an alternative to the quantified modal logic favoured by theorists such as Kripke, which he (Lewis) interpreted as allowing for the paradox that "one thing is allowed to be in several worlds" ("CT" 112). Where Kripke defined the name of an entity as a rigid designator, something that once specifically assigned to a particular entity is necessarily true of that entity in any possible world, Lewis gives the rigid-designator definition to "the attribute [an entity] shares with all and only its counterparts... the attribute which is its essence" ("CT" 121), which need not be its name – although it certainly can be – but may be some other specific property shared by all the counterparts of a given entity.

Lewis's emphasis on essential properties does owe something to "the standard descriptivist account descending from Frege and Russell... [in which] an associated cluster of descriptive attributes... serve[s] to define... the particular item" (Norris 231) as well as to Kripke's ideas on proper names, but differs in its insistence that being a *counterpart* to an entity in another possible world – that is, sharing a name and/or a set of properties with that entity – is not necessarily the same as being *identical* to that other entity ("CT" 125-28). Kripke's name theory was itself meant to alleviate the problems inherent in Russellian descriptivism's "failure... to provide any means of fixing reference" (Norris 232); however, as Norris's discussion of the two fictional counterparts of Kripke in Rebecca Goldstein's *The Mind-Body Problem* (Norris 225, 231-32, 241) demonstrates, an entity's name is itself a property of that entity. An entity can have a counterpart in one possible world that bears no other resemblance but a name; at the same time, it can have another counterpart in yet another possible world that has all the same properties but a different name. The same entity could conceivably have more than one counterpart in the same possible world, based on "ties of similarity" (D. Lewis, "CT" 126), which themselves are based on the distribution of the 'original' entity's properties; Goldstein's aforementioned counterparts of Kripke are examples of this possibility. A strict interpretation of Kripke's naming theory would identify only those entities that shared a name as counterparts, even if another entity had all the other properties associated with the 'original' in the actual world; a descriptivist interpretation would consider only those entities that shared the same properties as counterparts, even if another entity shared the name of the 'original.' Lewis's counterpart theory, by treating similar entities as counterparts rather than as identicals, allows for either possibility – similarity of names or similarity of properties – to pick out and define counterpart relations within and across possible worlds.

Lewis's shift from names to essential properties as the rigid designators of an entity and its counterparts, and his emphasis on counterpart relation rather than transworld identity, are but small parts of his contribution to the development of possible/fictional-worlds theory. His concept of possible worlds differs in one very significant way from previous treatments of the multiple-worlds model: whereas most theorists of possibility have more or less agreed, to varying extents, with Leibniz's belief that the co-existence of all possible worlds alongside the actual world "would obliterate all beauty from the universe and all choice" ("On Freedom" 94-95), Lewis believes quite the opposite. In his 1973 book *Counterfactuals* he makes the bold statement, "I believe that there are possible worlds other than the one we happen to inhabit" ("Possible Worlds" 182), thus literalizing what previous theorists have generally taken as metaphor. Lewis refers to his theory of possible worlds as "modal realism: the thesis that the world we are part of is but one of a plurality of worlds" (*Plurality* vii), although 'modal relativism' might be a more accurate term, because according to this theory, actuality is not a property possessed by one world only but by all worlds, from the perspective of each individual world. Lewis thus defines "actual" as "this-worldly" (*Plurality* 99): what we know as the 'actual world' is actual to us because we are in it; meanwhile, the inhabitants of another possible world would consider *their* world to be the actual one (*Plurality* 92-101).

In terms of fiction, we can thus differentiate between the *actual* world in which the work is produced and read, and the *textual* actual world described within the work, to use Marie-Laure Ryan's terms (21-22); one is the actual world to the author and reader, and the other is the actual world to the characters and/or narrator. Furthermore, each possible world is self-contained and has no direct influence on any others. "You can't get into a 'logical-space ship' and visit another possible world" (D. Lewis, *Plurality* 80), even in works of fantasy or science fiction which not only accept, as Lewis does, the existence of "possible non-actual worlds" (Maitre 14), but also involve travel to those other worlds and interaction between inhabitants of different worlds. Lewis would consider all the worlds in such a work to be part of the same larger world-set, in a manner similar to the atomist view of many worlds in one universe, but that universe is itself one of infinite possible universes, each with its own set of worlds and inhabitant entities. Lewis does recognize that, since we can only access other possible worlds through the imagination, we must represent them via linguistic and/or mathematical constructs; however, those constructs, to which he refers as "ersatz worlds" (*Plurality* 137), are merely representations, limited by the finite properties of language and human thought (cf. Sider 281-86). A linguistic representation of a possible world, such as a work of fiction or a set of statements in modal logic, can never *be* that entire world because "What can be described is limited by what we can have words for; whereas worlds can outrun our means of describing them" (*Plurality* 165).

While Lewis's concept of modal realism was influential on, and is useful for, the study of the textual-actual-world/readerly-actual-world distinction outlined by Ryan and others, his "full-blooded modal realism" (Norris 243) has not found nearly as much favour with modal logicians who regard his literalization of the possible-worlds metaphor as an unfalsifiable, and by extension, unnecessary, complication to the study of possibility. Indeed, in encouraging us to go beyond the limitations of language, the senses, and experience in order to categorize the full range of possible worlds and even possible universes, Lewisian modal realism/relativism also – albeit perhaps unintentionally – transcends another boundary, that of possibility itself, risking contradiction in assuming "that there exist things...that do not actually exist" (Loux 45).

Modal logic, following the publication of Lewis's *Counterfactuals,* and postmodern fiction have both taken the threat or promise of self-contradiction in Lewisian modal realism into account, to varying degrees, in their examinations of the nature of possibility. For example, Takashi Yagisawa has challenged Lewis's theory not by objecting to it in the usual manner, but by extending it to include "reference to possible *and* impossible worlds and their inhabitants" (176, emphasis in original), on the analogy of real and imaginary numbers. This reworking of modal realism posits worlds in which the basic laws of logic do not apply, where two contradictory options can occur in the same world-space, on the premise that, if a modal realist can make the unfalsifiable claim that all possible worlds equally co-exist, then it would be just as much of an unfalsifiable claim to say that impossible worlds exist alongside possible ones. Impossible or improbable worlds also form a key strategy in many works of what we commonly refer to as postmodern fiction, although the desire to subvert and/or expose the literary game is in fact as old as the game itself (Doležel, *Heterocosmica* 160-68).

Postmodern 'impossible fictional worlds' take both Lewisian modal realism and arguments such as Yagisawa's extension of Lewis's theory at their word to hypothesize about the existence of impossibilia alongside possibilia, to imagine a universe in which all options exist on equal footing. Such fictional worlds, of which the classic example is that of Jorge Luis Borges's "The Garden of Forking Paths," produce "contradictory, irreconcilable alternatives, all of them fully authenticated but none of them a fictional existent" (Doležel, *Heterocosmica* 164). Impossible-world theory and postmodern fiction, therefore, suggest that any attempt to break the bonds of possibility would be doomed to fall apart from its own weight; granting equal co-existence to conflicting possibilities in the same world, or to possibilities and impossibilities at the same time, ultimately negates all of these possibilities. However, the inner, psychological worlds of fictional and real entities alike are often characterized by an apparent exception to the law of non-contradiction: cognitive dissonance, the simultaneous co-existence of two incompatible belief systems in the same mind, when "we believe one thing in our heads, and another in our hearts.... But we try to believe in both of them at once" (Walker 13).

Fictionality and Intertextuality

With the theological and linguistic underpinnings of possible-worlds theory in mind (cf. Patterson 5), we may summarize the two guiding principles of the creation of a fictional world by the opening line of the Gospel of John, "In the beginning was the Word," and by Jacques Derrida's statement in *De la Grammatologie*, "Il n'y a pas de hors-texte" (227) – "there is nothing outside the text." To elaborate, according to a metaphorical reading of possible/fictional-worlds theory, a fictional world is brought into being by the author's words, yet is limited to those very words within the text; a fictional world is not the actual, infinite, physical world but, as Nicholas Rescher explains, "is the finite product of a finite mind" (*Imagining Irreality* 38). Even in a literalist view of possible worlds such as that of David Lewis, what is embodied in the fictional text is a finite part of a much greater world-space, and that small part is brought to our awareness through the author's words but is inaccessible by any other means.

Fictional worlds are possible worlds, but not all possible worlds are fictional worlds. Each possible world is defined by sets of assumptions and propositions held to be true in that world. Alvin Plantinga refers to these sets of propositions as "books" (259), and Lubomír Doležel calls them "encyclopedias" (*Heterocosmica* 177); both terms allude to the role of text in the definition of possible and fictional worlds. Where fictional worlds differ from other possible worlds in this respect is in having not merely a *book* – that is, a defining set of propositions – but also a *story* that develops from those propositions or takes them into consideration (cf. Rescher, *Imagining Irreality* 199-201). If we were to say, 'Let there be a world in which unicorns exist' to use Kripke's example (*Naming* 23-24), or 'Let there be a world in which swans are blue' to use Lewis's (*Plurality* 9), we would be describing possible worlds; if, on the other hand, we were to give a narrative, lyrical, or dramatic account of the experiences of, say, a unicorn or a blue swan – or other individuals in those worlds encountering these entities – we would be creating works of fiction and, thus, fictional worlds.

Yet, narrativity and/or performativity alone do not make a work fictional (cf. Ryan 3): newspaper articles and mathematical word problems, for example, are narratives, but they are, for the most part, not considered fictional narratives. The difference lies in intent: a newspaper article gives information about the actual world in narrative form; a word problem illustrates a mathematical concept using forms and examples more easily relatable to the everyday world; but a fictional narrative is an acknowledged work of imagination, created for the pleasure of the author and readers – although a secondary didactic intent may also be present in a fictional narrative as well as in a nonfictional one, and a secondary aesthetic intent may also be present in a nonfictional narrative as well as in a fictional one.

The intent of fiction also separates it from other counterfactual situations such as lying or misunderstanding. In *Imagining Irreality,* Nicholas Rescher divides counterfactual statements into three main categories, based upon the ways in which the statement diverges from actual fact:

> *inadvertently,* through what we would ordinarily categorize as falling into error;
>
> *knowingly and deliberately with a malign intent* through what we would ordinarily characterize as deceptions and lies;
>
> *knowingly and deliberately with a benign intent* – through endeavoring [to] amuse, divert, instruct, stimulate (to thought or action), or the like. (13; emphasis in original)

Only the strictest interpretation of truth value would consider a work of fiction to be equivalent to a lie, because when an author tells a fictional story, or actors put on a play, both the author/performers and the readers/audience are aware that the story or performance is a deliberate speech act and willingly suspend disbelief for the duration of the telling/performance (Norris 227); and here, it is also important to remember the distinction between 'truth of fiction' and 'truth in fiction' to which Kripke and Lewis have both alluded, as mentioned above. It is possible, however, that a reader who discovers that a favourite story is 'merely' fictional may initially feel he/she has been deceived, but even such a reader eventually realizes that it was never the author's intent "to deceive the reader into taking [works of fiction] as descriptions of the actual world" (Maitre 35) but in fact to entertain the reader. Indeed, a reader's mistaking a fictional world for the actual world can be taken as a compliment on the author's skill in describing that world.

Furthermore, while we read the text or, in the case of a dramatic work, see it performed, we temporarily imagine ourselves to be in the fictional world, and/or the fictional characters to be in the actual world, in a process many commentators have likened to a game of make-believe (e.g. Pavel 54-57; Crittenden 80-90; Ryan 22-23). Through these processes of figuratively placing ourselves in fictional worlds and fictional entities in our world, we are able to hypothesize about situations that *may* exist or have existed in the actual world at some point in time, in much the same way that philosophers use possible-world models "to identify and explain the subject matter of the actual world of our present experience" (Maitre 26).

Authors also bring actual-world entities into fictional worlds, but in different ways than readers do and for many different purposes. Among the effects of authorial insertions of actual-world people, places, and things into fictional worlds are verisimilitude, especially in a realistic novel; speculation on particular people and events of history, the defining feature of genres such as the historical novel or history play; radical reimagining of "even the most typical and well-known properties and life histories" of familiar historical figures and events (Doležel, *Heterocosmica* 17); or playful investigations into the nature of fictionality (Proudfoot 13). However, readers must remember that such entities, despite sharing names and properties with entities in the actual world, are not necessarily those entities themselves but fictionalized counterparts. Fictionalized counterparts of actual-world entities, especially those that appear in well-established and respected literary works such as Tolstoy's *War and Peace* or Shakespeare's history plays, may often end up overshadowing those actual-world entities in the public imagination and even influencing historians' conceptions of them (Hart 340). In some cases, this phenomenon can lead to its polar opposite, the organized attempts of historians and writers of historical fiction to discredit not only the fictional portrait but also everything that influenced it.

The possible-world model of fictionality not only allows us to account for the existence/non-existence paradox of fictional entities, or the presence and purposes of counterparts of actual-world entities and/or situations in a work of fiction; it also provides an ideal framework from which to observe and categorize intertextual references between different fictional works/worlds and between fictional worlds and the actual world. Plantinga's definition of the "book" of a possible world as the set of propositions true for that world ideally means "a maximal state of affairs" (258); that is, every conceivable proposition that could be, and is, true in that world. However, because possibility is infinite and human thought and language are limited, we cannot represent every single proposition about a world. Similarly, propositions that can be applied to the actual world at one particular point in time cannot be applied to a possible world in which "conceptual resources going beyond those available to the author" (Proudfoot 11) must come into play. To use Diane Proudfoot's example, a proposition such as "At some time there is a nuclear war" (11) would be absurd if applied to a Shakespearean fictional world – except, perhaps, in the case of a modernized production or adaptation – because the proposition is anachronistic for that world.

Thus, both to simplify matters and to avoid absurdity, "we reconstrue the central world of a textual universe... [and] the alternate possible worlds of counterfactual statements as conforming as far as possible to our representation of [the actual world]" (Ryan 51), unless the text explicitly specifies otherwise. This is what "Marie-Laure Ryan... terms the principle of minimal departure" (Palmer 35). For example, we would assume all the characters in a literary work are human unless we are dealing with a work of fantasy, science fiction, or mythology in which the characters could be animals, aliens, supernatural beings, or inanimate objects, and are specifically described as such in the text. We would similarly assume that the fictional world follows the same laws of logic and physics as the actual world, unless we are given clues that the text is a postmodern or fantastic work dealing with worlds that we would consider logically or physically impossible (Doležel, *Heterocosmica* 160-68; Maitre 29-34). Thus, once we take the principle of minimal departure into consideration, we need only specify which propositions about the possible/fictional world under discussion are different from the actual world, and these propositions may range from mere descriptions of fictional entities that do not exist in the actual world, to entire worlds that are virtually unrecognizable at first glance to actual-world readers.

The problem of anachronism that Proudfoot mentions, however, adds another dimension to the principle of minimal departure: the actual world from which the fictional world is a departure should be envisioned in terms of the author's society and experience rather than the reader's. Even so, what would be a minimal departure from the author's society may well require explanation to a reader from a different temporal and/or cultural milieu. This is a main reason for the plethora of 'explanatory' works on literary texts, such as Shakespearean plays or Victorian novels (see Hulbert et al. 22-23), which are meant to familiarize modern-day readers with the contexts in which the authors lived and wrote, and thus provide an actual-world basis for the fictional world embodied in the text.

Although fictional worlds are separate from the actual world, they are not wholly separate from each other; whether consciously or unconsciously, authors produce texts "in response to other texts" (Fokkema 5) as well as in response to other authors and/or readers. Though one reading of Derrida's typically ambiguous statement "There is nothing outside the text" in relation to fictional worlds suggests that a fictional world is a self-contained entity, fictional worlds do in fact depend on forces that exist outside the text: the author who produces the text, the reader who reads the text, and the actual world in which the author, text, and reader exist, are essential elements in the creation, definition, and endurance of the text and its fictional world. Similarly, literary texts do not exist in isolation from one another but are influenced by, and themselves influence, other texts (Fokkema 5-6) in ways ranging from subtle allusions to deliberate imitations, from serious commentary to parody and satire to revision or antithesis of the previous text, and all of these build upon the worlds embodied in earlier texts to create new and distinct worlds of their own which are still counterparts of the previous worlds.

Doležel and Lanier: Classifying Adaptations

Lubomír Doležel, in the final chapter of *Heterocosmica*, divides literary adaptations into two main categories: translation, the act of rewriting a work in a new language; and transduction, a broad category which "supersedes and absorbs intertextuality" (202) by accounting for virtually all the different ways in which authors, readers, and texts communicate with each other (203-06). Both translation and transduction have as their goal the restatement of a literary work in a different mode of communication. Where they differ is in that translations generally attempt to preserve as much of the original text's world as possible in the new text's counterpart world, with the primary difference between the two texts being the language in which they are written; translations will be discussed further in Chapter Three. Transductions, on the other hand, involve transformations of the source text's world into new and often vastly different counterpart worlds, meant to simultaneously defamiliarize the familiar and familiarize the unfamiliar. Doležel further classifies transductions into "three distinct types" (*Heterocosmica* 206): transposition, expansion, and displacement. These three types may themselves be combined within one text depending on the author's purpose in creating the adaptation.

Transposition places the familiar characters, plots, and/or themes of a source text into a different time or place setting, drawing upon elements of familiar fictional worlds while merging those elements with sociopolitical concerns of the adaptors' actual world(s) in order to demonstrate the simultaneous timelessness and "topicality of the canonical world" (Doležel, *Heterocosmica* 206) and make readers aware of events in the adaptors' parts of the actual world by translating those events into familiar terms. With respect to Shakespearean adaptations, transpositions are probably the most common type of transduction, as evidenced by the abundance of productions of the plays in every conceivable manner of non-Shakespearean dress; not to mention that the productions of Shakespeare's own time, even the history plays and the Roman tragedies, were generally done in what would have been 'contemporary' dress to his audience (Orgel, "Shakespeare Imagines" 551-54). These productions may be considered visual transpositions, retaining Shakespeare's original text but updating the costumes and settings, although play texts such as Restoration abridgments (B.A. Murray 63-68) or Victorian burlesques (Schoch 31-56) also combine the language and décor of their own time with those of Shakespeare's for, respectively, familiarizing or comical effect.

Other transpositions drastically 'modernize' the source text by assigning the source text's plot elements to characters and settings closer to the new text's author's sociohistorical milieu, and using the common language of that author's time and place. Examples of this type of transposition include Mary Elizabeth Braddon's 1863 novel *Eleanor's Victory,* an early example of the detective novel whose protagonist can be considered a Victorian female counterpart to Hamlet, and Ranulfo Concon's 2006 novel *Joker,* whose Hamlet-figure is an Australian teenager coping with the death of his best friend and the divorce of his parents. Even Shakespeare's *Hamlet* is itself a transposition, retaining the Danish setting of the original story as first set down by Saxo Grammaticus, but moving it forward from Saxo's sixth-century timeframe to the beginning of the seventeenth century, and presenting it as an analogue to Elizabethan/Jacobean Britain.

The broader category of expansion covers several different ways in which an author may attempt to fill in gaps and blanks in the source text and thus provide or reveal what the author of the source text chose to leave unsaid. There are several different ways in which the author of an expansion may go beyond the boundaries of the base text. Among these are *prequel,* in which the new text provides backstory to the source; *sequel,* which tells what came after the events of the source; and *role expansion,* which can either flesh out a minor or supporting character from the source text or invent a completely new character who happened to be present at the events of the source text but was not mentioned in that text.

Each type of expansion is represented in the case of *Hamlet* adaptations. For example, Lillie Buffum Chace Wyman's 1934 novel *Gertrude of Denmark;* Percy MacKaye's 1950 dramatic tetralogy *The Mystery of Hamlet, King of Denmark;* John Turing's 1967 novel *My Nephew Hamlet;* and John Updike's 2000 novel *Gertrude and Claudius* all present different versions of the stories of Hamlet's parents and uncle prior to the events of Shakespeare's play. On the other hand, Alethea Hayter's 1972 novel *Horatio's Version* is a sequel to the play, alternating between Horatio's diary entries and proceedings at Fortinbras's court. In their focus on secondary characters – albeit very important ones – from the original play, these texts are also examples of role expansion, as is the recent prevailing trend of adaptations told from Ophelia's perspective, such as Lisa Fiedler's *Dating Hamlet* and Rebecca Reisert's *Ophelia's Revenge*. Another such example is probably the most famous of all adaptations of *Hamlet*, if not of Shakespearean adaptations in general: Tom Stoppard's 1967 play *Rosencrantz and Guildenstern Are Dead*.

The broadest of Doležel's three main categories of transduction is displacement, which may involve elements of the two other categories or may choose to preserve certain essential characteristics of the source text, but has as its purpose the creation of "an essentially different version of the protoworld" (*Heterocosmica* 207), by radically changing some element of the base text in order to challenge it and/or its worldview. Each of these forms of adaptation can thus serve not only as new and original approaches to familiar works, but also as acts of literary and/or sociopolitical criticism within the more aesthetically pleasing and accessible form of another literary work. Indeed, all of the adaptations cited in the above paragraphs (and which will be discussed further elsewhere in this book) can be described as displacements of one sort or another. However, for the purpose of this study, I will divide displacement into two subcategories: parody and satire, and polemical revisionism, to borrow and adapt Doležel's term. While both of these subcategories may be, and often are, present in the same text, the difference is that, in general, parody and satire use their similarities to and departures from the source text for humorous effects, while polemical revisionism employs these tactics for more serious purposes.

As Douglas Lanier demonstrates in *Shakespeare and Modern Popular Culture*, Doležel's three categories of transduction – expansion, transposition, and displacement – may be further broken down into more specific types. Lanier's taxonomy of adaptations focuses mainly on works of fan fiction, adaptations written by readers[12] as hobby projects for distribution amongst fellow readers, usually on the Internet or in self-published newsletters and magazines, rather than 'published' in the more traditional sense, in forms such as novels or plays. The six categories into which Lanier classifies these works are equally applicable to more conventionally published adaptations as to the fan-fiction subculture he describes, because these adaptations are

---

[12] The term "fan fiction" itself implies that the reader producing the adaptation is a non-professional writer. See Hellekson and Busse.

themselves the product of reader/fan responses to the plays and/or their characters. His classification of different types of transductions is as follows:

> *extrapolated narrative,* in which plot material is generated from events mentioned but not developed in the 'master' narrative...;
>
> *interpolated narrative,* in which new plot material is dovetailed with the plot of the source;
>
> *remotivated narrative,* in which the new narrative retains the basic plotline or situation of the source but changes the motivations of the characters;
>
> *revisionary narrative,* in which the new narrative is told from a different point of view;
>
> *hybrid narrative,* in which narrative elements or characters from two or more Shakespearean plays [and/or other works] are combined.
> (Lanier 83; emphasis in original)

Lanier's classifications of extrapolated and interpolated narrative are analogous to Doležel's category of expansions; prequels and sequels may be described as extrapolated narratives or "diachronous transformations" (Rozett 6), while interpolated narratives form "synchronous transformations" (Rozett 6). Similarly, what Lanier describes as revisionary narrative is not necessarily 'revision*ist*' narrative – though it may be that too – but is essentially Doležel's classification of role expansion. The hybrid narrative is a special case, ranging from relatively subtle intertextual mixtures of various literary works to full-blown crossovers in which one might find, for example, characters from *Hamlet* and *Macbeth* meeting each other or following each other's plotlines (cf. Vining 47; Innes, *H&H* 44; Mark 69-70; Brode vi).

To Doležel's two overarching categories of adaptation, I argue it is possible to add a third, intermediary category: retelling, which combines elements of both translation and transduction. Like translations, retellings generally seek to preserve as much of the source text's world as possible, but unlike translations, retellings present the source text in a different genre rather than in a different language – though it is possible for a retelling to involve translation into another language as well as into another genre. In this way, retellings share with transductions a radical transformation of the source text, but the transformation is primarily one of form rather than of content. Retellings also differ from transductions in the general absence of or de-emphasis on sociopolitical interrogations, preferring to take the source text's worldview at its word, or at least explain it to the readers, when drastically changing the worldview would be disruptive to the unity of the original text.

The purpose of a retelling is, indeed, closer to that of a translation than of a transduction: both translations and retellings familiarize the source text to their readers by presenting that text in a mode of communication that the readers are better able to understand. Retellings are often meant as first steps toward the reader's learning to appreciate the source text in its original form, as is the case of the many retellings of Shakespeare's plays as works of juvenile fiction; but, as seen in the example of Charles and Mary Lamb's retellings (see Richmond 7-17), the adaptations may distinguish themselves as skillfully-written works in their own right that are equally enjoyed alongside the original.

As Shakespeare's *Hamlet* itself demonstrates, it is possible for an adaptation to displace the original, not merely in a metaphorical sense, but in a literal sense as well. Indeed, the possibility of an adaptation overtaking its original in the public imagination is one of the reasons many commentators have given for resisting adaptation. One example of this resistance to adaptation is George Eliot's 1879 dismissal of Shakespearean burlesque as "premonitory signs of a hideous millennium, in which the lion will have to lie down with the monkey that his soul naturally abhors" (qtd. in Schoch 20), with its invocation of the "reductive oppositions of 'high' and 'low' culture" (Schoch 20). Yet comparatively few objections have been made to Shakespeare's *Hamlet* having almost completely obscured its source texts, in part because of the position the play has held in literary history.

CHAPTER TWO

SHAKESPEARE AS ADAPTOR:
THE CASE OF *HAMLET*

> Is it not monstrous that this player here,
> But in a fiction, a dream of passion,
> Could force his soul so to his own conceit
> That from her working all the visage wann'd,
> Tears in his eyes, distraction in his aspect,
> A broken voice, an' his whole function suiting
> With forms to his conceit? And all for nothing,
> For Hecuba!
> What's Hecuba to him, or he to Hecuba,
> That he should weep for her?
>
> (*Hamlet* II.ii. 551-60)

The Historical and Literary Backgrounds of the Play

Looking at *Hamlet* as an adaptation of its source materials is a useful way into the appreciation of other texts that use the play as their source. This approach allows us to make comparisons between each writer's handling of his/her source texts in the creation of a new text and the fictional world that text embodies. A study of Shakespeare as an adaptor also serves as a reminder of the changes in public and critical opinion of adaptations between his time and that of the reader.

It is well known that virtually all of Shakespeare's plays and some of his longer poems were inspired by works of history, mythology, folklore, poetry, and popular fiction which he had read, as was usual for playwrights of his time. In addition, we must also remember that Elizabethan literary/dramatic culture did not have copyright laws as we are familiar with them (Smith 17-34) and generally privileged the spoken word over the printed one (Murphy, "What Happens" 1-15; Stallybrass and Chartier 35-56), as demonstrated by the fact that Shakespeare's contemporaries would speak of 'hearing' a play where present-day audiences would speak of 'seeing' one (e.g. *Hamlet* II.ii. 535-36). As well, because drama was not as highly privileged a literary genre at the time as it has since become, being regarded primarily as popular entertainment and having long been defined by adaptation of familiar material, 'originality' as we now think of it was not nearly as sought-after in plays of the English Renaissance as it would be in later literary works. As William F. Hansen points out, "Shakespeare's *Hamlet* is a revision of a dramatic treatment... of a retelling... of a literary treatment... of a Scandinavian legend" (67), an adaptation at least four times over and a great work in its own right.

The exact age, origin, and historical veracity of the Hamlet story are somewhat uncertain, which has allowed writers working from the sources as well as from Shakespeare some leeway in determining the story's time setting. Among adaptations of the Shakespearean text and its sources, Lars Walker's *Blood and Judgment* identifies the time of the original story as the beginning of the sixth century, the time in which the earliest complete version places it, while Graham Holderness's *The Prince of Denmark* places it in the early eleventh century, around the time that Christianity first came to Denmark.

On the academic rather than the literary side, Kemp Malone draws an interesting series of parallels between the Hamlet story and legendary histories of the British Isles that are Scandinavian in origin, such as the Anglo-Saxon epic *Beowulf* (59-99), which may be roughly contemporary to the timeframe of the Hamlet story, and "a Scandinavian warrior named Amhlaidhe... slayer of King Niall Glundubh" (54), mentioned in the Irish Annals of the years 904-917. Malone finally identifies Amleth/Hamlet as a Danish analogue to Onela, the Swedish king mentioned in *Beowulf* (52-76). Marion A. Taylor's study of the origins of Saxo Grammaticus's version of the Hamlet story gives it a more definite historical background, identifying Amleth/Hamlet's grandfather, Rorik the Dane, with the historical Rurik, "a frequent harrier of Christendom from 835 AD until the middle 870s" (37) who is best known as "the founder of modern Russia" (38), though acknowledging that Hamlet himself was most likely a legendary character even if he was connected to a known historical figure.

One of the earliest identifiable references to the Hamlet story occurs in Icelandic literature, in "a verse uttered by the tenth-century poet-adventurer Snæbjörn, in the *Prose Edda*" (M.A. Taylor 24). The allusion is not to any incident known to us from Shakespeare's play, but rather to "one of the riddling sayings of the hero Amleth" (Bullough VII. 5) that were preserved in the pre-Shakespearean historical/legendary accounts. Variations of the name *Amleth* or *Amlóði*, as a common noun rather than a proper name, occur in several Scandinavian languages, most prominently in Icelandic and Norwegian but less frequently in Swedish and Danish (Malone 52-58; Hansen

6), all of these variations having the common meaning of "a fool" (Hansen 6).[13] It is thus uncertain whether the proper name came first and came to be used as a generic term for a fool because of the character (cf. Malone 55), or whether the character was so named because of his pretending madness.

According to William F. Hansen, however, the name of the Shakespearean character may well have two different etymological origins. The name can be traced both to the original Scandinavian name, *Amlóði,* meaning 'fool,' and to the very similar English names *Hamlet* or *Hamnet* – the latter the name of Shakespeare's young son who died at the age of eleven in 1596 (Holden 150, 192-93).[14] As Hansen notes, E.G. Withycombe traced the origin of the English name to the Old German word *haimi,* meaning 'home' (162, note 10), like the common noun *hamlet,* meaning "a settlement... with too few dwellings to warrant a church" (De Grazia 44). Indeed, as Margreta de Grazia states, both meanings suit the Shakespearean character in that not only does he pretend madness, but he is also left landless by his father's death and uncle's succession, and seeks to regain his inheritance and property.

The plot itself, with its protagonist who feigns insanity, seeks revenge, and brings down a corrupt king, is common in the folklore, mythology, and legendary history of various cultures. The most notable such example for our purposes is the Roman historical account of Lucius Junius Brutus and the founding of the Roman Republic in about 509 BC, which may well have been the earliest known original for or analogue to the Hamlet story (De Grazia 68; Hansen 25-35; M.A. Taylor 26-28). The Brutus story as told by Livy was a primary source for Shakespeare's 1593 poem *The Rape of Lucrece,* not to mention that Lucius Junius Brutus's descendant, Marcus Brutus, is a major character in Shakespeare's *Julius Caesar.* Livy's account of Brutus, from his *Histories* of the first century BC, was also known to Saxo Grammaticus (Bullough VII. 6-7; Hansen 25) and, on the evidence of similar details, probably influenced his telling of the Hamlet story in his masterwork *Historiae Danicae* – the earliest surviving complete version of the story, and thus the most prominent, if distant, ancestor of Shakespeare's play (Hansen 31-37). Indeed, because the names *Amleth/Hamlet* and *Brutus* both mean 'foolish' or 'stupid' (Hansen 25; Bullough VII. 6; M.A. Taylor 9), many

---

[13] Kemp Malone notes that a cognate, "amlaye" (56), occurs in the Middle English poem *The Wars of Alexander,* but it is derived from the Gaelic *Amhlaidhe* rather than directly from the Scandinavian *Amlóði.*

[14] "The memory of his own son Hamnet" (Holden 192) could perhaps also account in part for the appeal of the Hamlet story, whose protagonist dies young and without continuing the line of descent, to Shakespeare.

scholars have argued that both stories belong to the same tale-type, which William F. Hansen describes as "the Hero as Fool" (16). In the case of Brutus, who was a known historical figure even if some of the details of his story are wholly or partly fictional, the legend probably grew around the meaning of his name, perhaps as a means of lending the name some dignity (Hansen 25). However, the reverse may be true for Hamlet, for as Hansen points out, "there is... no other instance from Germanic legend in which the name of a hero has passed into speech as a common noun" (6). Saxo Grammaticus himself, in fact, gives two other examples of "the wise-fool theme" (Bullough VII. 6) elsewhere in *Historiae Danicae*. It is also possible, as Taylor suggests, that *Amleth* is merely a translation of *Brutus*, and that the Scandinavian legend may thus be a transposition of the Roman one (26).

Saxo Grammaticus's *Historiae Danicae*

Saxo Grammaticus – the Latin title *grammaticus* means 'writer' – lived from 1150-1204. He began writing *Historiae Danicae*,[15] also known as *Gesta Danorum* (Deeds of the Danes), "at the end of the twelfth century" (Bullough VII. 5) but the work was not printed until 1514, in Paris. Because *Historiae Danicae* combines Latin, Icelandic, and Danish histories with oral tradition and mixes provable history with myth and legend, Geoffrey Bullough categorizes Saxo as "to Denmark what Geoffrey of Monmouth was to Britain" (VII. 6). Much like Geoffrey of Monmouth's *History of the Kings of Britain,* Saxo's *Historiae Danicae* was greatly influential on other contemporary and later historians as well as writers of imaginative literature. William F. Hansen notes that "five other early Danish accounts of Hamlet have come down to us" (147); all of these were first written in the thirteenth and fourteenth centuries and show varying degrees of influence from Saxo. *Historiae Danicae* consists of sixteen volumes; the story of Amleth/Hamlet is told in two of these. Book III, the most pertinent for Shakespeare's version, covers "Amleth's survival in his uncle's court, and... his revenge" (Bullough VII. 7). Book IV, meanwhile, tells of events that were either not related by Shakespeare or treated in an entirely different manner in the play than in the history.

In Saxo's version of the story, Amleth – the name by which he is known in Oliver Elton's 1894 English translation of Saxo's first nine books – is not prince of all Denmark as he is in Shakespeare's play and some of the known post-Saxo Danish histories, but rather is the son of a co-ruler of Jutland, although this discrepancy may have been influenced by "local patriotism...

---

[15] Hereafter cited as *HD*.

[because] Saxo... was probably a Zealander and in any case has a bias in favour of Zealand" (Hansen 151). The characters known to readers of Shakespeare as King Hamlet and Claudius began their literary lives as "Horwendil and Feng, whose father Gerwendil had been governor of the Jutes... appointed by Rorik to defend Jutland" (*HD* 60). As there is no evidence that Shakespeare knew any of the Danish histories other than translations of Saxo, we may theorize that his decision to make Hamlet's father ruler of all Denmark may have been influenced by the fact that in Saxo's history, Amleth's mother Gerutha, the earliest incarnation of Shakespeare's Gertrude, is Rorik's daughter (*HD* 62).

At least two of the post-Saxo Danish chronicles mentioned by Hansen (148-150) list Amleth/Hamlet as king of Denmark after his uncle; one, the thirteenth-century *Annals of Ryd*, further describes him as "a very clever man [who] slew the king of England in war and gained control of Denmark, England, and Scotland" (148). The position of the 'historical' Hamlet as ruler of Denmark, England, and Scotland gives an insight into the appeal of the story in Shakespeare's time; as Geoffrey Bullough observes (VII. 18-19), it was possible to read Amleth/Hamlet as an analogue of sorts to James I (James VI of Scotland), who married Anne of Denmark in 1589, and became king of England as well as of Scotland in 1603, two years after the generally-accepted first performance date of Shakespeare's play.

I shall return to the historical analogues and counterparts of the Hamlet story later in this discussion. To return for the moment to Saxo, the account of Hamlet in Book III of *Historiae Danicae* begins with the story of Horwendil's battle against the King of Norway (*HD* 60-61; cf. *Hamlet* I.i. 60-63; 80-107), known in Shakespeare's play as King Fortinbras but referred to by Saxo as Koll, or in Latin, Collerus. Interestingly, both Saxo's and Shakespeare's names for the Norwegian king form interlingual puns on the characteristics that Shakespeare assigns to Prince Fortinbras: the name *Collerus* sounds like the Latin word *colera*, which means 'bile' or 'anger' (*OED Online*), and the name *Fortinbras*, which Shakespeare used for both father and son, means "strength in arms" (*HD* 60) in French. Saxo draws no parallels between the Danish and Norwegian royal families as Shakespeare does, but does characterize both Horwendil and Koll as honourable men, both in their conduct in battle and in their agreement "that the conqueror shall give funeral rites to the conquered" (*HD* 61; cf. *Hamlet* V.ii. 395-403). Furthermore, Saxo emphasizes Horwendil's valuing not only of honour but of glory (*HD* 60), as was expected of Danish heroes, as well as "his boldness [which] did not fail" (*HD* 61). In this way, Saxo establishes the character of Horwendil as the sort of man his audience admired, and sets him up as a comparison and contrast both to his brother/murderer and to his son.

Saxo begins discussing the murder of Horwendil immediately after mentioning the marriage of Horwendil and Gerutha and the birth of Amleth (*HD* 62), implying that Feng's "jealousy" and his plan "to waylay his brother" (*HD* 62) must have developed over several years. This is because Amleth must be "old enough to appreciate what has happened and to develop a sophisticated strategy" (Hansen 71) in order for the story to make sense. The account of the murder given in *Historiae Danicae* also provides details of Feng's wooing of Gerutha which are not mentioned in Shakespeare's *Hamlet* but do have a coincidental yet unmistakable analogue in I.ii. of *Richard III:*[16]

> Also the man veiled the monstrosity of his deed with such hardihood of cunning, that he made up a mock pretence of goodwill to excuse his crime, and glossed over fratricide with a show of righteousness. Gerutha, said he, though so gentle that she would do no man the slightest hurt, had been visited with her husband's extremest hate; and it was all to save her that he had slain his brother, for he thought it shameful that a lady so meek and unrancorous should suffer the heavy disdain of her husband. Nor did his smooth words fail in their intent, for at courts, where fools are sometimes favoured and backbiters preferred, a lie lacks not credit. Nor did Feng keep from shameful embraces the hands that had slain a brother; pursuing with equal guilt both of his wicked and impious deeds. (*HD* 62)

The effect of this passage is to establish Feng as everything Horwendil is not; where the elder brother honours his promises, engages in fair fights, and earns the approval of his future wife and her father, the younger steals, cheats, lies, and murders in order to get what he wants. Marion A. Taylor reminds us, however, that Danish society of Amleth's time would probably have taken a different view of the marriage of Feng and Gerutha than either Shakespeare or Saxo did. Saxo's judgment of the marriage as "incest" (*HD* 62), which both Belleforest and Shakespeare followed, was influenced by Christian views of kinship and marriage, but in sixth-century Denmark "it was not only proper for a widow to marry her dead husband's brother, but usually compulsory to do so" (M.A. Taylor 51).

Saxo's and Shakespeare's accounts of Amleth/Hamlet's feigned madness also differ considerably in details. First of all, Saxo describes Amleth's appearance and behaviour in much blunter terms than Shakespeare does (*HD* 62-63; cf. *Hamlet* II.i. 74-97). As well, while Shakespeare does give his Hamlet a talent for wordplay, it is different than that of Saxo's Amleth,

---

[16] Cf. Brode, whose account of the marriage of Gerutha/Gertrude and Feng/Claudius (48-51) is directly based on *Richard III* I.ii.

whose propensity for making cryptic yet meaningful riddles reflects a long-standing tradition of Scandinavian folklore and literature as well as Old English heroic poetry.

Most of Amleth's riddles are obvious enough based on visual and metaphorical cues, but virtually all of them depend on puns in Danish and Icelandic that do not always translate accurately into Latin or English. For example, while Amleth's reference to "the meal, meaning the sand... ground small by the hoary tempests of the sea" (*HD* 64) does make sense based on the physical resemblance of white sand to flour, the riddle can also be explained as a pun on the similarity of "Old Icelandic *melr* 'sand' and *meldr* 'meal, flour'" (Hansen 128). It is this scene to which the Icelandic poet Snæbjörn refers in the earliest known allusion to the Hamlet story, a description of the sea as "the host-fierce mill... [that] long ago ground Amlóði's meal" (qtd in Hansen 129).[17] This is one of the more felicitous examples of Amleth's riddles in that it is equally understandable in any language because of its visual element, even when the pun is lost. Similarly, Amleth's "wooden crooks... sharp javelins to avenge his father" (*HD* 62), an analogue to a similar incident in the Roman story of Brutus (Hansen 27; cf. *HD* 69) but not present in Shakespeare's play, make sense by themselves as symbols of – and later, tools in – his plan for revenge, yet also have multiple meanings when comparing Saxo's Latin text both to Scandinavian languages and to English. "In Old Icelandic *krókr* 'crook' can also mean 'clever trick'" (Hansen 125), and in English, *crook* can refer both to a curved stick and to a dishonest or deceitful person (*OED Online*).

The situations in which Amleth gives his riddling answers not only provide the reader with examples of his true cleverness under his façade of "an utter lack of wits" (*HD* 62), but also show the ways in which he evades the suspicions of those around him:

> When they [Amleth's companions] averred that he had given a cunning answer, he answered that he had spoken deliberately: for he was loth to be thought prone to lying about any matter, and wished to be held a stranger to falsehood; and accordingly he mingled craft and candour in such wise that, though his words did lack truth, yet there was nothing to betoken the truth and betray how far his keenness went. (*HD* 63)

This passage may well be the ancestor of Polonius's remark in Shakespeare's Act II, scene ii, "Though this be madness, yet there is method in't" (205-06); as well as Hamlet's admission to Rosencrantz and Guildenstern, "I am but

---

[17] "*Amlóða mólu*" (Updike 33) in the original Icelandic.

mad north-north-west. / When the wind is southerly I know a hawk from a hand-saw" (*Hamlet* II.ii. 378-79).

The character in Saxo's narrative who inspired Shakespeare's Horatio also displays a talent for riddling puns in his only appearance in the story. He is identified only as "a foster-brother of Amleth, who had not ceased to have regard to their common nurture" (*HD* 63), and he is the one who warns Amleth of Feng's plot to "provoke his mind to the temptations of love" (*HD* 63). The way in which the foster brother warns Amleth of the plot seems absurd at first glance, until one realizes the metaphorical and punning aspects – which Saxo himself seems to have overlooked, as the passage describes and interprets the details more literally than metaphorically, thus making it more appropriate for a fantastic fictional world than a realistic one. Amleth's foster brother "found a straw on the ground and fastened it underneath the tail of a gadfly that was flying past" (*HD* 64) as a signal of Feng's intentions. Geoffrey Bullough interprets this odd detail as a warning "to beware of 'the sting in the woman's tail'" (VII. 12, n. 1). William F. Hansen, following Jørgen Olrik's and Hans Sperber's suggestions, tentatively links the straw to the Danish word "*agnbak* 'straw-back'... an old nickname for a... petty thief who stole grain from the sheaves of the field" (132) and the gadfly to the Old Icelandic word "*fluga*, which means literally 'fly' and figuratively 'bait'" (133). Kemp Malone suggests (211) that the gadfly might have been a literal translation of the foster brother's name, which Saxo did not mention. The foster brother himself differs from Shakespeare's Horatio in being a servant of Feng, perhaps making him a counterpart not only of Horatio but also, in different ways, of Laertes, Rosencrantz, and Guildenstern.

The woman whom Feng sends to tempt Amleth (*HD* 63-64) is the obvious inspiration for Shakespeare's Ophelia, but like Horatio's original, she has a much smaller role in Saxo's history than in Shakespeare's play. Also like the model for Horatio, she is identified as a foster sibling of Amleth: "both of them had been under the same fostering in their childhood; and this early rearing in common had brought them both into great intimacy" (*HD* 64). Saxo's text does not indicate what sort of attitude his society had to physical relationships between foster siblings, suggesting that either "he finds nothing very reprehensible in the encounter or prefers not to detract from the nobility of the hero" (Hansen 130). However, Saxo's description of the "erotic relationship" (Hansen 130) between Amleth and the woman, consummated in "a distant and impenetrable fen" (*HD* 64) where they will not be observed, is the opposite of Hamlet's deliberate outburst to Ophelia, "Get thee to a nunn'ry, why wouldst thou be a breeder of sinners?" (*Hamlet* III.i. 120-21), made in full knowledge that he is being spied upon.

Furthermore, Amleth's answer to the court that when "he had ravished the maid... he had rested upon the hoof of a beast of burden, upon a cockscomb, and also upon a ceiling" (*HD* 64) provides yet another example of his use of puns to tell the truth and still evade his questioners: although the Latin text does not mention it, "'horsehoof' and 'cockscomb'... are the popular names of certain plants in Denmark" (Hansen 134) and the "ceiling" reference probably implies thatch made from reeds. Amleth does thank his foster brother for sending him the warning of "a certain thing bearing a straw" (*HD* 64-65), but both the foster brother and the foster sister disappear from Saxo's narrative immediately upon having served their purposes.

Following the incidents of Hamlet's foster siblings, Saxo introduces us to "a friend of Feng, gifted more with assurance than judgment" (*HD* 65), the original of Polonius, but, like most of the other characters in the story, unnamed by Saxo. The history provides no overt reason why "Amleth should be closeted alone with his mother in her chamber" (*HD* 65) other than as a means to test Feng's suspicions, for there is no indication in Saxo's text of whether Gerutha had in fact requested him to see her as Gertrude does in Shakespeare's version (III.ii. 374-75). Although Amleth's address to Gerutha (*HD* 65-66) is very similar to Hamlet's haranguing of Gertrude (*Hamlet* III.iv. 34-196), the circumstances of the eavesdropper's death are told by Saxo in much blunter detail than they are depicted in Shakespeare's play. Rather than hiding himself behind a curtain, a common feature in castles of Shakespeare's time, he "lay down skulking in the straw" (*HD* 65) – which Bullough's notes identify as "possibly a straw mattress" (*HD* 65, n. 3) – prompting Amleth to imitate a crowing rooster in a nest before killing the interloper. Saxo makes no indication, as does Shakespeare (*Hamlet* III.iv. 26-33), of whether Amleth believed the King himself was spying on him, but recounts in grim detail what became of the spy's body:

> Then, cutting his body into morsels, he [Amleth] seethed it in boiling water, and flung it through the mouth of an open sewer for the swine to eat, bestrewing the stinking mire with his hapless limbs.... Amleth, among others, was asked in jest if he had come upon any trace of him, and replied that the man had gone to the sewer, but had fallen through its bottom[18] and been stifled by the floods of filth, and that he had then been devoured by the swine that came up all about that place. (*HD* 65-66)

---

[18] Hansen's translation is even more explicit: "Amleth... reported that the man had gone to the outhouse and fallen through the hole" (102).

Compared to Saxo's description, Shakespeare's reference to Polonius being "At supper.... Not where he eats, but where 'a is eaten; a certain convocation of politic worms are e'en at him" (IV.iii. 17-21) seems relatively euphemistic, though it does retain the morbid humour present in the earlier text.

The originals of Rosencrantz and Guildenstern appear very briefly in Saxo's text as Feng prepares to send Amleth away to Britain (*HD* 66; cf. *Hamlet* IV.iii. 39-68). But unlike the hapless sometime friends of Hamlet in Shakespeare's play who are presented as, essentially, pawns in a greater game, there are "no doubts about their being accomplices" (*HD* 67, n. 1) in Saxo's story, for they have known all along that the King's message "was an implement of destruction to another" (*HD* 67). Amleth's further addition to Feng's letter to the British king requesting marriage with his daughter,[19] which Shakespeare does not use, is introduced with the somewhat ambiguous statement that Amleth was not "satisfied with removing from himself the sentence of death and passing the peril on to others" (*HD* 67). This could suggest that the marriage proposal is Amleth's way of mitigating any guilt he might have felt over the death of the servants, or that changing Feng's request for his execution to a request for marriage would enhance the original revenge plot.

Shakespeare chooses to ignore Amleth/Hamlet's experiences in England, mentioning only what occurred on the voyage itself (*Hamlet* IV.vii.), even though Saxo indicates that Amleth "had passed a whole year with the king" (*HD* 69). Indeed, the British interlude in Saxo's tale serves primarily as a reminder of Amleth's wit and keen senses in his "role of the perceptive folktale hero" (Hansen 136), and William F. Hansen likens the episode to a Danish folktale – more specifically, from Jutland, as Amleth himself was said to be – in which three protagonists, not merely one as in Saxo, display similar perceptiveness and are rewarded for it (136-39). Amleth's remarkable guesses about the ignoble origins of both the king's feast (*HD* 67-68) and the queen mother (*HD* 68-69) do fit into the quasi-mythical fictional world of Saxo's history, but in their attribution of virtually supernatural deductive abilities to the protagonist, they would have been out of place in the world of Shakespeare's play – even though the Shakespearean fictional world does allow for the presence of the supernatural. Even so, some echoes of the British king's feast do appear in Shakespeare's text: Amleth's guess that the drink served at the feast was made of honey from "bees that had fed in the paunch of a dead man" (*HD* 68) could have informed Hamlet's remark, upon being questioned about the death of Polonius, that "a king may go a progress

---

[19] She is unnamed by Saxo, but the *Legend Chronicle* of the fifteenth century calls her "Ingaefreth" (Hansen 150).

through the guts of a beggar" (*Hamlet* IV.iii. 30-31; cf. Sjögren 21). Similarly, Amleth's presentation of the hollow sticks containing "the weregild [blood money] of the slain as though it were themselves" (*HD* 69) could possibly be a distant ancestor of the English ambassador's report at the end of Shakespeare's play "That Rosencrantz and Guildenstern are dead" (*Hamlet* V.ii. 371).

When Amleth returns to Denmark in Saxo's text, he arrives to behold his own funeral, the "pretended obsequies" (*HD* 66) he had requested of his mother before leaving for Britain. While Shakespeare does retain the funeral scene for his play, he makes it Ophelia's (*Hamlet* V.i. 218-99) rather than Hamlet's; however, Hamlet's conversation with the gravedigger who does not suspect he is indeed speaking with "he that is mad, and sent into England" (*Hamlet* V.i. 148) suggests Saxo's description of Amleth arriving "Covered with filth... whose last rites they were celebrating as though he were dead... in the flesh" (*HD* 69). The funeral also serves as the backdrop for Amleth's final act of revenge, at which he at last reveals the purposes of "the stakes he had long ago prepared" (*HD* 69): to secure the "knotted tapestry" (*HD* 67) in which he has bound the king and nobles, and to provide kindling for the fire he sets to burn down the palace (*HD* 70). Hamlet's and Laertes's switching swords during the final duel in Shakespeare's version (V.ii. 302-320) may have been suggested by Amleth's swapping Feng's sword for his own, which has "had both sword and scabbard riveted across with an iron nail" (*HD* 69), meant to 'protect' Amleth from his irrational behaviour but thereby leaving the king unable to defend himself.

Unlike Shakespeare's Hamlet, who dies in the process of avenging his father, Saxo's Amleth survives and thus does not require another person to "Report me and my cause aright / To the unsatisfied" (*Hamlet* V.ii. 339-40). The beginning of Book IV of *Historiae Danicae,* therefore, consists of Amleth's explanation of what has transpired (70-73), reminding the Danish people of Feng's treachery and tyranny and of Gerutha's "two-fold weight of ignominy, embracing one who was her husband's brother and murderer" (*HD* 72). He also has images of his previous exploits painted on a shield (*HD* 73), which he brings with him to the British court. However, following Amleth's two summaries of his adventures, the remainder of his story undergoes an ironic reversal, as his father-in-law, the British king, is revealed to have made "an old promise to avenge Feng" (*HD* 74). The British king's dilemma in keeping his promise to Feng yet honouring his son-in-law further serves to illustrate the various value systems which governed Saxo's society, as the king must choose between "the sanctity of his oath... [and] family bonds" (*HD* 75) while still respecting "the holy ties of hospitality" (*HD* 75). The British king ends up using a variation of the method Feng used when

sending Amleth to Britain in the first place: he sends Amleth as an envoy to
"a certain queen reigning in Scotland... [who] had always loathed her wooers,
and had inflicted on her lovers the uttermost punishment" (*HD* 75), only for
his plot to backfire when the queen, in admiration of Amleth's cleverness,
resorts to the same ruse and rewrites the letter to request "that she be asked
to marry the bearer" (*HD* 76). The queen has the distinctly German-sounding
name Hermutrude or Herminthrud, an example of the Danish tradition of "the
assigning of a German name" (Hansen 57) as a generic marker of
foreignness, and perhaps also a hint at Shakespeare's transformation of
Hamlet's mother's name, *Gerutha,* into *Gertrude.*[20]

Amleth's marriage to Hermutrude while he is still married to the British
princess – by whom he has a son (*HD* 77) – places him, like Feng before
him, in a questionable marriage situation, this time bigamy rather than incest
(see Hansen 188, note 41). However, Amleth's first wife, though "slighted
by the wrong of having a paramour put over her" (*HD* 77), still loves him
enough to warn him of her father's plot against his life. In battle against his
father-in-law, Amleth resorts to another clever ruse: arranging "some of the
dead bodies of his comrades... just as if they were about to engage" (*HD* 78)
to intimidate the British army into surrendering.[21]

The final fate of Saxo's Amleth prefigures that of Shakespeare's Hamlet
in that both meet their ends avenging the wrongs done to their mothers (cf.
Hamlet V.ii. 327) as well as to themselves. Amleth's final adversary is
Wiglek, successor to Rorik, who "harassed Amleth's mother with all manner
of insolence and stripped her of her royal wealth, complaining that her son
had usurped the kingdom of Jutland" (*HD* 78) and eventually challenged
Amleth to battle. Wiglek's challenge once again illustrates the Scandinavian
heroic values of honour and glory, even at the cost of the hero's own life, as
Amleth insists that by going into battle "he would not tarnish the
unblemished lustre of his fame by timidly skulking from his fate" (*HD* 79).
Amleth also displays concern for Hermutrude's fate should anything happen
to him; however, Hermutrude ends up an analogue to Gerutha/Gertrude in her
declaration "that the woman who dreaded to be united with her lord in death

---

[20] Hansen points out, however, that the name *Gertrude* "was known to both England and...
Denmark" (85) at the time Shakespeare wrote *Hamlet*. Malone notes that both Gerutha and
Hermutrude may have owed something to the Scandinavian legends of Yrsa, wife of Onela
(100-16; 230-41), and of "Offa...and his wife Þryð" (115).

[21] The closest, though unrelated, Shakespearean analogue to this detail is probably IV.iv-vi.
of *Macbeth*, in which "Birnam wood / Do come to Dunsinane" (V.v. 43-44).

was abominable"[22] (*HD* 79) only to offer herself to Wiglek upon Amleth's death. Hermutrude's marriage to Wiglek prompts a comment from the narrator on the mutability of women (*HD* 79), which Shakespeare would abridge to the single line, "Frailty, thy name is woman!" (*Hamlet* I.ii. 146); and the story itself ends with a brief elegy to Amleth and a reference to his burial place in Jutland, which has since been identified with "some two dozen different sites" (Hansen 189, n. 49), though most probably meant is "Ammelhede... in eastern Jutland" (Hansen 145).

François de Belleforest's *Histoires Tragiques*

Saxo's text did influence later Danish historical writings as well as works produced by authors elsewhere in Europe, especially following its first printing in Paris in 1514. Several anecdotes told by Saxo, especially the Hamlet story, were retold by the French writer François de Belleforest, who, as Julie Maxwell notes, was "Royal Historiographer of France [from] 1568-79" (518), in his anthology *Histoires Tragiques*,[23] published in seven volumes "between 1564 and 1582" (Bullough VII. 10). Belleforest's version of the Hamlet story, the one that apparently had the most direct influence on Shakespeare (Stabler, "Melancholy" 207), appears in the fifth volume of 1570 and was reprinted at least ten times over the next thirty years; in the wake of Shakespeare's play's popularity, it was translated into English in 1608 (Bullough VII. 11; M.A. Taylor 47; Maxwell 518) under the title *The Hystorie of Hamblet.* Although the title page of this work bears the legend "Imprinted by Richard Bradocke, for Thomas Pavier"[24] (*Hystorie* 81), the translator is unknown.

If Saxo's version of the Hamlet story shows intersections of the pagan and Christian worldviews, Belleforest's is more obviously a Christianized moral tale – in effect, a polemical revision of Saxo's text. This revision is demonstrated in his opening description of Danish society of Hamlet's time:

> Faut savoir que longtemps auparavant que le royaume de Dannemarch receut la foi de Jésus, et embrassast la doctrine et saint lavement des chrétiens, comme le

---

[22] Cf. the dialogue between the Player King and Queen in *Hamlet* III.ii. 154-228, but especially 179-80: "In second husband let me be accurs'd! / None wed the second but who kill'd the first."

[23] Hereafter cited as *HT*.

[24] Pavier also published editions of Thomas Kyd's *The Spanish Tragedy* and *The First Part of Hieronimo,* other texts that influenced Shakespeare's *Hamlet,* in 1602 and 1605, as well as, with the assistance of William Jaggard, unauthorized quarto editions of eight of Shakespeare's plays in 1619 (G.W. Williams 591).

peuple fut assez barbare et mal civilisé, aussi leurs Princes étaient cruels, sans foi ni loyauté, et qui ne jouoient qu'au boute-hors, tâchans à se jetter de leurs fieges, ou de s'offencer, fut en la robe ou en l'honneur, et le plus souvent en la vie, n'ayans guère de coutume de mettre à rançon leurs prisonniers, ains les sacrifoient à la cruelle vengeance, imprimée naturellement en leur âme. Que s'il y avait quelque bon Roi ou Prince... bien que le peuple l'eut en admiration (comme la vertu se rend admirable aux vicieux même) si est-ce que l'envie de ses voisins était si grande, qu'on ne cessait jamais jusqu'à tant que le monde fut dépêché de cet homme ainsi debonnaire. (*HT* 150)[25]

The prevalence in Belleforest's story of moral digressions and marginal comments on "the cruelty of the Danes" (*Hystorie* 85, note 4), as well as comparisons to similar examples from Biblical and classical histories, places a much greater critical distance – in more than one sense of the term – between his actual world and the world of the text than we find in Saxo, whose occasional and relatively mild criticisms of pre-Christian society do not overshadow "the patriotic pride of a Dane" (M.A. Taylor 49) evident in his narrative. Where Saxo takes great effort to set up the characters in his story as models of his society's views of good and evil, Belleforest constantly dismisses the characters as rude, uncivilized, and superstitious, and presents the textual world as an example by contrast to his actual world. By doing so, he hopes he will inspire his readers

non de les imiter, étant l'imitation peu de chose, mais à les surmonter, tout ainsi que notre Religion surpasse leur superstition, et notre siècle est plus purgé, subtil, et gaillard, que la saison qui les conduisant. (*HT* 191)[26]

---

[25] "You must understand, that long time before the kingdom of Denmark received the faith of Jesus Christ, and embraced the doctrine of the Christians, that the common people in those days were barbarous and uncivil and their princes cruel, without faith or loyalty, seeking nothing but murder, and deposing (or at the least) offending each other, either in honours, goods, or lives; not caring to ransom such as they took prisoners, but rather sacrificing them to the cruel vengeance naturally imprinted in their hearts: in such sort, that if there were sometime a good prince or king among them... although the people held him in admiration (as virtue is admirable to the most wicked) yet the envy of his neighbours was so great, that they never ceased until that virtuous man were dispatched out of the world" (*Hystorie* 85). All spelling in citations of Belleforest and the *Hystorie* has been modernized except where indicated.

[26] "not only to follow (imitation being a small matter), but to surmount them, as our religion surpasseth their superstition, and our age more purged, subtle, and gallant than the season wherein they lived and made their virtues known [literally, 'conducted themselves']" (*Hystorie* 124). The English translator seems less judgmental than Belleforest at this point.

Probably the most remarked-upon difference between Belleforest and Saxo, as well as the most obvious example of Belleforest's polemical revision of Saxo, is the contrast in their attitudes toward the remarriage of Amleth/Hamlet's mother. While both regard the remarriage as incestuous, a viewpoint that thus came down to Shakespeare, Belleforest does not follow Saxo's characterization of Gerutha (or Geruthe, as he spells her name) as a relative innocent in the matter whose "only fault [was] that she entered into a marriage with a brother-in-law" (M.A. Taylor 49). Rather, he dismisses her as

> celle malheureuse, qui avait reçu l'honneur d'être l'épouse d'un des plus vaillans et sages Princes de Septentrion, souffrit de s'abaisser jusques à telle villenie, que de lui fausser la foi: et qui pis est, épouser encore celui, lequel était le meurtrier tyran de son époux legitime: ce qui donna à penser à plusieurs, qu'elle pouvait avoir causé ce meurtre pour jouir librement de son adultère. (*HT* 153-54)[27]

He also makes the accusation, apparently unique to his version, that "Fengon, enhardi pour telle impunité, osa encore s'accoupler par mariage, à celle qu'il entretenait execrablement, durant la vie du bon Horwendille" (*HT* 153)[28]. Belleforest's charge against Geruthe leads Marion A. Taylor to note with some indignation that "Gertrude... has been turned from a good pagan woman into a criminal by the Christians" (47), influenced by long-standing feelings of misogyny which were still very much evident by the time Shakespeare wrote *Hamlet*. Interestingly, Belleforest's account of Amleth's and Geruthe's confrontation appears to be the first version of the work to hint at a possible Oedipal undercurrent to their relationship, as we are told that she sees "la vive image de sa vertu et sagesse en cet enfant, representant le hault coeur de son père" (*HT* 162).[29] But this passage also contains an element unique to Belleforest: unlike Saxo and Shakespeare, he allows Geruthe the chance

---

[27] "the unfortunate and wicked woman, that had received the honour to be the wife of one of the valiantest and wisest princes in the north, imbased herself to marry him, that had been the tyrannous murderer of her lawful husband; which made diverse men think that she had been the causer of the murder, thereby to live in her adultery without control" (*Hystorie* 88). The adjective "wicked" appears to be the addition of the translator, as Belleforest only uses the word "malheureuse" (unfortunate). Cf. *Hamlet* III.iv., and perhaps also *Richard III* I.ii. 227-63.

[28] "Fengon, boldened and encouraged by such impunity, durst venture to couple himself in marriage with her whom he used as his concubine during good Horvendile's life" (*Hystorie* 88).

[29] "the lively image and portraiture of his virtue and great wisdom in her child, representing his father's haughty and valiant heart" (*Hystorie* 98). Bullough suggests this passage may have influenced "the pictures at III.iv. 53-67" (*Hystorie* 98, n. 3).

to speak in her own defence. She insists – contrary to the narrator's assertions – that not only is she innocent in her first husband's death, but also that Fengon had forced her into marriage (*HT* 162-63; *Hystorie* 98-99).

Amleth's second wife, Hermutrude, also suffers under the misogyny of Belleforest's worldview. While Saxo had merely stated that she wanted to marry Amleth because "wedlock with the old she utterly abhorred, and desired the embraces of young men" (*HD* 75), Belleforest calls her an "Amazonne sans amitié, parant l'estomach à Cupidon" (*HT* 184),[30] and describes her intention: "priver la princesse Anglaise d'un mariage, que seule elle se pensait meriter" (*HT* 184).[31] Furthermore, Belleforest points out that not only did the Scottish queen give herself willingly to Wiglere – Belleforest's counterpart to Saxo's Wiglek – upon Amleth's death, but that "Hermetrude avait intelligence avec lui, et lui avait promis marriage, pourveu qu'il ostait des mains de celui qui la detenait" (*HT* 188).[32]

Much like his treatment of Geruthe and Hermutrude, Belleforest's judgment of Amleth himself is also influenced by the Christian moral framework of his fictional world. Although he favourably compares Amleth's pretended madness to that of "le Roi David, qui faignist le forcenué entre les Roitelers de Palestine, pour conserver sa vie" (*HT* 155),[33] he is quick to remind his readers that revenge, especially against a king, is contrary to the laws of both God and man, except in the case of "tyranny and treason" (Stabler, "Melancholy" 211; cf. *HT* 155; *Hystorie* 91). He further dismisses Amleth's "feats of clairvoyance" (Stabler, "Melancholy" 207) while in England as the result of demonic influence:

> veux que ce temps là tous ces pays Septentrionaux, étans sous l'obeissance de Sathan, il y avait une infinité d'enchanteurs.... il se trouve infinité que savent plus de choses que la sainteté de la religion chrétienne ne permet. (*HT* 168)[34]

According to A.P. Stabler ("Melancholy" 207-08), this passage and other such references may have influenced Shakespeare's Hamlet's suspicion, "The

---

[30] "Amazon without love, disdaining Cupid" (*Hystorie* 119).

[31] "deprive the English princess of her spouse, whom she thought fit for no men but herself" (*Hystorie* 119).

[32] "Hermetrude... had secret intelligence with him, and had promised him marriage, so that he would take her out of the hands of him that held her" (*Hystorie* 122).

[33] "King David that counterfeited the mad man among the petty kings of Palestine" (*Hystorie* 90).

[34] "for that in those days, the north parts of the world, living as then under Satan's laws, were full of enchanters... there are many that knew not what the Christian religion permitteth" (*Hystorie* 103).

spirit that I have seen / May be a devil, and the devil hath power / T'assume a pleasing shape" (*Hamlet* II.ii. 598-600), and thus his determination to prove Claudius's guilt.[35] Indeed, Belleforest's Amleth has no such need to prove Fengon's guilt, since Fengon had killed Horwendille in public, "at a banquet with his friends" (*Hystorie* 87).

Belleforest's view of Amleth's Denmark as a society ruled by superstition and (by the standards of his time) false belief sets up the possibility of supernatural elements active in the everyday world of his text. However, the most obvious such element familiar to us from Shakespeare's play, the ghost of Hamlet's father, does not actually appear in Belleforest's text, except for two brief and presumably metaphorical references to "les ombres de Horwendille" (*HT* 160; cf. Stabler, "King Hamlet's Ghost" 18-19). Similarly, the majority of Amleth's riddles – with the exception of the replies he gives to the British king (*HT* 166-72; *Hystorie* 103-07) – are also omitted, though that is most likely due to the difficulty of translating them into French. With these transformations of Saxo's text and its world, Belleforest's textual world begins to resemble that of a Senecan revenge tragedy, albeit one placed "in a predominantly Christian frame of reference" (Stabler, "Melancholy" 212), more than that of a Danish legendary history.

The strongest resemblances between Belleforest and Shakespeare come in the account of "L'Harangue d'Amleth à la Reine Geruthe sa mère" (*HT* 159)[36] and the death of Fengon's spy. In Belleforest's French text, the eavesdropper (still unnamed) hides "sous quelque loudier" (*HT* 158)[37] through which Amleth runs his sword, but the post-Shakespearean translation in the *Hystorie* not only places him "behind the arras" (94; *Hamlet* III.iii. 27) but also has Amleth say, "A rat, a rat!" (94; cf. *Hamlet* III.iv. 23) upon discovering his presence. Amleth's treatment of the spy's body follows Saxo's description (*HT* 158; *Hystorie* 94), but his address to his mother expands upon that in Saxo by "emphasiz[ing] the incest" (Bullough VII. 95, n. 6) as well as the animalistic aspects of Geruthe's second marriage. Belleforest, unlike Saxo or Shakespeare, also foreshadows Amleth's being sent to England, as Amleth asks his mother, "N'est-ce pas me trahir, quand... vous n'ayez su ou daigné trouver les moyens de sauver votre enfant,... plutôt l'exposer aux Anglais que le laisser la proye de votre infame adultere?"

---

[35] Bullough also likens Belleforest's references to demons to "the Witches in *Macbeth*" (*Hystorie* 104, n. 4).

[36] Chapter III of the *Hystorie* (93-101); cf. *Hamlet* III.iv.

[37] Under a quilt (Bullough VII. 94, note 2), an intermediary between the straw of Saxo's text and the curtain of Shakespeare's.

(*HT* 160-61).[38] While Saxo, Belleforest, and Shakespeare all emphasize the "Repentance de la Reine Geruthe" (*HT* 158) in her response to her son, Belleforest introduces a detail that appears in the First Quarto version of Shakespeare's play but not in the Folio or Second Quarto versions (Bertram and Kliman 172-76). According to Belleforest and the First Quarto of the play, Geruthe not only accepts her son's explanation "That I essentially am not in madness, / But mad in craft" (*Hamlet* III.iv. 187-88), but assures him that "puisque l'esprit étant sain, je vois les moyens plus aisez de la vengeance de ton père" (*HT* 162).[39]

Although Belleforest does not always share Saxo's valuing of honour and glory, and at times shows that he "does not understand the age of saga and its ethical code" (Bullough VII. 11), he does produce an eloquent restatement of the Danish belief that "la gloire est le salaire des vertueux" (*HT* 164)[40] in Amleth's final speech to Geruthe, which both Bullough and Stabler have read as the possible original of the best-known passage in Shakespeare's play, "the 'To be or not to be' speech" (Bullough VII. 100, n. 4; cf. Stabler, "Melancholy" 210-11). Belleforest's version of the speech begins with a passage justifying revenge against Fengon as being "ne... trahison ni felonnie, lui n'étant point mon Roi ni seigneur... mon vassal, qui s'est forfait desloyaument contre son seigneur et souverain prince" (*HT* 164).[41] But it is in Amleth's declaration:

> il faut ou qu'une fin glorieuse mette fin à mes jours, ou que les armes au poing, chargé de triomphe et victoire, je ravisse la vie à ceux qui rendent la mienne malheureuse, et obsurcissent les rayons de celle vertu que je tiens du sang et mémoire illustre de mes predecesseurs (*HT* 164-65)[42]

that we see the inspiration for Hamlet's pondering "Whether 'tis nobler in the mind to suffer / The slings and arrows of outrageous fortune, / Or to take arms against a sea of troubles, / And by opposing end them" (*Hamlet* III.i.

---

[38] "Is not this as much as if you should betray me, when you... have not once sought, nor desired to find the means to save your child... by sending him into... England [literally, 'exposing him to the English'], rather than to leave him as a prey to your infamous adulterer?" (*Hystorie* 96).

[39] "seeing that thy senses are whole and sound, I am in hope to see an easy means invented for the revenging of thy father's death" (*Hystorie* 99).

[40] "glory is the reward of the virtuous" (*Hystorie* 100).

[41] "neither... felony nor treason, he being neither my king nor my lord, but... my subject, that hath disloyally behaved himself against his lord and sovereign prince" (*Hystorie* 100).

[42] "it must necessarily follow, that either a glorious death will be mine end, or with my sword in hand, (laden with triumph and victory) I darkened the beams of that virtue which I possessed from the blood and famous memory of my predecessors" (*Hystorie* 100).

56-59). However, where Shakespeare's version can be, and has been, read as a reference either to suicide or to vengeance, Belleforest's is more clearly a statement of vengeance with just cause, a theme to which he returns several times in his story.

Like Saxo, Belleforest makes the final part of the story into an ironic reversal, but he does so in two ways. The first, as we have seen, is Amleth's second marriage, which Saxo also treats in detail; the second is that Belleforest specifically identifies Wiglere as "son oncle, et fils de Rorique, ayant osté les trésors royaux à Geruthe sa sœur" (*HT* 187).[43] Thus, just as Amleth finds himself in a questionable marriage after having dealt with that of his mother, he now also becomes the target of a plot by yet another ambitious uncle, this time on his mother's side of the family rather than his father's.[44] However, Belleforest does not make much of Wiglere's relation to Amleth nor its parallel to that of Fengon; rather, he expands upon Saxo's treatment of Hermetrude's unfaithfulness as a significant factor in Amleth's downfall (*HT* 188-90; *Hystorie* 121-23). The parallel between Wiglere and Fengon disappears entirely in Shakespeare's treatment, as Wiglere becomes Fortinbras, who is more a counterpart to Hamlet than to Claudius.

Unlike Saxo, Belleforest makes explicit references to various literary, mythical, and historical incidents that form parallels to the story, several of which have been discussed above. However, the most interesting intertextual reference in Belleforest's account is the comparison of Amleth to his Roman counterpart – and perhaps his original – Brutus (*HT* 155; *Hystorie* 90), described in a marginal note as "reputé sage pour contre faire le fol" (*HT* 155).[45] Near the end of his story, Belleforest also acknowledges that "Saxon grammairien a écrit ce discours" (*HT* 190), thus presenting his history as a retelling of Saxo's original.

The Revenge Tragedy, *The Spanish Tragedy*, and *Hamlet*

Belleforest's account of Amleth/Hamlet was a significant step in the transposition of Saxo's 'legendary history' of early medieval Denmark to the concerns of Renaissance Europe. Its popularity with readers was in part due to the enduring appeal of the revenge narrative in Western literary/dramatic

---

[43] "his uncle, and son to Roderick, having taken the royal treasure from his sister Geruthe" (*Hystorie* 121).

[44] Gunnar Sjögren cites a reference in the *Danish Rhymed Chronicle* of 1495 that refers to Wiglek/Wiglere as "Amleth's second stepfather" (14), who kills Amleth because "he wanted the kingdom for himself" (14). Another version of the story places the fight between Wiglek/Wiglere and Amleth "on the Sound of Denmark... not far from Elsinore" (Sjögren 18).

[45] "esteemed wise for counterfeiting the fool" (*Hystorie* 90, n. 4).

tradition, marked by a desire on the part of readers/audiences for fictional worlds in which justice was swift and decisive, with little or no "dissatisfaction with the state's ability to intervene in an effective manner" (Simkin 2), a dissatisfaction that was, and is, all too common in the actual world. The revenge story also allowed for the representation of the inner psychological worlds of character and reader/spectator alike, acknowledging "that at the core of human nature there is a volcano of smouldering rage" (Hallett and Hallett 7) which requires socially-acceptable outlets for both expression and comprehension.

At the same time, the tragic nature of the revenge narrative served as a reminder of the costs of vengeance and thus, to some degree, as a potential deterrent. As Katharine Eisaman Maus observes, the protagonists of English revenge tragedies are generally unable to enjoy the fruits of their labours because "their own deaths follow so quickly upon the wreaking of vengeance that they have no time to install themselves in place of their enemies" (89). The death of the revenge tragedy's hero in the process of obtaining vengeance is itself an outgrowth of the fictional world's moral framework in which "Providence... requires the avenger's death" (Hallett and Hallett 98) to atone for the loss of innocents during the enactment of revenge, as well as a reminder to the reader/audience of the dangers of taking the law into one's own hands.

In their study of the characteristics and appeal of the revenge tragedy in sixteenth- and seventeenth-century English literature, Charles and Elaine Hallett identify a series of motifs and symbols which have become, in effect, the constitutive properties of the genre of Elizabethan/Jacobean revenge tragedy and the fictional worlds such works embody:

> those conventional elements of the Elizabethan stage – the ghost, the madness, the delay, the play-within-a-play, the multiple murders, and the avenger's death – which have been recognized as appearing with such surprising frequency in the revenge tragedies as to be particularly characteristic of them. (8)

According to the Halletts, these symbols draw attention to the supernatural, psychological, and metafictional nature of the revenge tragedy. The appearance of a ghost or related entity, such as the Greek Furies, spurring the protagonist to action suggests the presence both of "a force in the universe" (8) demanding the restoration of order and justice, and of "the revenger's own passion... push[ing] the revenger into madness" (9), ironically disregarding rationality and/or the law in order to accomplish his/her goal. The use of a play-within-a-play is an analogue to the protagonist's questioning of his/her actual world, as well as a self-referential acknowledgment "that every play creates its own world and defines its own reality" (Hallett and Hallett 10). Just as the author of the play creates a fictional world to illuminate some aspect(s) of his/her actual world, so does the protagonist of the play create his/her own fictional world, embedded in the fictional world in which he/she operates, to represent the changes in his/her internal world. However, the multiple-world constructs of both madness and metatheatricality also illustrate the danger of "confusing the real world with a world created out of [the character's] own psyche which he has projected upon it" (Hallett and Hallett 10). This sort of confusion is represented in the play's world by the excesses to which the revenger is prepared to go, and in the actual world by the frequent objections of certain readers who fear that fictional/dramatic representations of "violence and revenge" (Joseph 121) may inspire other readers/audience members to imitate these behaviours in reality.[46]

The revenge tragedy as it existed in Elizabethan England was greatly influenced by the plays of Seneca, especially after their translation into English in Thomas Newton's *Seneca, His Ten Tragedies* in 1581 (Bullough VII. 159-65; cf. Bullough VII. 24-26; Joseph 121-24). Indeed, in Shakespeare's *Hamlet*, the First Player's recitation of "the rugged Pyrrhus" (II.ii. 450-64, 468-97, 502-18) appears to have been based on Jasper Heywood's translation of Seneca's *Troas* (Bullough VII. 163-65). Many of the common features of revenge tragedies identified by the Halletts appear in Seneca's plays; however, in part because Seneca wrote for recitation rather than for performance as we are familiar with it, these plays are also characterized by "black and white character drawing, ferocious villains, milkwhite victims, ghastly descriptions, Byronic [or, more properly, proto-Byronic] defiance, [and] flamboyant repartee" (Beare 113), as well as long narrative passages "to permit the audience to visualize the events it does not actually see" (P.B. Murray 12). In adopting and adapting the Senecan form for use in English drama, Elizabethan playwrights did borrow many of the excesses, language-wise and plot-wise, of Seneca's writing, but they also borrowed dramatic conventions such as the five-act structure, the use of soliloquies and choruses (Beare 113-14), and narrative passages to condense the sweeping action of the play into the time and space available.

The first great revenge tragedy in English literature was Thomas Kyd's *The Spanish Tragedy,*[47] believed to have been written around 1587 and first

---

[46] Such a reading, which runs contrary to the Aristotelian concept of catharsis, does raise the question of exactly who – reader, author, character, or critic – is confusing the fictional world with the actual one. Compare the amateur actors' comments in *A Midsummer Night's Dream* III.i. 9-46.

[47] Hereafter cited as *ST.*

published in 1592 (Cairncross xiii, xxxi). While much has already been said about the similarities between this play and Shakespeare's *Hamlet* (see e.g. Bullough VII. 15-18; Joseph 121-34; Erne 146-56), a comparison of these two plays as counterpart texts is still useful in tracing the development of the Shakespearean fictional world. Though not a Hamlet play in itself, *The Spanish Tragedy* marked the introduction of several key elements in the fictional world familiar to us from Shakespeare's play, both directly and through the 'missing link' between the two texts, the so-called *Ur-Hamlet* (Hunt 22-30), which was so named "following the usage of German scholars in analogy to Goethe's *Ur-Faust*" (Erne 146).

Like those of Saxo and Belleforest, Kyd's fictional world is a hybrid of pagan – in this case, classical Greco-Roman – and Christian worldviews. This combination of worldviews is displayed most prominently in the opening scene, in which the ghost of Andrea describes his descent into the underworld and his meeting with the judges of the dead (*ST* I.i. 18-85) in terms very reminiscent of Book VI of Virgil's *Aeneid* (Cairncross 60). By contrast, although the ghost of Hamlet's father alludes to the "sulphurous and tormenting flames" (*Hamlet* I.v. 3) of either hell or purgatory, depending on the reading, he also admits he is "forbid / To tell the secrets of my prison-house" (*Hamlet* I.v. 13-14) and "this eternal blazon must not be / To ears of flesh and blood" (*Hamlet* I.v. 21-22). The presence of a personification of Revenge as Andrea's companion and fellow "Chorus in this tragedy" (*ST* I.i. 91) further connects Kyd's fictional world to those of Seneca by transposing the classical figures of "Nemesis and the Furies" (Hallett and Hallett 21) into the Renaissance world. At the same time, Kyd's use of two ghost-figures, one the victim of a particular crime and the other an embodiment of a general concept, also powerfully illustrates the process by which a single act – Andrea's death in the previous play, *The First Part of Hieronimo*[48] (*Hieronimo* xi. 107-11; *ST* I.ii. 22-84) – sets in motion a series of all-consuming events. Unlike King Hamlet, Andrea never speaks directly to any of the characters and serves primarily as a framing narrator connecting the spiritual to the physical world, and the textual world(s) to the actual world. Despite the lack of direct interaction between Andrea and the other characters, his simultaneous absence as a living man and presence as a ghost

---

[48] The questions of which play appeared first and whether Kyd wrote both plays need not concern us here. Andrew Cairncross treats both plays as Kyd's, with the extant text of *Hieronimo* a memorial reconstruction similar to the first quarto of Shakespeare's *Hamlet* (xiv-xxxiii). Lukas Erne, following the views of Rudolf Fischer and F.S. Boas, believes that *Hieronimo* is a reworking, probably even a parody, of *The Spanish Tragedy* and/or a lost original.

is still felt throughout the play, especially after the murder of his successor in both life and death, Horatio (*ST* II.iv. 50-63).

Whether Shakespeare named Hamlet's confidant Horatio after Kyd's character is uncertain, but both characters do serve similar functions in their respective texts. Both are "faithful friend[s]" (Bullough VII. 17) to their texts' respective avenger-figures (see e.g. *ST* I.iv.; *Hamlet* I.ii. 160-75), although Kyd's Horatio ends up a victim in need of revenge himself, while Shakespeare's lives to tell the tale.

The parallels between Kyd's and Shakespeare's avenger-protagonists, Hieronimo and Hamlet, are much more obvious, as both not only seek revenge for the deaths of loved ones but also come to question whether justice is obtainable or even possible in their respective worlds. At the beginning of *The Spanish Tragedy*, Hieronimo becomes "an officer of the law... in favour of legal justice or the justice of the heavens" (Cairncross xxvii), only to have the King favour Andrea's murderer Balthazar over Horatio (*ST* I.ii.); and with Horatio's murder in Act II, scene v, Hieronimo rejects justice in favour of personal vengeance, declaring, "To know the author were some ease of grief / For in revenge my heart would find relief" (40-41). Both Hieronimo and Hamlet also display signs of madness, a common trait for the protagonists of revenge tragedies, although it is far more certain that Hieronimo's madness is indeed genuine (e.g. *ST* III.xii. 5-6; cf. III.xiiA. 42-53). Indeed, some early printings of the play gave it the subtitle *Hieronimo Is Mad Again*.

Hieronimo's greatest influence on Hamlet, however, is evident in both dramatists' use of soliloquies to establish and develop their protagonists' characters, as well as their use of plays within plays as means of enacting revenge. Hieronimo's two great speeches, "Oh eyes!... / Oh life!... / Oh world!" (*ST* III.ii. 1-52) and "Vindicta mihi!" (*ST* III.xiii. 1-45), are in many ways ancestors of Hamlet's "To be or not to be" (*Hamlet* III.i. 55-87): all three speeches occupy central positions in their respective plays both literally and figuratively, and each outlines the ways in which each character evaluates and questions the working of his respective world (P.B. Murray 124-30). As Peter B. Murray notes, all three passages compare the characters' "two related desires for suicide and revenge, for self-destruction and for destruction of others" (92). But where they differ is that, although it takes both Hieronimo and Hamlet the remainder of their respective plays to accomplish their goals, the reasons for their delays – aside, of course, from dramatic necessity – are different. Horatio's murder occurs in the middle of *The Spanish Tragedy*, and Hieronimo's plan to avenge him – and Andrea – with the help of Bel-imperia occupies much of the rest of the play;

conversely, King Hamlet's murder occurs before the start of *Hamlet,* and the main action of the play concerns Hamlet's inaction and delay.

Shakespeare's expansion of the various nameless secondary characters in Saxo's and Belleforest's histories owes something to Kyd's use of the Duke of Castile's family as parallels to Hieronimo's, especially to the Duke's children, Bel-imperia and Lorenzo, as possible counterparts to Ophelia and Laertes. However, Bel-imperia, as her name suggests, is a far less passive character than Ophelia, as she goes so far as killing Balthazar and then herself as part of Hieronimo's revenge plot (*ST* IV.iv. 59-67), while Lorenzo bears a more noticeable resemblance to Laertes in his willingness to resort to murder to uphold his family's honour (*ST* III.x. 35-39; cf. *Hamlet* IV.vii.). In a similar fashion, Hieronimo's wife Isabella provides a partial inspiration for Ophelia's madness, with her reaction to the death of her son (*ST* III.viii., IV.ii.; cf. *Hamlet* IV.v.).

Both Kyd and Shakespeare use the device of a play-within-a-play as an example and comment on embedded fictional worlds as well as on the overlap of the fictional and actual worlds. In both cases, the protagonists are inspired to incorporate plays into their revenge plans when they see or hear representations – a painting for Hieronimo, a dramatic passage for Hamlet – of the fall of Troy (*ST* III.xiiA 80-161; *Hamlet* II.ii. 450-605). But where Hamlet means for his play to "catch the conscience of the King" (II.ii. 605) and trick him into admitting his guilt, Hieronimo uses the play itself as the instrument by which he and Bel-imperia gain revenge for Horatio's and Andrea's deaths by killing Lorenzo and Balthazar during the actual performance (*ST* IV.iv. 11-67) and revealing the initial crime afterward in order to justify ending the play with an actual murder-suicide (*ST* IV.iv. 73-152). In this way, Kyd subverts the expectations of both characters and audience by deliberately breaking down the boundary between fictional worlds, while Shakespeare does so only in a figurative sense.

Hamlet and Shakespeare's Contemporary History

The aesthetic appeal of the revenge tragedy was not the only, nor even the most significant, reason for the popularity of the Hamlet story in Shakespeare's England. As previously mentioned, the story "would have considerable topicality... after the execution of Mary Queen of Scots" (Bullough VII. 18), the marriage of Mary's son James VI to Anne of Denmark, and James's accession to the English throne as James I. Shakespeare, of course, was no stranger to fictionalized analogies between historical and contemporary events, as his history plays and Roman tragedies demonstrate; and, indeed, several scholars, beginning with James Plumptre in 1796 (Johnston 180-186), suggest that he may have intended Hamlet as a counterpart of James I and/or of the Earl of Essex, who, prior to his failed rebellion and execution in 1601, was known to have supported James's claim to the English throne (Winstanley 38).

While the traditional, idealized portrait of Hamlet is at first glance difficult for many readers then and now to reconcile with the rather unromantic James, there are in fact several reasons for treating them as possible counterparts. The most obvious such reason centers on the death of James's father, Lord Darnley, who "was assassinated... by the Earl of Bothwell in February [1567].[49] In May, the same year, Mary Stuart married that very Earl of Bothwell, the murderer of her husband" (Schmitt 16). Though more recent treatments of Mary's life, such as Retha M. Warnicke's 2006 biography, have stated that Bothwell probably forced her into marrying him (146-62; cf. Belleforest, *HT* 162-63), popular sentiment among English and Scottish Protestants of the time held that Mary herself may have been involved in the murder or at least approved of it (Winstanley 67; Schmitt 16; Warnicke 144-45, 174-77). This belief was not only due to her "o'erhasty marriage" (*Hamlet* II.ii. 57) to Bothwell, but also to her falling-out with Darnley after another incident that has an echo in Shakespeare's *Hamlet*: the murder of her advisor, David Rizzio, in March 1566, while she was pregnant with the future James I. According to James Anthony Froude, Rizzio's murder by agents of Lord Darnley took place "in a closet... in the queen's presence" (qtd. in Winstanley 111; cf. Warnicke 112-20). This is very similar to the death of Polonius as Shakespeare describes it in Act III, scene iv. of his play; furthermore, the Italian-born Rizzio's position as a foreigner at court also provides him with another similarity to Polonius, whose name means 'from Poland.'[50] As for Bothwell, he spent the latter years of his life, following Mary's abdication and during her long imprisonment in England, as a prisoner in Denmark, where he went insane and died in 1578 (Bullough VII. 126, n. 1; Warnicke 212-13). According to William Preston Johnston, "When Bothwell was captured in 1567, he was taken before Eric Rosencrantz, Governor of Bergen" (219), and one of the witnesses to his death in prison was "one 'M. Gullanstarn'" (219), an alternate spelling of *Guildenstern*.

---

[49] Schmitt's original text has 1566, in keeping with the practice in Renaissance Britain of beginning the year in March.

[50] More specifically, Polonius may be from Danzig (Gdánsk); as Sjögren (46-49) and Hansen (84-85) both point out, "Danskers" (II.i. 7) means both 'from Denmark' and 'from Danzig.'

The lives and deaths of Mary's husbands and herself quickly inspired numerous occasional ballads and verses; one in particular bears some resemblance to portions of Shakespeare's *Hamlet*. Shortly after Mary's execution in 1587, "John Gordon, a relative of the Queen and... First Gentleman of the Chamber to Henri III" of France (Bullough VII. 19), wrote a Latin poem addressed to James VI, entitled *Henrici Scotorum Regis Manes ad Jacobum VI Filium,* or *The Shade of Henry, King of Scotland* [i.e. Lord Darnley], *to His Son James VI.* Although it is uncertain whether Shakespeare knew this poem, its dominant image of a murdered king calling upon his son for revenge is a definite foreshadowing to the Ghost in *Hamlet*, as well as a Scottish analogue to the well-known anthology of English historical poetry (and source for Shakespeare's history plays), *A Mirror for Magistrates* (Bullough VII. 19).

Darnley's ghost, as narrator of the poem, accuses both Mary and Bothwell of his murder, in a similar manner to the accusations of King Hamlet's ghost against Claudius:

> And thou my wife, dearer to me than breath,
> Whose heart so changed against me on behalf
> Of a vile rascal pardoned in despite
> Of Lords' just anger and the People's wrongs!
> To thee, the evil life of such a boor
> Was aphrodisiac until, forgot
> Both royal fame and queen's decorum, thou,
> First trying me with poison, drov'st out fear
> Soon from thy mind, then murdered'st me with flames! (J. Gordon 125-26)

Both Gordon and Shakespeare refer to the respective murderers, Bothwell and Claudius, in similar terms – as "vile adulterer" (J. Gordon 126) or "that incestuous, that adulterate beast" (*Hamlet* I.v. 42) – though they differ over how directly each queen, Mary or Gertrude, was involved in her respective previous husband's murder. Gordon notes that Mary had "lived / Near twenty years 'neath watchful guard, [and] at last /... felt the headsman's axe" (126-27) both for Darnley's murder and for her intent (real or perceived) "to raise her steel against / Her cousin-german" Elizabeth I (126). Because of this, Gordon asserts that further vengeance against Mary would be unnecessary. However, Shakespeare's Ghost's insistence that Hamlet "leave [Gertrude] to heaven, / And to those thorns that in her bosom lodge, / To prick and sting her" (*Hamlet* I.v. 86-88), does not explicitly tie Gertrude to King Hamlet's murder, but only to her remarriage to Claudius.

Gordon never directly mentions James's claim to the English throne, so whether he intended his poem to encourage James to assert his claim as

Elizabeth I's successor is uncertain. He seems more obviously to have meant the poem as an exemplum, much in the manner of the poems in *A Mirror for Magistrates*, combining direct advice to the poem's addressee with a narrative account of the incident from which the poem's lesson is drawn. Darnley's advice to James is to honour his father's example,[51] and defy Bothwell's supporters, by avoiding the mistakes Mary made:

> to seek
> Justice o'er all, and ne'er despise the gods.
> Fly the approach of prudent flatterers, prudent fly
> As well as canst the sting of envious tongues.
> What aids the realm, or profit shall demand,
> Or gives the people health, be strong to urge.
> Ignore the rest, secure from rumours base;
> Vain, Son, thy work if aught thou seek beside.
> Nor should thy mother's death move thee so deep
> As thou rejoic'st thy sire's death is avenged.
> (J. Gordon 127)

Although Gordon's poem shows definite parallels to Shakespeare's depiction of the ghost of King Hamlet, it is unusual among contemporary views of James I as an avenger in its focus on his father's murder. His status as "the direct successor of the queen who sixteen years before had his mother executed" (Schmitt 18) – even though Elizabeth had "reluctantly agreed [to the execution] under pressure from her advisors" (Warnicke 254) after a considerable delay – was far more commonly emphasized. Elizabeth's admitted reluctance (and the sincerity, or not, thereof) aside, however, a play dealing directly with Mary's execution would have been considered too politically sensitive during a time of "extreme tension and incertitude... caused by the issue of the succession to the crown" (Schmitt 17). This was especially so because of the possibility that literary/dramatic treatments might seek to portray Elizabeth as the villain of the piece, the Claudius to Mary's King Hamlet, much as Gordon's poem did with Bothwell and Darnley.

Thus, both of James's parents appear to have left their mark upon Shakespeare's King Hamlet. By drawing upon Darnley's murder and Mary's marriage to Bothwell to flesh out the characters of King Hamlet, Gertrude, and Claudius, Shakespeare could "make [Claudius, Bothwell, and/or Mary] appear... as the victim of a just retribution" (Johnston 173). Also, by playing, albeit prudently and indirectly, on Mary's execution and James's relationship

---

[51] Bullough, however, notes that Gordon's fictionalized and idealized Darnley "assum[ed] an innocence which he lacked in life" (VII. 18).

to both queens, he could lend his voice, through the medium of a fictionalized counterpart world, to the succession debate while still avoiding explicit mention of "the taboo of the queen" (Schmitt 12). The Pyrrhic victory of Hamlet followed by the triumph of Fortinbras could also help to symbolize James's accession as a peaceful form of revenge, a striking contrast to the violent end of the play.

But it is James's wife, Anne of Denmark, who was probably a more immediate influence on the Hamlet story as it was known to Elizabethan/Jacobean audiences. As mentioned above, the marriage of James and Anne could be read as a gender-reversed real-world parallel of sorts to Amleth's two marriages to princesses of England and Scotland. Even the actual circumstances of James and Anne's marriage have parallels to Shakespeare's telling of the Hamlet story. Their difficult voyages between Scotland and Denmark (E.C. Williams 15-28) bear some resemblance to Hamlet's journey through stormy and pirate-infested waters to England (*Hamlet* IV.vi. 13-22), and, as Gunnar Sjögren notes, "James... married Anne... in Oslo, the capital of Norway. The wedding ceremony was later repeated at Kronborg, Elsinore" (20). Shakespeare's reference to the Danes' proverbial fondness for drink (*Hamlet* I.iv. 7-38) has been read as a possible, if remote, allusion to the death of Anne's father, Frederick II, "in 1588, from an excess of alcohol" (Sjögren 37). Furthermore, the union of Denmark and Norway under Fortinbras at the end of the play displays some similarities to the union of England and Scotland under James I – despite the relative lack of violence surrounding James's accession – making him a counterpart to both Hamlet and Fortinbras. Aside from their similarities to James, Hamlet and Fortinbras could also have been seen by contemporaries as the semi-legendary ancestors of Anne of Denmark, "just as Richmond [in *Richard III*]... was the ancestor of Queen Elizabeth, and... Banquo [in *Macbeth*]... was... of James I" (Sjögren 20).

The reasons for treating Hamlet and James as counterparts go beyond historical and biographical parallels. Many adherents of the Hamlet/James counterpart theory have also noted the similarities in their personalities, belief systems, and actions; the most comprehensive and compelling study of these similarities appears in Lilian Winstanley's *Hamlet and the Scottish Succession*. Winstanley notes that Hamlet's "hesitancy and delay combined with sudden vigour in emergencies is just precisely the character of James I as it appeared to his contemporaries" (76), including Elizabeth I, who in her letters often criticized him for showing too much mercy to his enemies (Winstanley 77-83). Both Hamlet and James also shared an interest in philosophy and theology, especially the Protestant side of the Catholic/Protestant debates of the time; indeed, James himself wrote a treatise on demonology that, while well known as an inspiration for the witches in *Macbeth,* may also have partly influenced Hamlet's ponderings of the nature of his father's ghost (*Hamlet* II.ii. 598-603; cf. Schmitt 25; Stabler, "Melancholy" 207-08). In addition, the odd discrepancies between the traditional characterization of Hamlet as a brooding young man of about sixteen (Roth par. 18-28) and his descriptions in Act V as thirty years old (*Hamlet* V.i. 162), "fat, and scant of breath" (*Hamlet* V.ii. 287), while most likely indicating a conflation of time similar to those in Shakespeare's history plays and in Saxo Grammaticus's history (De Grazia 83), also serve to evoke both James I and Richard Burbage, the first actor to play Hamlet. Both Burbage and James were in their thirties "when *Hamlet* was first produced" (Winstanley 96), and James was often described by contemporaries as having "a ridiculous pot-belly on stick-like legs, with a hanging tongue and the eyes of a dullard" (Schmitt 26).

For the more romantic aspects of Hamlet's character that bear little or no resemblance to James's, Shakespeare appears to have found another historical counterpart, and one suggested by the majority of the adherents of the Hamlet/James analogy theory: "the influence exerted by the personality and destiny of the Earl of Essex" (Schmitt 22). Winstanley notes that Essex, like Hamlet, was characterized as studious, melancholy, and "irresolute almost to the point of insanity" (142), especially around the time of his unsuccessful rebellion against Elizabeth I that probably coincided with the writing of *Hamlet.* Furthermore, he also shared with Hamlet an interest in the theatre both as an art form and "for political purposes" (Winstanley 145), the most infamous example being his commission of a production of Shakespeare's *Richard II* on February 7, 1601, "the very eve of his ill-starred rebellion" (Baker 803). It is quite possible that Shakespeare, who was fortunate to escape blame (though not censorship) in this incident, had this performance and Elizabeth's reaction "I am Richard II; know ye not that?" (qtd. in Hulse 99) in mind as he made Hamlet say, "The play's the thing / Wherein I'll catch the conscience of the king" (*Hamlet* II.ii. 604-05). Even Hamlet's and Rosencrantz's seemingly out-of-place digression on the theatrical fashion of the day (*Hamlet* II.ii. 329-62) alludes to the consequences of the performance, as Shakespeare's company was temporarily barred from performing in London and had to tour the smaller towns.

Shakespeare's use of Polonius's family as counterparts to Hamlet's may also have been partly inspired by members of Essex's circle, with Laertes as an analogue to Sir Walter Raleigh (Winstanley 148-50) and Ophelia a possible reference to "Elizabeth Vernon, the wife of [the Earl of] Southampton, and Lady Essex" (Winstanley 131; cf. Sjögren 69-70). This may to some degree explain Shakespeare's expansion of what were very minor characters in Saxo's history into full-blown parallel characters and plotlines to the play's main storyline. As well, Essex's last words before his execution, "Lift my soul above all earthly cogitations, and when my soul and body shall part, send Thy blessed angels to be near unto me, which may convey it to the joys of heaven" (qtd. in Schmitt 58, n. 17), are very reminiscent of Horatio's elegy to Hamlet at the end of the play, "Now cracks a noble heart. Good night, sweet prince, / And flights of angels sing thee to thy rest!" (*Hamlet* V.ii. 359-60).

Of course, Shakespeare's play is more than merely a sum of contemporary allusions transposed to an earlier foreign setting; and recognizing parallels between the fictional world of *Hamlet* and the actual world of Shakespeare, Essex, and James I is not simply a return to the sort of "mimetic interpretation... to assign to a fictional entity an actual prototype" (Doležel, *Heterocosmica* 6) that fictional-world theory was meant to resist. Identifying these parallels also does not and should not mean reductively reading the play as 'Stuart propaganda,' the way some historians have attempted to reduce Shakespeare's history plays and their sources to 'Tudor propaganda' (see Murph 2-23). William Preston Johnston seems mostly to regard the contemporary political undercurrents of *Hamlet* in this manner, arguing that Shakespeare – especially considering Essex's use of *Richard II* – could have meant *Hamlet* for a similar purpose to its own interpolated play, the Mousetrap: "A play that should stir the minds and hearts of the Court, then the centre of intellectual and political activity... to palliate, excuse, or justify, such a doubtful political act as the execution of a sovereign of a sister country" (173-74), or even to remind Elizabeth of her role in Mary's execution. Winstanley agrees with Johnston about the parallels between *Hamlet* and the Mousetrap, but sees the play's "political motive... [as] simply the endeavour to excite as much sympathy as possible for the Essex conspirators, and for the Scottish succession" (180). While reading *Hamlet* as a political allegory is certainly possible in its original context, treating it as the dramatic equivalent of a *roman à clef* of the stories of Mary Queen of Scots, James I, and the Earl of Essex, in much the same manner that the Mousetrap functions in the world of *Hamlet* itself, "would be not only unartistic but also politically impossible" (Schmitt 21). Rather, the Hamlet/James/Essex connections are more properly examples of what Carl Schmitt calls "irruptions" (23) of the actual world into the fictional world: concerns of one informing the other in ways that enrich both the fictional text and the actual context. According to this reading, Shakespeare chose the Hamlet story as a way of commenting upon his contemporary history from the safe critical distance of a similar yet sufficiently different fictional world, and he also used his actual world as inspiration to make the fictional world presented in the earlier versions of the Hamlet story more relevant for his immediate audience.

As time passed and the play became known beyond its immediate audience, writers and directors saw the need to continue the adaptation processes that helped to create the play and its world. This was especially the case for the reception of Shakespeare's plays in the non-English-speaking world, where the difference between languages was often equaled by that between dramatic traditions. Translations of *Hamlet* thus continue another process that shaped the Shakespearean text and its world: not only are they more links in the chain of adaptation, but they also follow up on the successive translations of the Hamlet story, from Scandinavian oral tradition, to Saxo's Latin history, to Belleforest's French morality tale, to Shakespeare's English tragedy.

CHAPTER THREE

TRANSLATIONS AND/AS ADAPTATIONS

> His name's Gonzago, the story is extant, and written in
> very choice Italian. You shall see anon how the murtherer
> gets the love of Gonzago's wife.
>
> (*Hamlet* III.ii. 262-64)

The Possible Worlds of Translation

Translations have much in common with adaptations, and indeed can be
regarded as instances of adaptations themselves, because both are ways in
which writers create new literary worlds from the raw material of existing
texts. However, a distinctive feature of translation as opposed to other forms
of adaptation is that in producing a translation, the translator creates two new
counterpart worlds at the same time: one in which the characters and/or
narrator (where present) of the original text speak in the translator's language,
and one in which the author of the original text writes according to the
linguistic and cultural norms of the translator's society. Depending on the
approach and purpose of the translation, a third counterpart world in which
the translator writes according to the linguistic and cultural norms of the
original author's society can also come into being. While translations
generally seek "to preserve the fictional world in its extensional structuring
and, as far as possible, its intensional structuring as well" (Doležel,
Heterocosmica 205) – that is, to retain as much of the denotative and
connotative meanings of the original as prosodic, linguistic, and cultural
differences will allow – translations transform the original as much as they
preserve it, and translators, especially when treating a well-established
original text such as *Hamlet*, can use this paradox to their advantage in
seeking to transform not only the fictional world of the text but their actual
world as well. In this way the translation can become an act of either
conformity to or resistance against the sociocultural and/or linguistic norms
under which it is produced.

In a study of French translations of Shakespeare's plays, Romy Heylen
notes that the aims of translators can be characterized in two different modes,
referred to as "exoticizing/naturalizing" or "historicizing/modernizing" (16-

17). The former is a scale of cultural accessibility, and the latter of sociohistorical accessibility; and in each case, the translator must navigate the "different sets of cultural norms and values" (Heylen 21) of his/her own society and that of the author of the original text. Like all adaptations, translations may range from those that attempt to remain as culturally neutral as possible – though of course no translation can ever be considered completely neutral – to those that, much like Hamlet's reworking of the "very choice Italian" (*Hamlet* III.ii. 263) play *The Murder of Gonzago* into the Mousetrap, "deliberately distort or appropriate the source-language work to suit the translator's political or cultural agenda" (De Lotbinière-Harwood 98). However, the most significant challenges to translators are the inherent differences between the source and target languages. Each language has not only its own grammatical, syntactic, and semantic systems but also its own prosody and poetic forms, and these are often as unlike each other as Platonic and Aristotelian metaphysics, to use Yves Bonnefoy's characterizations of the respective essences of French and English (cf. Heylen 105-08).

All of these factors contribute to the decisions of translators over whether to adhere as closely as possible to the literal meaning of the text and ignore poetry entirely, to attempt to recreate something of the source text's prosody in the target language, and/or to create an equivalent to the source text using the target language's usual prosodic forms. In the case of a Shakespearean text being translated into a language other than English, there is also the question of whether to use the sixteenth-century form of the target language or the translator's contemporary form.

On his experiences translating Shakespeare into Spanish, Manuel Ángel Conejero says:

> we are talking about putting the dictionary aside and picking up our paintbrushes in order to put *Hamlet* on an easel. Translating is not the copying, but the redrawing of a text in a different linguistic code; that is to say rewriting. (68)

Examining versions of *Hamlet* in languages other than English, from Jean-François Ducis's French Neoclassical version to Robert Gurik's political satire *Hamlet, Prince du Québec*, and from Leandro Fernández de Moratín's prose-dramatic Spanish translation to Marcos Mayer's prose-narrative retelling in *Shakespeare Para Todos*, allows us to compare and contrast how writers in different times, places, and languages have reworked Shakespeare's original text and the fictional world it embodies in order to meet the literary and/or sociopolitical concerns of their respective societies.

Ducis and Moratín: Early Translations

Whether even to call Jean-François Ducis's 1769 version of *Hamlet* a French translation of the play is controversial, because Ducis spoke no

English and in fact based his play on Pierre-Antoine de la Place's prose translation in *Le Théâtre Anglais* (1745); indeed, Ducis himself referred to his *Hamlet* as a "tragédie... imitée de l'anglais" (19). It was, however, the first French adaptation of the play to be widely performed; as Joseph McMahon notes, "the public faithfully applauded it for eighty-two years and 203 performances at the Comédie Française" (15). The play underwent several revisions between 1769 and 1812, and its success earned Ducis a place in the Académie Française – ironically, as a replacement for Voltaire, whose attitude toward Shakespeare translations in general and Ducis's adaptations in particular was ambivalent at best.

Though it may not qualify as a translation in the strictest sense of the term, Ducis's transformations not only of Shakespeare's language but also the play's form and plotline qualify his *Hamlet* as what Michel Garneau labels a "tradaptation" (qtd. in Lieblein, "Langue" 255). These transformations were necessary, both because of Ducis's lack of direct experience with English, and because of the strict rules governing French drama of the time: under the direction of the Académie Française, drama was expected to follow the Neoclassical model, itself inspired by the examples of Greek tragedy. Neoclassicism was based on the principles of *vraisemblance* (authenticity and accuracy), *convenance* (poetic justice), and *bienséance* (decorum and propriety) (cf. Pemble 33), and was also expected to adhere to the Aristotelian unities of time and place. The Neoclassical era did produce many of France's best-known playwrights, including Corneille and Racine; however, by the time of Ducis, Neoclassical tragedy was suffering from many of the same defects as other examples of moralistic and formulaic literature: it "was compact, claustrophobic, and static" (Pemble 34).

The enduring appeal of the definitely non-Neoclassical Shakespeare in England and abroad seemed paradoxical to French writers such as Voltaire, who regarded him as a genius while simultaneously criticizing his flagrant disregard for classical literary models. Ducis recognized that in order to make France safe for Shakespeare, he would have to make Shakespeare safe for France – in short, to reimagine him as a Neoclassical writer even as his plays were being put forth as an alternative to Neoclassicism. Ducis's version of *Hamlet* thus, to use Heylen's terms, attempts to naturalize and modernize the original text to the concerns of his audience. If Ducis's approach to popularizing Shakespeare in France seems revolutionary to some and sacrilegious to others, it should be remembered that English writers of his time were themselves reworking the plays to fit their dramatic conventions, and many of these reworkings were as different from their 'originals' as Ducis's was from his (McMahon 15).

Ducis's *Hamlet* eliminates much that is familiar to readers of Shakespeare's text – for example, most of the wordplay, the play-within-the-play, the comic relief, and the mass deaths at the end – leaving a drastically abridged counterpart to Shakespeare's fictional world: a bare-bones version of the plot and only eight named characters. Much of the action is narrated by these characters in dialogue, with only certain key events being enacted on the stage itself. The play also follows the traditional prosodic form of French drama, transforming Shakespeare's blank verse (unrhymed iambic pentameter) into alexandrine verse (twelve-syllable lines with rhyming couplets).

Ducis describes Hamlet as "roi de Danemarck" (19) rather than merely as the prince; at the time the play takes place, he is first in line to the throne but has not been officially crowned. Similarly, Claudius is "premier prince du sang"[52] (19) but not specifically identified as Hamlet's uncle or stepfather nor yet actually married to Gertrude; and in a particularly drastic change from the original, Ophelia is Claudius's daughter rather than Polonius's, although Polonius is present in this version. Ducis also renames Horatio Norceste, and gives Gertrude a lady-in-waiting named Elvire, so that all three main characters have their own confidants, in keeping with Neoclassical conventions which discouraged the use of soliloquies. The ghost never appears onstage, although there are frequent references to his appearances in the kingdom (e.g. Ducis 20, 25).

Interestingly, banishing the ghost offstage makes Hamlet's apparent madness more ambiguous in Ducis's version than in Shakespeare's, despite Ducis's admitted "trepidation at displaying a mad king [or prince] on the French stage" (McClellan 133) in his adaptations of both *Hamlet* and *King Lear*. While the stage directions do indicate that Hamlet sees the ghost, the audience never does, leaving the impression that Hamlet is talking to himself. Hamlet himself does not appear until II.v., having first been discussed by the other characters; and his description of his father's ghost and narration of Claudius's crime (Ducis 26; cf. *Hamlet* I.ii. 189-257) are contrasted with Norceste's account of the death of the king of England (Ducis 26), which serves as an analogue both to the Hamlet/Fortinbras parallels of the original play and to the Mousetrap (Jusserand 420).

The circumstances of King Hamlet's death are also different for Ducis than for Shakespeare. Where Shakespeare never quite makes clear how much Gertrude knew of Claudius's crime, in Ducis's version Gertrude herself poisoned her first husband at Claudius's instigation, and throughout the play she expresses remorse at having done so (e.g. Ducis 24), in a more sincere echo of Claudius's prayer in Shakespeare's Act III, scene iii. By contrast, Claudius "is cautious, scheming, cruel, as the conventional usurper was supposed to be" (Bailey 15), as the play's opening lines make abundantly clear:

---

[52] First prince of the blood; i.e. a high-ranking nobleman. All translations in this chapter are mine except where indicated.

> Oui, cher Polonius, tout mon parti n'aspire
> En détrônant Hamlet, qu'à m'assurer l'empire.[53]
>
> (Ducis 19)

The characterizations of, and contrasts between, the guilt-ridden Gertrude and the conspiring Claudius exemplify the Neoclassical fictional world's emphasis on the punishment of vice, both via the conscience and in the couple's final fate (Ducis 38-39).

Neoclassical fictional worlds equally stress the rewards of virtue, as exemplified in the principle of *convenance*, and in the case of Ducis's play, this is illustrated in his treatment of Hamlet and Ophelia, who are significantly different from their Shakespearean originals. We have already seen that in this play, "Hamlet never puts an antic disposition on" (Bailey 15); in addition, Ducis gives a very different reason than Shakespeare's for Hamlet's hesitation to avenge his father. That reason is tied to the Neoclassical emphasis on "gloire" and "devoir" (Ducis 36); and in the latter case, specifically to the "Cornelian conflicts between love and duty" (Monaco 69) that arise from Ophelia's relationship to Claudius. Though Hamlet is obliged to avenge his father's death by killing Claudius, he is hesitant to do so out of respect for Ophelia, as her reaction to Hamlet's confessions to her in Ducis's Act V, scene ii shows:

> Mon devoir désormais m'est dicté par le tien;
> Tu cours venger ton père, et moi, sauver le mien.
> Je ne le quitte plus; de tes desseins instruite,
> Je vais l'en informer, m'attacher à sa suite,
> Jusqu'au dernier soupir lui prêter mon appui,
> Et, s'il meurt, l'embrasser, et périr près de lui.
>
> (Ducis 36)[54]

This dialogue between Hamlet and Ophelia reminds the readers/audience that Ophelia is a potential obstacle to Hamlet's revenge and removes her from the remainder of the play's action. At the same time it softens the blows of Shakespeare's original in eliminating both Hamlet's outbursts at Ophelia

---

[53] Yes, dear Polonius, all my options aspire
In dethroning Hamlet, but to assure me the empire.

[54] My duty in future is dictated to me by thine;
You go to avenge your father; I, to save mine.
I will not leave him anymore; of your instructed designs,
I go to inform him, to attach myself to his retinue,
Until the last sigh, to lend him my support,
And, if he dies, to embrace him, and perish beside him.

(*Hamlet* III.i. 94-149) and her subsequent madness (*Hamlet* IV.v.), neither of which would have been acceptable in a Neoclassical dramatic world.

The climax of Ducis's *Hamlet* (Ducis 36-39) combines several elements from Shakespeare's play – the Mousetrap, the reappearance of the ghost during Hamlet's meeting with Gertrude, and the death of Claudius and Gertrude – all redone in ways more acceptable to French Neoclassical custom. Since Ducis eliminated the ghost as a character, he instead has Hamlet address an urn containing his father's ashes (Ducis 36-37) in the presence of Gertrude, thereby confronting her with her part in the crime and daring her to confess:

> Où mon père est-il? D'où part la trahison?
> Qui forma le complot? Qui versa le poison?
> > (Ducis 37)[55]

Gertrude's 'confession' takes the form of fainting in a chair; while Hamlet accepts this act as her confession, he is reluctant to kill her, even when urged on by the ghost. Instead, in an echo of Shakespeare's Ghost's admonishment to Hamlet to "leave her to heaven" (*Hamlet* I.v. 86), he reminds her that her crimes can be forgiven:

> Votre crime est énorme, exécrable, odieux;
> Mais il n'est pas plus grand que la bonté des dieux. (Ducis 38)[56]

Ducis's play ends with Hamlet defeating and killing Claudius in battle, after which Gertrude publicly confesses, "Le monstre conseilla, mais je permis le crime" (Ducis 39)[57] and then commits suicide. Hamlet is thus left alive to rule Denmark, though most likely without Ophelia by his side, "because [he] sacrifices his love for Ophelia to avenge the deaths of... his parents" (Bailey 75), and so his revenge brings him, at most, a bittersweet victory.

Critical and popular response to Ducis's *Hamlet* was mixed. Despite its long-standing popularity with French audiences who appreciated its mixture of the Shakespearean plot with Neoclassical models, many writers and thinkers who were familiar with Shakespeare regarded Ducis's version as "*Hamlet* travestied to defend the dignity of French tragedy" (Bailey 23). Others, such as Diderot, seemed equally disdainful of "Shakespeare's

---

[55] Where is my father? From whence came this treason?
Who made the plot? Who poured the poison?
[56] Your crime is enormous, execrable, odious,
But it is not greater than the kindness of the gods.
[57] The monster [Claudius] advised it, but I allowed the crime.

monster... [and] Ducis's scarecrow" (qtd. in Bailey 18) while still praising those elements of both plays that were dramatically effective. Ducis's *Hamlet* fell out of favour during the years of the French Revolution, but with the dawning of the nineteenth century, he revised it to include, among other things, a paraphrase of the most famous passage of Shakespeare's text,[58] the "To be or not to be" soliloquy (Ducis 31; cf. *Hamlet* III.i. 55-89), which had not been as prominent in the first version. The revised play continued to be performed until the middle of the nineteenth century.

Both despite and because of its significant differences from the Shakespearean text, Ducis's *Hamlet* became influential elsewhere in Europe as well, especially in Spain. According to Ángel-Luis Pujante and Keith Gregor, "not only was Spain the first country in which such a translation [i.e. a translation of Ducis's *Hamlet*] was produced, but there are no less than four extant versions of the play" (129). These translations were the first Spanish versions of *Hamlet,* as Ducis's had been among the first French versions. However, the reasons for the delay between the writing of *Hamlet* and the translation were different in Spain than in France, as Spanish literature of the sixteenth and seventeenth centuries already boasted a strong dramatic tradition: "the age of Lope de Vega and Calderón saw the growth of a national popular theatre in which foreign plays were virtually... absent" (Pujante and Gregor 130), and translating Shakespeare into "the Castilian of Lope de Vega" (Conejero 29) would merely be the exchange of one language's classical literary forms for another. But by the time of Ducis's French *Hamlet,* Spanish drama was as influenced by Neoclassicism as French drama, and it is primarily for this reason that *Hamlet* entered the Spanish literary community through Ducis's version before it did through the Shakespearean 'original.'

The first direct translation of *Hamlet* into Spanish was undertaken in 1798 by Leandro Fernández de Moratín, who published it under the name Inarco Celenio. It was never performed in his lifetime, but did become influential on future Spanish translators (see e.g. Campillo Árnaiz 26-33; Tronch-Pérez 54-56). Structurally it follows the practice of Neoclassical plays in designating act and scene breaks whenever a character enters or exits, with the result that Hamlet's soliloquies take up entire scenes in themselves. As well, just as Ducis had renamed Shakespeare's Horatio as Norceste, Moratín gave Rosencrantz, Guildenstern, and Osric the names Ricardo, Guillermo, and

---

[58] The reference here to Shakespeare's text is more precisely to the composite of the First Folio and Second Quarto texts, which is usually followed by textual editors today. The "To be or not to be" passage appears in a very different form in the First Quarto text. See Bertram and Kliman 123-25.

Enrique, respectively. These choices of character names are especially interesting in that they are the Spanish equivalents of the English names *Richard, William,* and *Henry,* suggesting cross-references to Shakespeare himself and to his history plays.

Moratín's translation restores virtually all of the characters and plot elements that did not appear in Ducis's French version but had been used in varying degrees in the Spanish versions of Ducis's play (Pujante and Gregor 135-36). Its most significant differences from the Shakespearean texts are linguistic ones, as the prosody and wordplay present in the source texts proved difficult to reproduce accurately in Spanish. As an example of the latter, Moratín translated Hamlet's first line in the Second Quarto and First Folio texts, "A little more than kin, and less than kind" (*Hamlet* I.ii. 65), as "Algo más que deudo, y menos que amigo"[59] (Moratín I.iv.), while his response to Claudius immediately after, "I am too much i'th' sun" (*Hamlet* I.ii. 67), ignores the pun on *sun* and *son,* becoming "estoy demasiado a la luz"[60] (Moratín I.iv.). But the problems of multiple meanings were not the only reasons for such alterations: the world of Moratín's *Hamlet* still straddles the border between the 'Shakespearean' and 'Neoclassical' fictional worlds, and as such is strongly influenced by the Neoclassical rules of propriety and decorum. In the introduction to his translation, Moratín criticized Shakespeare for including in his plays "diálogos más groseros, capaces sólo de excitar la risa de un populacho vinoso y soez"[61] (Moratín 3), and in many places in the translation, "sexual puns are remarkably bowdlerized" (Campillo Árnaiz 33). Probably the most obvious evidence of this sort of translation decision occurs in Moratín's version of Hamlet's and Ophelia's sexually-charged banter before the performance of the Mousetrap play (*Hamlet* III.ii. 112-21), which appears as follows:

> HAMLET. ¿Permitiréis que me ponga sobre vuestra rodilla?
> OFELIA. No, señor.
> HAMLET. Quiero decir, apoyar mi cabeza en vuestra rodilla.
> OFELIA. Sí, señor.
> HAMLET. ¿Pensáis que yo quisiera cometer alguna indecencia?
> OFELIA. No, no pienso nada de eso.
> HAMLET. Qué dulce cosa es...

---

[59] A little more than a debtor, and less than a friend.

[60] I am too much in the light.

[61] "coarse dialogues that could only raise a laugh in the rude and drunken populace" (Campillo Árnaiz 27).

OFELIA. ¿Qué decís, señor?
HAMLET. Nada. (Moratín III.xi.)[62]

With the abridgment of Hamlet's remark, "What a fair thought it is to lie
between maids' legs" (*Hamlet* III.ii. 118), the punning reply "Nothing"
(*Hamlet* III.ii. 121) becomes less apparent, except to a reader who is familiar
enough with the English version to fill in the missing portion of the line.
Even so, Moratín shows more tolerance for risqué dialogue than French
Neoclassical writers/translators such as Ducis, especially in passages where
such meanings would be equally apparent in Spanish and in English. This is
illustrated in his version of the dialogue between Hamlet, Rosencrantz, and
Guildenstern in II.ii. 228-36 of Shakespeare's text:

GUILLERMO. No, no servimos de airón al tocado de fortuna.
HAMLET. ¿Ni de suelas a su calzado?
RICARDO. Ni uno ni otro.
HAMLET. En tal caso estaréis colocados hacia su cintura: allí es el centro de
los favores.
GUILLERMO. Cierto, como privados suyos.
HAMLET. Pues allí en lo más oculto... ¡Ah! Decís bien, ella es una prostituta.
(Moratín II.viii.)[63]

Moratín's concerns for "la modestia de los lectores" (263, n. 7) aside, his
translation of *Hamlet* is semantically quite close to the English original,
producing what Barbara Folkart characterizes as a "translation driven by the
notion of fidelity...[to] the source text's denotations" (11). Rather than
attempting to reproduce the distinctive rhythm and prosody of the

---

[62] HAMLET. May I sit on your lap?
OPHELIA. No, my lord.
HAMLET. I meant to say, rest my head in your lap.
OPHELIA. Ay, my lord.
HAMLET. Did you think I meant to commit something indecent?
OPHELIA. No, I think nothing of that.
HAMLET. What a sweet thing it is...
OPHELIA. What did you say, my lord?
HAMLET. Nothing.
[63] GUILLERMO. No, we serve only as a button in Fortune's cap.
HAMLET. Nor the soles of her shoe?
RICARDO. Not one or the other.
HAMLET. In that case, you would be located around her waist; there is the centre of her
favours.
GUILLERMO. Faith, as her privates.
HAMLET. Well then, there in the most secret... Ah! You speak well, she is a prostitute.

Shakespearean text, or even to "castilianize" (Conejero 29) the text by using the counterpart forms of Spanish poetry in place of the English ones, his version concentrates more on the meanings of the words than on the verse forms used to deliver them, and thus the majority of the text is in prose.

Where Moratín does attempt to use the typical prosodic forms of Spanish drama of his time is in his rendition of the First Player's speech (Moratín II.x.; *Hamlet* II.ii. 450-518) and the Mousetrap (Moratín III.xiii.; *Hamlet* III.ii. 149-260), both of which display "the metrical variety characteristic of Spanish verse drama...mixing hendecasyllables and either octosyllables or heptasyllables" (Tronch-Pérez 55); as well as in the songs Ophelia sings after she has gone mad (Moratín IV.xii-xiii., xvii.; *Hamlet* IV.v.) and those the gravediggers sing while at their work (Moratín V.i.; *Hamlet* V.i. 61-64; 71-74; 94-97). This mixture of verse with prose gives an archaic flavour, when comparing the verse with the 'modernized' prose, to the Player's speech and the Mousetrap, emphasizing their status as embedded fictional worlds as well as examples of the type of dramatic verse to which Shakespeare – or Shakespearean translation, in Moratín's case – forms a counterpart and an alternative; these would, perhaps, be the Spanish equivalents of a post-Shakespearean English writer using Shakespearean verse in the midst of a prose play.

Gurik and Mayer: (Post)Modern Translations

Thanks to the works of Ducis and Moratín, and others after them, *Hamlet* became as familiar to the French- and Spanish-speaking worlds as it was to the English-speaking world, and it was this familiarity that made it attractive to many writers, especially in the latter half of the twentieth century, as the source text for adaptations which presented vastly different fictional worlds from those of Shakespeare and his early translators. A large number of such adaptations also used these fictional worlds as models of the sorts of improvements they wished to see made to their actual world. The French-Canadian writer Robert Gurik, for example, appropriated *Hamlet* as a means of resistance to the "double colonization of Quebec" (Lieblein, "Langue" 255) by English Canada and France. As critics such as Leanore Lieblein ("Pourquoi" 101-03) and Annie Brisset (182-257) point out, Gurik's use of *Hamlet* was but one example of the fashion in Québécois literary circles of translating and/or adapting Shakespeare for postcolonial and nationalist ends; indeed, Michel Garneau coined the neologism "tradaptations" to describe his translation of *Macbeth* into the Québécois dialect rather than into 'standard' French. Gurik's 1968 play *Hamlet, Prince du Québec* utilizes a fairly semantically accurate prose translation of Shakespeare's original text, albeit altered as the revision's political undertones required, as the basis for an allegory of the nationalist movement in Quebec, with each character in the play standing in for a specific political figure. Hamlet himself represents Quebec, specifically "le Québec avec toutes ses hésitations, avec sa soif d'action et de liberté, corseté par cent ans d'inaction"[64] (Gurik 5); with Claudius and Gertrude representing, respectively, English Canada and the Catholic Church, both institutions which exert a great deal of power over the French-Canadian population. Other characters represent important people in both provincial and federal politics of the day – for example, Laertes and Polonius represent Pierre Elliott Trudeau and Lester B. Pearson, while Ophelia and Horatio represent Jean Lesage and René Lévesque. Rosencrantz and Guildenstern, as representatives/representations of the Bilingual and Bicultural Commission, repeat each other's lines: one in English, one in French. The Ghost signals the specific political event which inspired Gurik to write his satire: he symbolizes France in general and Charles de Gaulle in particular, both quoting from and embodying de Gaulle's infamous "Vive le Québec libre" (Gurik 30) speech in Montreal in 1967. The presence of explicit political references in Gurik's play – indeed, in the first production, the actors were dressed as combinations of Shakespeare's characters and the Canadian political figures they were meant to satirize, and the stage directions consistently list both the character and the actual-world entity he/she represents – illustrates the vast difference in purpose between Gurik's adaptations and those of earlier writers such as Ducis and Moratín. Where Ducis and Moratín were attempting to 'domesticate' Shakespeare for their respective audiences by creating hybridized fictional worlds of, in their cases, Shakespearean Neoclassicism and/or Neoclassical Shakespeare, Gurik envisioned alternatives to the actual world as well as to the fictional world. His play calls up a possible world in which Quebec exists as an independent political entity, which he hoped would be brought about in part through an alternative fictional world where Shakespeare's characters embody "an unmistakable call for self-determination" (Hoenselaars 16).

Gurik's adaptation is in fact a play-within-a-play, creating a three-layered structure of the actual world of the audience and two textual worlds that begin separately but do come together at certain crucial points. The play and its fictional world(s) are introduced by a framing scene in which the two gravediggers play cards and discuss their plight as working-class Québécois unable to find better employment because, as one of them says, "j'ai pas

---

[64] "Quebec with all its hesitations, with its thirst for action and liberty, constrained by one hundred years of inaction" (Lieblein, "Re-making" 180).

d'instruction et puis j'parle pas anglais" (Gurik 10).[65] In contrast to the other characters in the play who speak 'standard' French, the gravediggers speak working-class Québécois French, and they begin the play with a folk song about the defeat of Montcalm at the Plains of Abraham in 1745 (Gurik 9), an event long mythologized by French-Canadian nationalists as the beginning of anglophone dominance of Canada. The two cards held up by the gravediggers, "dame de cœur, roi de pique" (Gurik 9),[66] introduce the main action of the play, which begins at the equivalent of Shakespeare's I.ii. 42, with Laertes requesting "la permission d'aller à Ottawa" (Gurik 12),[67] rather than to France as in the Shakespearean original.

Throughout the play, Gurik intersperses specific political and historical references within what is otherwise a close translation of Shakespeare's text, demonstrating that a translation need not be drastically removed, linguistically speaking, from the original to be subversive. Several times, Hamlet repeats the provincial motto of Quebec, "Je me souviens" (e.g. Gurik 14); and the ghost appears at "le balcon" (Gurik 17), a reference to the balcony of the Montreal City Hall where de Gaulle made his speech. At various points in the play, a radio voice describes other historical events of colonialism and/or resistance such as the Vietnam War (Gurik 19-20), terrorist attacks by the Front de Libération du Québec (Gurik 24-25), English-Canadian reactions to de Gaulle's visit to Quebec (Gurik 33-34), and ethnic slurs against English- (Gurik 55) and French-Canadians alike (Gélinas 29). The book Hamlet reads in Gurik's I.viii. (39) is labelled "100 ans d'injustice" (Gurik 39),[68] a common separatist slogan during Canada's centennial in 1967; and Horatio's warning in the original that the ghost might "assume some other horrible form / Which might deprive your sovereignty of reason" (*Hamlet* I.v. 74) acquires a double meaning in Gurik's translation "il vous prive de la souveraineté de la raison" (Gurik 27),[69] in which "sovereignty" refers both to reason and to political self-determination. The manner of the former king's death also acquires a polemical meaning, as the ghost informs Hamlet, "ton oncle muni d'une orange... força le fruit dans ma bouche jusqu'à l'étouffement" (Gurik 29).[70] The orange is a reference to "la

---

[65] I have no education and besides, I don't speak English. Marc Gélinas's English re-translation renders this line in heavily French-accented English: "I never go to de school and me goddamn I no spick Ingliss" (Gélinas 2).

[66] "Queen of de hearts, king of de spade" (Gélinas 1).

[67] "permission that I go to Ottawa" (Gélinas 3).

[68] One hundred years of injustice. Gélinas translates the title as "One Hundred Years Lost" (18).

[69] Gélinas makes the political allusion more explicit in his re-translation, "some other horrible form which might deprive you of your sovereignty" (11).

[70] "thine uncle armed with an orange... forced the fruit into my mouth until I died" (Gélinas 12).

fraction réactionnaire de l'anglophonie, les inconditionnels de la Couronne britannique qu'on appelle les Orangistes" (Brisset 185),[71] and the action itself represents the sentiment among many of Gurik's contemporaries of having "l'anglophonie" stuffed down their throats.

Probably the most memorable use Gurik makes of Shakespeare's text is his use of Hamlet's "To be or not to be" speech as an expression of the divided loyalties felt by many French-Canadians of the 1960s: "Être ou ne pas être libre! Voilà la question" (Gurik 51), juxtaposed with Ophelia holding a book entitled "Un pays, d'un ocean à l'autre" (Gurik 51)[72] – to which Hamlet replies dismissively, "Encore une chimère; décidément vous ne changerez jamais" (Gurik 52).[73] The answer Gurik gives for his version of Hamlet's famous question in this play is most definitely "être libre," as demonstrated by the fact that his Hamlet's last words incorporate those spoken by the ghost in this fictional world and de Gaulle in the actual world, "Il faut que ma mort serve aux autres. Il faut... que vive... un... Qué... bec... libre" (Gurik 95).[74]

Gurik's text does not only call for the freedom of Quebec from English-Canadian political domination: in its use of a classic English literary work as its model, and one that was dismissed by Voltaire and many other French intellectuals as a "monstrous farce" (Bailey 25) both before and after Ducis's popularization, it also signals a liberation from French cultural domination. This may not be apparent at first reading, because unlike many other Québécois translators/adaptors of Shakespeare during this period (Drouin 5-6), Gurik kept the use of the Québécois dialect to a minimum. However, the inherent irony for English readers of using an English text to resist English influence has its counterpart for French readers in the fact that Gurik chose to parody an English text rather than a French one in order to assert French-Canadian independence (cf. Drouin 1-6). The play thus represents the distinctness of Quebec both from its cultural ancestor France and from its geographical and political neighbour English Canada, as well as the influence of both in creating that distinctness. Gurik even symbolizes the complex relations between the actual and fictional worlds of his play with his rendering of Shakespeare's lines, "Married with my uncle, / My father's brother, but no more like my father / Than I to Hercules" (*Hamlet* I.ii. 151-

---

[71] The reactionary faction of the Anglophones, the supporters of the British Crown who were called the Orangists.

[72] One country, from one ocean to the other; reference to Canada's national motto, 'From sea to sea.' Gélinas translates it as "One Country, One Nation" (27).

[73] Another pipe-dream; certainly you will never change. In Gélinas's version: "The words have gelled, your mind is stuck, mesmerized by fear and the power of the buck" (27).

[74] "My death must serve those who follow on. For it must... must live... 'Vive the Quebec Libre'" (Gélinas 53).

53), as "Mariée avec mon oncle, mais qui ne ressemble pas plus à mon père que moi à *Shakespeare*" (Gurik 14; emphasis mine).

With its firm grounding in and explicit presentation of the sociopolitical currents of its time and place, Gurik's play is very much an example of Lubomír Doležel's category of polemical revisionism. At first the play seems to have little in common with a later Spanish adaptation that appears in Marcos Mayer's 1997 anthology of prose retellings, *Shakespeare Para Todos*. But as the collection's title – which means "Shakespeare for Everyone" – indicates, it too is an adaptation with a purpose, but one closer to those of Ducis and Moratín than to that of Gurik. Where Gurik's play has the specific audience and actual-world objectives of French-Canadian nationalists in mind, Mayer's retelling is addressed to Spanish-speaking lay readers, primarily young students who may be encountering the plays for the first time. *Shakespeare Para Todos* also shares with Moratín's translation a departure from the examples of more firmly established doubly-adapted works, for just as Moratín was working against translations of Ducis's *Hamlet,* so is Mayer's a work distinct from the numerous translations of Charles and Mary Lamb's *Tales from Shakespeare,* the best-known prose retellings of the plays.[75]

Mayer's retelling completely omits the Fortinbras subplot, concentrating on Hamlet's plan to avenge his father. However, the rest of the familiar story is present, told through narration as well as through translations of the Shakespearean dialogue. Like Moratín, Mayer presents the Shakespearean text in prose, preferring semantic accuracy to prosodic equivalency; but Mayer's adaptation takes the form of a narrative rather than a play. Since the first scene of Shakespeare's play, in which the guards discuss seeing the ghost, does not appear in Mayer's version, the story uses description of setting to establish the scene:

> El húmedo gris de las rocas que formaban el castillo de Elsinor – allá en la lejana Dinamarca donde, según algún funcionario de la Corte, algo olía a podrido – se traslucía por detrás de la imagen del Rey que acababa de morir.[76] (Mayer 42)

Mayer's choice of prose over verse also extends to the embedded texts and text-worlds of the Mousetrap and the various characters' songs and recitations. The Mousetrap itself is narrated except for two speeches (Mayer 51-54; cf. *Hamlet* III.ii. 149-260), while the songs are omitted entirely.

---

[75] Though translations of the Lambs' retellings are fairly common in Spanish as well as in French, other prose retellings have also been translated.

[76] The damp grey of the rocks that made up the castle of Elsinore – that was in faraway Denmark where, according to some official of the court, something smelled rotten – was revealed behind the image of the King who had just died.

Mayer interprets the character of Hamlet himself not so much as indecisive, as many other adaptations would have it, but as plagued by doubt: for example, on the death of King Hamlet, the story says, "La versión official establecía que había muerto envenenado, al ser mordido en su jardín por una serpiente, pero las dudas atormentaban el corazón de Hamlet"[77] (42-43). This suggests that, in Mayer's view, Hamlet already suspected foul play behind his father's death, even before the ghost reveals the truth about "su muerte, occurida en condiciones muy differentes de lo que se contaba en el palacio real"[78] (Mayer 44). Mayer's association of Hamlet with doubt also extends to the description of the relationship of Hamlet and Ophelia as "una relación ambigua" (44) – a phrase that is itself ambiguous, as it raises the question of how far their relationship truly does extend, as well as that of whether they are indeed in love in the first place.

Mayer's treatment of the Hamlet-Ophelia relationship contrasts Moratín's in an interesting way, considering that *Shakespeare Para Todos* is intended for young readers. Where Moratín glosses over many, but not all, of the double entendres in their dialogue before the Mousetrap, Mayer leaves more of these in his translation, with the exception of Hamlet's notorious line, "Do you think I meant country matters?" (*Hamlet* III.ii. 116). Most notably, he leaves in the full version of Hamlet's comment in III.ii. 118 as well as the ensuing pun on "nothing." His version of the scene is as follows:

> – Señora, ¿me permite que repose en su falda? – y se sentó a sus pies, apoyando la espalda contra las piernas de Ofelia.
> – No, señor – respondió Ofelia, casi sin abrir los labios.
> – Quiero decir reposar la cabeza en su falda.
> – Sí, señor – contestó Ofelia, mortificada por un trato que parecía no comprender.
> – ¿Piensa que quería decir alguna cosa desagradable?
> – No pienso nada, señor.
> – Linda idea la de reposar entre las piernas de una doncella – agregó Hamlet por lo bajo.
> (Mayer 50-51)[79]

---

[77] The official version established that he had died of poisoning, having been bitten in his garden by a snake, but the doubts tormented Hamlet's heart.

[78] His death, which had occurred under very different circumstances than he [Hamlet] had been told in the royal palace.

[79] "Lady, shall I lie in your lap?" and he sat down at her feet, resting his back between Ophelia's legs.
"No, my lord," replied Ophelia, almost without opening her mouth.
"I mean to ask to rest my head in your lap."
"Ay, my lord," answered Ophelia, mortified by a manner that appeared unintelligible.
"Do you think I wanted to ask you something disagreeable?"

Mayer is also clearer on whether Ophelia's death was intentional, for although he does not refer to her funeral having been abridged, the gravediggers are said to be "indignados de que aquella joven desconocida recibiera una sagrada sepultura habiéndose suicidado"[80] (63; cf. *Hamlet* V.i. 1-29).

Mayer's retelling of the play's final two scenes, which are shorter than their counterparts in the Shakespearean text, emphasizes the tragic nature of both his fictional world and Shakespeare's. However, Mayer's proves to be the more tragic – in the commonly used sense of an unhappy ending, rather than in the strict dramatic sense – of the two. Although Hamlet has spent the duration of the play trying to avenge his father's murder, it is not until Mayer's Hamlet finds Yorick's skull that the enormity of the situation truly impresses itself upon him: "La muerte tenía nombre ahora, el de alguien a quien Hamlet había conocido"[81] (62). It is his elegy over Yorick's skull and his sadness at Ophelia's death, rather than the Shakespearean Hamlet's encounter with Fortinbras's army (*Hamlet* IV.iv.), that provide the Hamlet of *Shakespeare Para Todos* with the determination he needs to carry out his duty to his father. But the climax of Mayer's story provides little, if any, hope of resolution, being not only without Fortinbras to restore order, but perhaps even without Horatio to keep Hamlet's memory alive:

> – Que el Cielo te absuelva. Te sigo – respondió Hamlet mirando el rostro de Laertes que empezaba a empalidecer. – Soy muerto, Horacio.
> Pero también Horacio bebía de la copa fatal para acompañar a su amigo.
> – Cuenta todo con todos los incidentes, grandes y pequeños... – fueron las últimas palabras del Principe. – Lo demás es silencio.[82]
>   (Mayer 64-65; cf. *Hamlet* V.ii. 332-58)

In Mayer's version, Hamlet does not attempt to stop Horatio when he finds "yet some liquor left" (*Hamlet* V.ii. 342) in Claudius's cup, and the

---

"I think nothing, my lord."
"A fair thought [literally, a beautiful idea] it is to lie between a maid's legs," answered Hamlet in a low voice.

[80] Indignant that some young stranger was receiving a sacred burial when she had committed suicide.

[81] Death had a name now, that of someone Hamlet had known.

[82] "May Heaven absolve you. I follow," replied Hamlet, looking at Laertes's face, which had begun to turn pale. "I die, Horatio."
But Horatio too drank from the fatal cup to follow his friend.
"Tell everyone about all the incidents, great and small," were the last words of the Prince.
"The rest is silence."

implication is thus that Horatio will die soon after Hamlet, leaving nobody to explain the preceding events.

These French and Spanish versions of *Hamlet* each display the paradoxes of intercultural contact, of the relationship between actual and fictional worlds, and of the relationship between fictional worlds themselves. Even as a work produced in one culture closely influenced by that of a neighbouring society, or a work produced as an adaptation of an earlier text, struggles to assert itself against the other and/or the 'original,' it demonstrates that that contact between cultures and between text worlds is in fact necessary for such a work to exist in the first place. These texts also demonstrate the power of a fictional world to transform or at least influence the actual world in which they are produced and read/performed. Ducis's creation of Neoclassical counterparts to both Shakespeare and his play helped open the world of French literature to dramatic possibilities outside of Neoclassicism even as it reimagined Shakespeare and *Hamlet* in ways that were more acceptable to French culture. Moratín's translation of *Hamlet* into Spanish represented an intermediary between Shakespearean drama, "the Castilian of Lope de Vega" (Conejero 29), and Neoclassicism as practiced in both Spain and France. While Gurik's vision of an independent Quebec has not (at this writing) come to pass, his appropriation of *Hamlet* for French-Canadian nationalist ends does present a vivid picture of the alternative worlds of both politics and literature by translating those worlds into a language and form in which they could be better understood. And though Mayer's purpose in translating the Shakespearean text and its world for Spanish student readers is not an overtly political one but rather a desire to clarify the "enigma de su persistencia a lo largo del tiempo" (7), it illustrates that even adaptations whose differences from the original are more structural than ideological embody distinctive worlds of their own.

CHAPTER FOUR:

EXPANSIONS: *HAMLET* WITHOUT THE PRINCE

> Remember thee?
> Ay, thou poor ghost, while memory holds a seat
> In this distracted globe. Remember thee?
> Yea, from the table of my memory
> I'll wipe away all trivial fond records,
> All saws of books, all forms, all pressures past,
> That youth and observation copied there;
> And thy commandment all alone shall live
> Within the book and volume of my brain,
> Unmix'd with baser matter.
>
> (*Hamlet* I.v. 100-109)

The supercategory of adaptations that Lubomír Doležel labels transductions, consisting of expansions, transpositions, and displacements, is too broad to be covered in a single chapter, and so the remainder of this book looks at each of these smaller categories in turn. The category of adaptation that Doležel calls "role expansion" and Douglas Lanier calls "revisionary narrative" is a useful place to begin a discussion of transductions of *Hamlet* precisely because of the play's reliance – a common trait of Shakespearean tragedy – on a single dominating character. This type of adaptation repositions the fictional world to the perspective of characters who were secondary or even very minor in the source text. Such adaptations have the effect of providing the reader with the everyman's, antagonist's, and/or ally's views of major events; they may also be ways of filling in backstory for these characters to make them far more interesting than their smaller roles in the source text had allowed. No matter which character is foregrounded in these adaptations, what they all have in common is a reorientation of the Shakespearean fictional world in ways that bring the formerly dominant figure of Hamlet onto the margins while privileging the voices and experiences of those characters Shakespeare chose to leave undeveloped or less developed. Much like Hamlet's promise to remember his father's ghost, these adaptations help to keep the characters around him "within the book and volume" (*Hamlet* I.v. 108) of the public imagination.

Hamlet Before the Prince: Claudius, Gertrude, and King Hamlet as Main Characters

In keeping with a long-standing tradition of heroic poetry and drama, Shakespeare's *Hamlet* begins *in medias res,* following the death of King Hamlet and the coronation of Claudius. Authors of prequel texts to Shakespeare's play use this beginning point and what is known of the characters from the play to create fictional worlds reflecting the authors' and/or characters' perceptions of what led to the "rotten... state of Denmark" (*Hamlet* I.iv. 90) at the beginning of the Shakespearean text. Such texts are examples of "the most magic of all transformations that fiction can accomplish: past made present. What is distant, backgrounded, fragmentary, and ghostly in [the source text] becomes close, continuous, human in [the adaptations]" (Doležel, *Heterocosmica* 213). This strategy allows writers to present their interpretations of the formative influences on the Shakespearean protagonist and also develop Hamlet's parents and uncle as significant characters and centres of fictional worlds in their own right.

A common element of the majority of prequels to *Hamlet* is their focus on the triangle of King Hamlet, Gertrude, and Claudius. King Hamlet especially serves as inspiration to the authors of prequel texts because he appears in the play only as a ghost, and even then only to four[83] characters; what little we do know of him in the Shakespearean world comes primarily from Hamlet's fond and often idealizing reminiscences (e.g. *Hamlet* I.ii. 139-42; III.iv. 55-63) as well as from the Ghost's dialogues with his son (*Hamlet* I.v. 9-92; III.iv. 110-15). Even in the play's primary source texts, Saxo Grammaticus's *Historiae Danicae* and François de Belleforest's *Histoires Tragiques,* the king – known as Horwendil in Saxo and Horwendille in Belleforest – is not as fully developed a character as the rest of his family, serving for the most part as an emblem of the ideal ruler as it was understood in the society of medieval Denmark (*HD* 60-61; *HT* 151-54). Although the histories do provide more detailed descriptions of the king's wife and brother, called Gerutha and Feng by Saxo or Geruthe and Fengon by Belleforest, they are still treated in far less detail than Amleth/Hamlet himself. Saxo and Belleforest define Feng/Fengon mainly by envy for his brother's success and determination to take what he wants by any means necessary, "showing that

---

[83] This is assuming that Gertrude does not actually see the Ghost when he appears to Hamlet in III.iv. 102-36.

goodness is not safe from those of a man's own house.... when a chance came to murder [Horwendil], his bloody hand sated the passion of his soul" (*HD* 62). Furthermore, his decision to send Amleth to England demonstrates that, "desirous to hide his cruelty, he chose rather to besmirch his friend than to bring disgrace on his own head" (*HD* 66).

But while Saxo's and Belleforest's respective characterizations of the two royal brothers are very similar to each other, their treatments of the queen are somewhat different. Saxo describes Gerutha as "meek and unrancorous" (*HD* 62) and willing to help her son even in very small ways. By contrast, Belleforest describes Geruthe as "malheureuse" (*HT* 153) – which in the 1608 post-Shakespearean[84] English translation was expanded to "this unfortunate and wicked woman" (*Hystorie* 88) – and even accuses her of having been Fengon's mistress "durant la vie du bon Horwendille" (*HT* 153), though she insists in private conversation with Amleth that she had been forced into doing so (*HT* 162-63; *Hystorie* 98-99).

Many role expansions of Hamlet's parents and uncle use their fictional worlds to explore whether, as Belleforest's insinuation would have it, a relationship may have developed between Gertrude and Claudius before the death of King Hamlet, and thus that Claudius's murder of his brother may have been as much to eliminate a rival for Gertrude as it was to obtain power. Even if they do not explicitly take the Ghost's characterization of Claudius as an "adulterate beast" (*Hamlet* I.v. 42) at his word, many fictional treatments of the Claudius-Gertrude relationship have more or less followed or been informed by 'traditional' views of Claudius as a schemer motivated by power and love or lust, and Gertrude as a self-sacrificing enabler. Other adaptations focus on the relationship between the royal brothers, Claudius and King Hamlet, tracing the authors' interpretations of the beginning of their rivalries in both love and politics. But whether they focus on Gertrude, King Hamlet, Claudius, or all of these characters, such adaptations range from largely traditionalist reworkings of the Shakespearean plot to more revisionary/revisionist approaches whose presentations of the characters and plot differ from those with which we have become familiar from the play.

The American writer Lillie Buffum Chace Wyman published her novel *Gertrude of Denmark*, which she described as "an interpretive romance," in 1924, though it may have been written earlier (Rozett 85). While on the surface it appears to be a straight retelling of Shakespeare's play in narrative prose with an emphasis on Gertrude's role in the story, it is also a polemical revision – perhaps more properly a revision with polemical undertones – meant as a reply to the traditional, male-dominated academic discourse of

---

[84] The commonly accepted date for Shakespeare's *Hamlet* is c. 1600-01 (Evans 53).

Wyman's time. As Courtney Langdon states in the novel's introduction, "settled opinions are squarely challenged, and... orthodox notions are put again upon the defensive" (vii). Indeed, Wyman was no stranger to the challenging of literary or sociocultural orthodoxies, as her mother was a leading figure in the nineteenth-century American feminist and abolitionist movements (Rozett 74-77) and she herself was familiar with other women writers' interpretations of Shakespeare such as Mary Cowden Clarke's short stories in *The Girlhood of Shakespeare's Heroines*[85] and Anna Jameson's and Helena Faucit's essays. On one level, *Gertrude of Denmark* is an exploration of Victorian depictions of "Holy mother-love" (Clarke 225) in both fictional and actual worlds; on another, it is a fictionalized treatment of "the alienation experienced by misrepresented and largely ignored women in a world both dominated and imaginatively recreated by men" (Rozett 74).

Wyman's novel begins similarly to Shakespeare's play: with the appearance of a ghost. In this case, Gertrude's ghost appears to the narrator, informing her that Shakespeare "left out some record of our thoughts and omitted to tell some things that would have revealed me more truly than I am shown in his pages" (4). Just as the Ghost directed the Shakespearean Hamlet to "Revenge his foul and most unnatural murther" (*Hamlet* I.v. 25), and Hamlet himself implores Horatio at the end of the play "To tell my story" (*Hamlet* V.ii. 349), so does Gertrude's ghost charge the narrator with presenting her side of the familiar tale. The appearances of Gertrude's ghost to the narrator provide a framing narrative, a form of mediation between the storyworld and that of the readers, as well as establishing the narrator's ambivalent attitude toward the Shakespearean fictional world. Gertrude's ghost says upon meeting the narrator for the first time:

> Shakespeare was a wizard on earth, but we others were not that when we lived in the flesh; coming and dwelling here as spirits does indeed give us the opportunity to learn some things of which we were ignorant before. But it does not make us, like him, know and understand everything pertaining to human life. (Wyman 5)

This admiring but hyperbolic sentiment, not unmixed with a sense of irony, continues throughout Wyman's novel, as both the narrator and Gertrude's ghost refer to Shakespeare as "the Great Wizard" (Wyman 6), and it is not always clear whether the nickname is an affectionate term or the opposite.

---

[85] Although Gertrude appears in Clarke's story about Ophelia, "The Rose of Elsinore," Clarke did not make her into a main character.

Wyman describes her Gertrude in idealized, bordering on angelic, terms typical of the heroines of romance literature (2); the birth of Hamlet only adds to this idealization, as both King Hamlet and Claudius describe her as "the most sacred creature on earth" (10) and remark that "She looks like the Holy Mother" (10)[86] when she holds the young Prince on her lap. Later in her life, she also develops a motherly attitude toward Ophelia (e.g. 37-38), which receives its fullest expression in her elegy on Ophelia's death (*Hamlet* IV.vii. 164-83; qtd. in Wyman 181), a passage which Wyman interprets as "a strange psychical experience" (180) awakened by tragedy after years of having "lived among conventions...[which] sufficed to quiet all impulse towards self-expression" (180). Of the relatively few incidents in Wyman's novel not taken directly from the play, most are flashbacks and reminiscences of Hamlet's boyhood (e.g. 14-15, 78-79, 144-45) which, as Martha Tuck Rozett notes (Rozett 75-76), may have been partially inspired by incidents from Wyman's own life as both daughter and mother. These moments in the novel are thus examples of the actual world influencing the fictional world, analogous in some ways to the "irruption of time into play" (Schmitt 23) that influenced the writing of the play itself.

Wyman's focus on Gertrude's relationship with Hamlet demonstrates that, even though Gertrude is the centre of her fictional world, the centre of Gertrude's world is "Hamlet... [who is] always with her – Hamlet first and last and all the time" (10) as, indeed, he has been to generations of readers and scholars of Shakespeare's play. She is genuinely concerned with her son's mental state, fearing he has truly gone insane with grief for his father (Wyman 125-45). Even Claudius's jealousy of the happy relationship between King Hamlet and Gertrude is in part influenced by the young Prince's central role in his parents' lives: on the one hand, he regards the young Hamlet as Gertrude's "intensest passion [which] so had prevented her husband from being the object thereof" (Wyman 11), but on the other "he hate[s] it, since its existence made him realize the more how far from the center of Gertrude's life was his own abiding place" (Wyman 11). But the most telling feature of Gertrude's concern for her son is that it is the primary reason she gives for wanting to marry Claudius after King Hamlet's death. Upon realizing that Hamlet has set up the Mousetrap play (Wyman 97-105; *Hamlet* III.ii. 154-270) as an attack on Claudius's marriage to her, though not knowing the full intent of the play, Gertrude indignantly says to herself, "Stupid child!... Why can't he divine why I married his uncle? Must he be told everything and have the words spelled to him, ere he can understand?"

---

[86] Indeed, the title page of Wyman's novel prints this quotation under a drawing of the Mother and Child.

(Wyman 101). According to Wyman, Gertrude marries Claudius both to protect Hamlet's right to the throne, knowing she is unlikely to have any other children while a younger wife might, and to protect her own position at court, fearing the possibility of having to live "a guarded life... of royal widowhood in a convent" (18).

Wyman's narrator insists repeatedly throughout the novel on Gertrude's innocence both in King Hamlet's death and in her remarriage (e.g. 114-15), in contrast to Belleforest's Geruthe, who maintains her innocence even as the narrator accuses her of complicity (*HT* 153, 163), as well as to the interpretations favoured by critics, such as A.C. Bradley (Rozett 82), who did believe in the existence of an extramarital affair between Claudius and Gertrude. For example, Wyman's narrator reads the confrontation between Hamlet and his mother in Shakespeare's Act III, scene iii. as proof that "No accomplice in either murder or adultery would thus have sought to probe the heart of her victim's son" (29). The Ghost's accusations against Claudius (*Hamlet* I.v. 42-83; Wyman 51-53) can, as Wyman notes, be read as a possible suspicion of guilt on Gertrude's part, but when the narrator brings up this possibility, Gertrude's ghost insists to her that "Whatever Claudius may have done.... He would never have made his mistress the queen of Denmark" (Wyman 53). But to Wyman, the strongest proof of Gertrude's innocence can be found in Claudius's confession: in his admission that he cannot repent because he will not give up "those effects for which I did the murther, / My crown, mine own ambition, and my queen" (*Hamlet* III.iii. 54-55), he is also "proclaim[ing] before Heaven, that he had not possessed his brother's wife while that brother was alive" (Wyman 115).

The confession is but one of the ways in which Wyman presents a more nuanced, and more sympathetic, Claudius than his counterpart in the Shakespearean texts and the interpretations of those texts by previous critics and readers. She notes that "he has been written of or ignored as though he possessed no idiosyncrasies whatsoever, and as if he might be pictorially represented on canvas by one shapeless, shadeless smirch of complete blackness" (152).

As previously noted, one of Claudius's principal motivations has been envy of his older brother's position and happy marriage. Wyman further develops the sibling rivalry between Claudius and King Hamlet through interpolated details unmentioned but hinted at by Shakespeare in Hamlet's "counterfeit presentment of two brothers" (III.ii. 54) and reminiscent of the latter two plays of his first tetralogy. Like Edward IV and Richard III, King Hamlet and Claudius are contrasted in physical appearance as well as in age, with the elder brother tall, strong, and handsome, and the younger "slightly hunched and curved in unbeautiful lines"[87] (Wyman 117; cf. *3HVI* III.ii. 153-95; *RIII* I.i. 14-31) and often dismissed by king and prince alike as "Sir Knight of Dwarfshire" (Wyman 118). Gertrude is the only member of the royal family to pity Claudius "because he had not been born with the right disposition" (Wyman 8), and her compassion does foster genuine feelings in him (see e.g. Wyman 176-77), even though she herself "did not love Claudius except in ordinary sisterly fashion" (Wyman 8). However, neither Wyman's Claudius nor Shakespeare's can be truly said to act out of "the bitterness of soul arising from physical malformation" (Marriott 213), as Richard does. Rather, Wyman attributes Claudius's actions against first his brother and then his nephew, and even his "o'erhasty marriage" (*Hamlet* II.ii. 57), primarily to desperation (150) but also, to some extent, to "that over development of aestheticism, which rots downward into the heart of man, and turns the love of anything... and of any person... into self love and the desire for gratification" (177).

The converse of Wyman's sympathetic treatments of Claudius and Gertrude is that the reputations of both Hamlet and his father suffer by comparison. On the one hand, Gertrude's ghost speaks fondly to the narrator of the genuine affection between herself and her first husband, though she adds the qualifying admission that both King Hamlet and Claudius "let me see them only when they were comporting themselves virtuously" (Wyman 5). The King himself, while he was alive, also displayed love and admiration for her (e.g. Wyman 10). But on the other, King Hamlet is frequently insensitive, even rude, to his younger brother Claudius (e.g. Wyman 9, 117-18), an attitude he passes on to his son. As well, where Claudius had always treated Gertrude as an equal both before and after their marriage, King Hamlet often "treated her mainly as a lovely plaything" (Wyman 133), presumably due to the age difference between them. Yet Wyman finds no evidence supporting that the Ghost suspected his wife's infidelity while he lived, and thus interprets his suspicions of Gertrude as out of character.

Just as Wyman accuses previous Shakespearean critics of being too unsympathetic to Claudius, so does she also charge them with being overly "enamoured of Hamlet" (241), and thus those critics fail to realize that the behaviours of those around him, far from being wholly antagonistic, could simply be read as sincere reactions to "a man and especially a prince who becomes insane" (241; cf. *Hamlet* III.i. 188). Indeed, she herself often doubts

---

[87] Wyman's comparison between Claudius and Richard III may also be a play on the literal meaning of the name *Claudius*, which comes from the Latin word *claudus*, meaning 'lame' (*Behind the Name*). Cf. Wain, "King-crowning is toward. And the crooked Feng / is made straight" (13), though here the imagery is metaphorical.

Hamlet's sanity, both because of his bitterness to Ophelia, Gertrude, Laertes, and Osric (e.g. 211-13), and because of his willingness to condemn Rosencrantz and Guildenstern to death, an act which places him "on the road towards extreme depravity" (Wyman 206), not unlike Claudius. Furthermore, in contrast to those interpretations of Hamlet which consider hesitation his tragic flaw, Wyman regards him as "incarnated Doubt" (222; cf. Mayer), finally characterizing him as

> a monstrous egotist, who could question all things in the Universe, himself included, but who could not see the answers to his questions, because his egoism imposed itself... between the eyes of his mind and everything in the Universe, not excluding himself. (222)

In this way, Wyman questions Hamlet's status as the centre of the Shakespearean fictional world, as well as the previous reputations of Gertrude and the other characters whom we have previously seen for the most part through his eyes. The narrator feels compelled to apologize to Gertrude for being "unable to gloss over her son's imperfections with inappropriate and unproved generalities of characterization" (226); however, while this statement is a definite response to previous Hamlet-centric and patriarchal readings of the play, it also shows sympathy both to Gertrude's "righteous sense, which made her defend a person from false accusation" (227) and even to Hamlet himself, despite all the flaws the narrator sees in his character.

Wyman chose the form of the "interpretive romance," a hybrid of romantic fiction and literary analysis, for her novel as a means of making academic discourse more accessible to lay readers, and especially to those women readers who were not involved in literary criticism, in a form the readers would find more aesthetically pleasing. In her focus on the oft-overlooked character of Gertrude as an archetype of "the self-sacrificing mother" (Rozett 72), she also familiarized the Shakespearean character for a reading public of wives and mothers, acknowledging both the similarities and differences between the actual world of the American middle and working classes and the fictional world of the Danish nobility.

Wyman's idealizing of Gertrude as a mother-figure while simultaneously questioning the Victorian image of the mother as 'the angel in the house' stands in sharp contrast to a later polemical revision of Gertrude by a woman writer: Margaret Atwood's 1983 short story/character sketch "Gertrude Talks Back." Wyman and Atwood are similar in both being feminist writers offering their interpretations of a prominent female character in the play, but their Gertrudes are very different from each other. Where Wyman follows Gertrude's life from her first marriage to her death, Atwood chooses a very specific timeframe, Gertrude's confrontation with Hamlet in her bedroom

(*Hamlet* III.iv.), for her text. The story is meant as an interpolation into the Shakespearean scene, representing Gertrude's inner psychological world at the moment her son acccuses her of having "my father very much offended" (*Hamlet* III.iv. 10). But, far from being frightened and worried by her son's behaviour, Atwood's Gertrude maintains a steadfast and often flippant attitude, which is emphasized by the fact that hers is the only voice we actually hear in the story. Though the reader is meant to fill in Hamlet's dialogue from Act III, scene iv of the play while reading the story, it is never made clear whether Gertrude is in fact speaking directly to him or merely thinking to herself while he questions her.

Atwood's Gertrude questions King Hamlet's insistence on naming their only son after himself, a decision she dismisses as "selfish" (167) while admitting that "I wanted to call you George" (167) – a more characteristically English, rather than Danish, name. She further insists that what Hamlet interprets as hand-wringing in either terror or guilt is really "drying my nails" (167). In response to Hamlet's description of "The counterfeit presentment of two brothers" (*Hamlet* III.iv. 54), she presents her own contrast of her two husbands, which is very different from the contrast her son makes between them. Where Shakespeare's Gertrude never speaks of her feelings toward either King Hamlet or Claudius, and Wyman's finds favour in both but for different reasons, Atwood's states unequivocally that she finds Claudius far more satisfying because "your Dad just wasn't a whole lot of fun.... You have no idea what I used to put up with" (167-68). In this way, Atwood's Gertrude frankly confesses her sexuality and that of both her husbands, but in a way that contradicts reader expectations, because her confession seems to be directed to her son. The informality of Atwood's dialogue further contrasts her Gertrude to Shakespeare's, who generally speaks in the formal tones and prosody associated with the nobility.

The Gertrude of "Gertrude Talks Back" also undercuts the idealized images of Hamlet and Ophelia that are familiar to most readers, even without their being present. Interestingly, in contrast to other contemporary treatments of the Hamlet story – not to mention the source texts of Saxo and Belleforest – which do posit a full sexual relationship between their counterparts of Hamlet and Ophelia, Atwood regards the couple as inexperienced, a reading much favoured in Victorian treatments such as Clarke's and post-Victorian treatments such as Wyman's. In a modern and ironic twist on Polonius's belief in the play that Hamlet is "Mad for... love" of Ophelia (*Hamlet* II.i. 82), Gertrude here believes that Hamlet's madness may be due to sexual frustration, which leads her to remark that "A real girlfriend would do you a heap of good. Not like that pasty-faced what's-her-name.... Any little shock could push her right over the edge" (Atwood 168). In this way too, Atwood's realistic and unsentimental Gertrude is a marked departure from the more sympathetic Gertrude – to both characters and readers – portrayed by earlier writers.

But the most obvious difference between Atwood's Gertrude and her counterparts in both the Shakespearean text and fellow adaptations is one that, in its way, hearkens back to Belleforest's dismissive characterization of her as an "unfortunate and wicked woman" (*Hystorie* 88). In Atwood's story, Gertrude, not Claudius, is the real murderer of King Hamlet: she admits in the story's closing sentences, "It wasn't Claudius, darling. It was me" (168). Atwood's text implies that Gertrude had killed her first husband precisely because she felt unsatisfied in her first marriage: as she says, "every time I felt like a little, you know, just to warm up my aging bones, it was like I'd suggested murder" (168). However, because the story presents us only with Gertrude's voice, with Hamlet's presence implied by relationship with the play yet silenced by the dominating first-person perspective, the reader does feel sympathy for Gertrude's actions. She also becomes a feminist counterpart of sorts to Hamlet himself – and perhaps to the Shakespearean Claudius as well – in that her decision to kill her first husband out of frustration can be viewed as an act of revenge for being taken for granted.

Atwood's short story is one of the relatively few revisions of *Hamlet* that blames someone other than Claudius for King Hamlet's death. Even those adaptations that reverse the 'polarity' of the Shakespearean text and its sources to present Claudius as a sympathetic protagonist do not entirely deny his role in murdering his brother; what they seek to do instead is understand his reasons for doing so. While there are not, as far as I am aware, enough pro-Claudius – and by implication, anti-Hamlet – adaptations to form a basis for a 'King Claudius Society' (cf. Murph 2-23), adaptations such as John Turing's[88] 1967 novel *My Nephew Hamlet* and John Wain's 1972 poem *Feng* do present their counterparts to Claudius in a much more sympathetic light than Shakespeare or his source texts did, often casting doubt in the process on the traditional images of King Hamlet, Gertrude, and/or their son.

Turing's novel is presented as an English translation of Claudius's journal before and during the events depicted in Shakespeare's play, supposedly 'originally' a highly encrypted work "changing from Danish to Latin, and occasionally to French... sometimes more than once within the compass of a single sentence" (xiii) – a reference to the languages in which Saxo and Belleforest wrote. Much like Wyman's *Gertrude of Denmark, My Nephew*

---

[88] John Turing was the brother of scientist Alan Turing, best known for his code-breaking efforts during World War II and his work in artificial-intelligence research. *My Nephew Hamlet* is dedicated to Alan.

Hamlet is meant as a 'corrective' to the Shakespearean view of events on the grounds that "for long have scholars been encouraged to put Shakespeare beyond the bounds of wholesome criticism and to assume, contrary to reason and the evidence, that the great man never made mistakes" (Turing ix). In Turing's fictional world, Claudius emerges as a more complex and forward-thinking character who is more a victim of circumstance than anything, in contrast with "his much detested martial brother... [and] the silly, amiable, and sensual but courageous Gertrude" (xii).

Many times throughout Turing's text, Claudius does appear to be the most sensible member of the Danish court. King Hamlet spends more time arranging pageants and parades (Turing 4-7) and ironically comparing himself to Julius Caesar – even to the extent that he celebrates his birthday on the Ides of March (Turing 4) – than he does actually ruling the kingdom, while Polonius is only slightly less bombastic than he is in the play. King Hamlet's captain of the guard is a "master of the drill book who knows all and understands nothing, Crappswein by name" (Turing 5), the name alone being an obvious clue to the disapproval Claudius feels for him and his office. Claudius, meanwhile, alternates between observing and commenting on the behaviour of those around him and making (somewhat anachronistic) improvements to his living quarters such as "the central heating system I ordered... last autumn... an insurance against the unspeakable Danish climate" (Turing 15) or an alarm to warn him of the presence of "the palace spies" (Turing 19). He reveals that the celebrated victory of King Hamlet over "the sledded Polacks on the ice" (*Hamlet* I.i. 63; Turing 16-17) was more the result of inclement weather than of any military prowess on the King's part, while the Polish soldiers themselves "were no more than a parcel of mercenaries engaged to support the army of the late King Fortinbras of Norway" (Turing 16). The account given by the poets (Turing 18) – and, presumably, which in this fictional world would have eventually come down to Shakespeare – should thus, in the world of *My Nephew Hamlet*, be taken as dramatic licence at best and propaganda at worst.

Turing's Claudius is entirely innocent of one charge many previous writers have laid against him: he did not have an affair with Gertrude prior to King Hamlet's death and indeed only marries her on the suggestion that "Your safety and hers depends on it.... Together you may crush your enemies" (Turing 60). In fact, Claudius is shocked to hear that palace gossip has been linking him to "the fastidious and inconsequent Gertrude" (Turing 33), as he is already in love with Penelope, great-niece of his physician Stavridos, whom he considers more intelligent.

Gertrude, meanwhile, is once again a relatively marginal figure in comparison to the central role she takes for Wyman and Atwood. She is concerned for the well-being of Hamlet (e.g. Turing 56-58) and Ophelia (Turing 78-79), and is friendlier to "those nitwits Rosencrantz and Guildenstern" (Turing 95) than Claudius desires to be, but we learn little of her other than through Claudius's often dismissive yet affectionate comments in his journal. As in many previous and subsequent treatments of the differences between her two marriages, Turing's Gertrude admits to being unsatisfied by King Hamlet, but her disappointment here is due to overindulgence rather than indifference on his part: she confesses to Claudius, "Your brother bored me stiff with his demands" (Turing 71), and hopes that her new husband will not do the same.

The text of *My Nephew Hamlet* is far less clear, however, over whether Claudius did in fact murder his brother. The journal entry that would have been for the day of King Hamlet's death (Turing 49) is partly missing and partly obscured; and when Claudius does speak of himself, Stavridos, and the coroner as "the assassin, his principals, and his accomplices" (Turing 50), it is uncertain whether this is truth or rumour. His interruption of the Mousetrap play (Turing 116; *Hamlet* III.ii. 265-95) comes more out of indignation at being accused of murdering King Hamlet than out of guilt for having done it; and even his prayer following the play (Turing 120-23; *Hamlet* III.iii. 36-72) is interpreted here as asking to be absolved of "that suspicion, already bred in my brother's lifetime, that his life was threatened" (Turing 121). He is also aware of Hamlet's presence during the prayer (Turing 121-23) and knows of his intentions, regarding him now not so much as a madman per se but as "a cool, shrewd, and calculating maniac" (Turing 127).

The Hamlet of Turing's text, in fact, has never appeared entirely sane, even before King Hamlet's death; Claudius observes that, between Hamlet's "vivacity and charm... mischievous cavortings with turns of phrase...engaging flights of fancy" and "black moods... long spells of brooding melancholy and fits of savagery... it seems... that there are two beings in one" (Turing 40). Claudius and Gertrude themselves suppose Hamlet's behaviour to be a combination of the stresses of high nobility, unrequited feelings for Ophelia, and the influence of "that hot-bed of vice and so-called liberal thought, the University of Wittenberg" (Turing 75). Stavridos, on the other hand, follows the example of many literary critics and stage directors in implicitly suggesting that Hamlet may have unhealthy preoccupations with his mother, as hinted at in his constant references to the myth of Oedipus (e.g. Turing 30-32), though very little is in fact made of this possibility. Furthermore, Hamlet has formed a friendship and most probably a political alliance with Fortinbras, who in Turing's text is also a student at Wittenberg, and may be planning to use the uncertainty in Denmark and Norway to their advantage (e.g. Turing 26, 137).[89] As the novel progresses, Claudius becomes more certain that Hamlet is in fact feigning madness and that his actions stem from "his dearest ambition... the throne. He is very proud, revengeful, and ambitious. The throne offers him satisfaction in all three respects" (Turing 104).

The presence or absence of supernatural forces, an important element of the Shakespearean fictional world, is uncertain in Turing's. Claudius himself admits to wavering between skepticism and belief, especially as he too has occasionally felt "the ghostly presence of [his] brother" (Turing 83) in moments of great stress; while Penelope dismisses science, religion, and superstition alike as human attempts at "For ever theorizing and trying to trim the universe to fit their [i.e. the theorists'] own neat conceptions and absurd notions" (Turing 33). But the more prominent manifestations of Hamlet's famous statement "There are more things in heaven and earth... / Than are dreamt of in your philosophy" (*Hamlet* I.v. 166-167) are in the form of prophecies rather than of ghostly visitations. For example, although Claudius dismisses mythology as "far from my taste.... Primitive garbage" (Turing 30), he recognizes Stavridos's reference to the Oedipus myth as a story of "him who divined the riddle of the Sphinx and thereby delivered Thebes" (Turing 30), referring to Hamlet's role in the Shakespearean text as a restorer of order even at terrible cost to himself. However, it is Penelope, despite her declaration of skepticism several pages before, who delivers the most ominous – to Claudius, and obvious – to the reader – prophecy: she warns him shortly after King Hamlet's death that he is "to be assassinated!... You were born to dig your own grave, Claudius... it will not endear you to your nephew" (Turing 42, 43). It is with this prophecy in mind that Claudius pursues his various acts against Hamlet, not so much out of evil intent, as the Shakespearean text would have it, but out of desperation, as in Wyman's version. His final journal entry combines his disappointment over not being able to arrange a proper funeral for Ophelia (cf. *Hamlet* V.i. 1-29, 218-42) with his concern that Hamlet has not only returned to Denmark but is most likely in league with Fortinbras: "In this, as in all else, I have failed. Forgive me" (Turing 138).

In contrast to Atwood, who blames Gertrude rather than Claudius for King Hamlet's murder, and Turing, who leaves the identity of the murderer deliberately uncertain, John Wain openly accepts the malign nature of his (text's) counterpart to the Claudius role in his 1972 poem cycle *Feng*. His

---

[89] Claudius refers to the alliance of Hamlet and Fortinbras as "the Primrose League" (Turing 14), a reference to the supporters of Benjamin Disraeli in Victorian Britain as well as to Ophelia's warning to Laertes about "the primrose path of dalliance" (*Hamlet* I.iii. 50).

protagonist, called by the name he has in Saxo's *Historiae Danicae,* is
portrayed as a "sick and hallucinated person who seizes power and then has
to live with it" (Wain vi); the common theme of the seventeen short poems
is Feng's desire to explain why he has done the things he has done. Like
Turing's Claudius, Wain's Feng disapproves of his older brother's
preoccupation with war and conquest, but where the Claudius of *My Nephew
Hamlet* constantly protests that, though he sometimes wished his brother
dead, he did not in fact want it to happen (e.g. Turing 52), the Feng of
Wain's poems justifies his actions with the realization that defeating a king
in battle – as Horwendil has done in Norway – is just as much an act of
regicide as killing him in his orchard: "Horwendil / king-killer / stamps his
red seal / of approval, on all / king-killing" (Wain 5).

As in the fictional worlds of "Gertrude Talks Back" and *My Nephew
Hamlet,* the world of *Feng* is mediated through the eyes of a first-person
narrator, and it is his perspective that colours the fictional world, and the
characters who populate it, for the reader. Wain's Feng differs from his
counterparts in previous adaptations in that he displays no obvious affection
for Gerutha, speaking of her only as "A chattel, a transmitted thing /... / she
moved on dull, obedient feet / like the mild cow some peasant drove" (44).
Both partners regard the marriage as a duty, though Feng also realizes that
marrying his brother's widow is the culmination of the process by which
"When I killed Horwendil...I turned myself into him" (32). In this way, Feng
also realizes that he is just as much a madman as Amleth himself, but where
"Amleth's madness is a mask: / behind it his revenge-thoughts grow cool as
cress /... / My insanity is to be the cold king / with the curtains of his mind
drawn tight together, / sitting at council with shadows, talking to ghosts"
(Wain 21, 22). But madness is not the only trait Feng and Amleth share:
several times, Feng confesses that "I love the dark girl who loves Amleth"
(Wain 23), Ophelia's unnamed counterpart in Wain's fictional world. Just as
his indignation over what he regards as Horwendil's savagery leads him "to
fratricide and regicide" (Wain 5), so does his desire for the young woman
lead him, in the final poem of the cycle, to rape her (Wain 54-55), with the
implication that he is again imitating the actions of another – in this case,
Amleth himself (cf. *HD* 63-64).

Wain's text does not present the alethically dyadic fictional world (Doležel,
Heterocosmica 114-23) present in Shakespeare's *Hamlet,* in which the
supernatural domain is not only present but can make contact with the
physical one. Instead, the contrast present in the world of *Feng* is between
civilization and nature, and the action focuses on each one's disregard for the
other. Reflecting upon Horwendil's battle against the King of Norway and the
festival which followed, Feng notices the total lack of concern among "the

wild swans and the deer... / [who] do not know that they have changed their nation" (Wain 4) as they move about over the land for which two kingdoms fight; at the same time, he is reminded that "these fools will treat the soil as if / it were as white and worthless as the snow" (Wain 1; cf. *Hamlet* IV.iv. 17-22) in the pursuit of their "childish game" (Wain 1). At the moment at which he murders his brother, he reminisces about his summer hunting seals "without, I hope, unnecessary brutality" (Wain 7) – a concern as much "of our own time and place" (Wain vi) as of the society depicted in the poem – while at his coronation, he ponders the vast differences between "the falcon's freedom, the fish-hunting / heron's stance, his stilted silence, / the coney's casualness in coming and going" (Wain 15) and the rules, customs, and ceremonies by which human societies operate (cf. *HV* IV.i. 230-84). All of these examples speak to character and reader at the same time, though in different ways. For Feng, the observation of nature helps him to justify his behaviour by analogy to that of animals who take what they want, when they want it. For the reader, the poems serve as reminders that actual-world society frequently loses track of the world around it and of which it is a part, especially emphasizing that animals, unlike people, take only what they need, only when they need it.

The contrasts between civilization and nature, and between law and desire, in the world of *Feng* further illustrate that this is "a world where the only reality is Power" (Wain 33) and that "to have Power, these beings... will barter everything in the world and if necessary gamble away the world itself" (Wain 34). This is, of course, a theme running through the majority of Shakespeare's writing, and one that especially drew Wain to the Hamlet story and its similarities to his own time, "an age in which raving madmen have had control of great and powerful nations" (Wain vi). It also brings the motivations of Hamlet and Fortinbras – the latter of who does not appear in Wain's text – into question: are they truly seeking revenge for their fathers to restore the natural order of things, or are they too part of the eternal struggle for power, and thus no better than Feng himself?

One question Wain's text does not answer, other than through Feng's disapproving comments, is what sort of character Horwendil is. Similarly, Atwood's and Turing's texts, when they do speak of the late king at all, show him in a negative light, and even Wyman's 'traditional' view of Hamlet's parents leaves King Hamlet in the background. However, King Hamlet does have the distinction of having inspired what is perhaps the longest *Hamlet* adaptation: the American playwright Percy MacKaye's 1949 tetralogy of plays known as *The Mystery of Hamlet, King of Denmark, or What We Will*. The four plays were MacKaye's last completed works and were performed only once (Rozett 89); in the afterword to the complete

edition, he mentions planning to write a sequel to *Hamlet* (MacKaye 655),
but he never did so. MacKaye himself considered *The Mystery of Hamlet* "a
profound work of poetry" (Van Waveren 659) serving as a simultaneous
tribute to his wife and father (cf. Rozett 90-94); however, later critics such
as Ruby Cohn dismissed it as a "blend of incompetence and pretentiousness"
(187), while Martha Tuck Rozett takes a slightly more balanced view of its
combination of "psychological realism... [with] melodramatic, fantastic,
mixed-media effect" (99).

The Mystery of Hamlet is very much concerned with possible worlds, not
only as a counterpart world to *Hamlet* but also as a text constructed of
multiple worlds. Even in its orthography it makes note of "the passing from
the visible to the invisible world" (MacKaye x) as well as the intersections
of its textual world with that of Shakespeare's play, all of which are indicated
with marginal emblems. The plays also contain embedded fictional worlds of
plays within plays and texts within texts, in a manner similar to the presence
of the Mousetrap play in *Hamlet* itself. Most notable among these are a
performance at court of the *Norwich Grocer's Play* (MacKaye 164-75), a
medieval dramatization of the story of Adam and Eve, in which Claudius
himself plays the serpent; and the royal priest/tutor Padre Celestino's
recitations of and commentaries on excerpts from Dante's *Divine Comedy*
(MacKaye 189-203), which underscore the tetralogy's central theme of the
redemptive power of both earthly and divine love.

In addition to the Danish royal family themselves, Yorick is also a
significant figure in the first half of the tetralogy as King Hamlet's jester and
confidant, making him a counterpart to the Fool in Shakespeare's *King Lear*
as well as to Horatio in *Hamlet,* while also providing an explanation behind
Hamlet's elegy over the skull (*Hamlet* V.i. 184-95). Gertrude too has a
confidante: Moll Cowslip, "the midwife who delivers Hamlet" (Rozett 96) at
the end of the first play (MacKaye 75-77) and continues to play a major role
until her death at the end of the fourth (MacKaye 615). But the most
remarkable and unusual character of MacKaye's tetralogy who has no overt
counterpart in Shakespeare is Gallucinius, an enigmatic figure representing
the intersection of the physical and spiritual worlds, in much the same way
that King Hamlet, as the Ghost, represents such intersections in the world of
Shakespeare's play. However, Gallucinius's part in MacKaye's plays, and the
significance of his role, are even more ambiguous and less readily apparent
than the Ghost's in Shakespeare's. At times Gallucinius seems to be a
messenger of doom, as in his warning to King Hamlet of his eventual fate at
the hands of his brother (e.g. MacKaye 14-22). At other times, he is a

demonic – or perhaps daimonic[90] – figure urging Claudius toward a "choice between love and hatred" (Rozett 98; cf. MacKaye 81-84), which leads to the death of Yorick's daughter Angela (MacKaye 104) and eventually to the deaths of the entire royal family at the end of the Shakespearean text. Elsewhere in the plays, Gallucinius appears as what is his most likely role in MacKaye's fictional world, "the carrier of much of the four plays' Christian symbolism" (Rozett 95), which is most powerfully expressed in his first appearance to King Hamlet:

> Mine is the eerie, transsubstantiating
> Cry of the primal energy – to warn
> And waken all drowsy earth-dwellers to insight
> Of their solar birth. My aim, at Elsinore,
> King Hamlet, is to show thee to thyself.
>   (MacKaye 13)

The opening scene of MacKaye's first play thus calls back to the appearance of the Ghost to the Shakespearean Hamlet, in more ways than one, as Gallucinius uses interpolated passages from Shakespeare's play (*Hamlet* I.iv. 1-91, I.v. 1-92; qtd. in MacKaye 14-16, 19-21) to show not only King Hamlet to himself, but Prince Hamlet to his father. This scene also suggests Hamlet's insistence to Gertrude that he will "set you up a glass / Where you may see the inmost part of you" (*Hamlet* III.iv. 19-20).

Having both been visited by different manifestations of the same spiritual entity, King Hamlet and Claudius become counterparts to each other in another way: they represent different aspects of madness, which here can be defined in terms of both anger and insanity. From the beginning of the first play, we are told that King Hamlet sleepwalks (MacKaye 8), an allusion to Lady Macbeth, and his dreams and visions of ghosts that occur throughout the tetralogy are visual and auditory reminders of his divided loyalties as king, husband, and father. In the second play he is a loving father to the young Prince Hamlet, whom he teaches the virtues of "Love and Memory" (MacKaye 151; cf. *Hamlet* I.v. 95-104). The King begins the third play as a symbol of the transition between old order and new, as indicated by the peasant family's mistaking him for both Odin and Jesus, figures of, respectively, war and love. However, as he learns of the developing

---

[90] At the beginning of the fourth play, MacKaye does refer to Gallucinius as "King Hamlet's Daemon" (497), with both meanings – malevolent entity and guardian spirit – implied.

relationship between Claudius and Gertrude (MacKaye 313-16), he becomes
jealous not only of them but also of the time Prince Hamlet spends away

> from his familiar
> Heaven of childhood and the cherishing
> Arms of our schooling love, to seek far hostels
> Of homeless learning, in the vexing lore
> Of magic, and the erudite ignorances
> Of the university. (MacKaye 404; cf. Turing 75)

It is with his disapproving reactions to Hamlet's tales of life at Wittenberg,
including, in an example of fictional worlds intersecting, having met "the
most learned Doctor Faustus" (MacKaye 461), that King Hamlet begins his
own descent into madness. Unlike that of his son, however, his madness is
clearly genuine. He also reverts from representing the new order of divine
love, to representing the old order defined by the desire for revenge, on
overhearing Claudius and Gertrude meeting in a mirrored room "which shows
us what we are" (MacKaye 485), which alludes to Hamlet's reminder to the
Players that "the purpose of playing... was and is, to hold as 'twere the
mirror up to nature" (*Hamlet* III.ii. 20-22).

   The contrast between the feigned madness of Shakespeare's Prince Hamlet
and the genuine madness of MacKaye's King Hamlet is most powerfully
illustrated in the middle of MacKaye's fourth play, as the king destroys his
son's books (550-56) and mumbles in his sleep of "hunting for... poison....
/ My own dear brother – / For whom – I pray – he may be damned – /...
/ Mean, mean, incestuous beast – / 'Vengeance is mine,' saith the Lord"
(MacKaye 564-65; cf. Kyd, *ST* III.xiii. 1-45). As Martha Tuck Rozett points
out, "the maddened King has invited his own destruction and described the
means by which it will occur" (100). Ironically, the King's madness makes
Claudius into a more sympathetic character by comparison, as MacKaye
contrasts King Hamlet's rage and single-minded desire for revenge with
Claudius's more tortured passion for Gertrude and envy of his brother.
Claudius thus becomes a counterpart to Shakespeare's Macbeth as well as to
Marlowe's Dr. Faustus (see e.g. MacKaye 228-29; cf. Rozett 98) – the latter
of whom Prince Hamlet is said to know personally, a familiarity that makes
these two characters counterparts to their authors, Shakespeare and Marlowe.
As for Prince Hamlet, he at first has no desire to take his father's throne,
either as regent during the elder Hamlet's madness or as king following his
father's death, wishing instead to marry Ophelia (MacKaye 632-33), until
Gertrude reveals that the way in which she intends "to free thee / From the
immense responsibilities / Of state, and loose thee to thy dearest aim – / Thy
quest of quiet with Ophelia" (MacKaye 637) is to marry Claudius herself.

The news of his mother's impending remarriage creates an ominous and all-too-familiar change in Hamlet's attitude toward Ophelia, symbolized in the letter he writes to her which begins "Return to thy nunnery!" (MacKaye 645); and with this, MacKaye's fictional world feeds back into Shakespeare's for the final time, as the last scene of *The Mystery of Hamlet* is in fact the second scene, as it appears in the Second Quarto and First Folio texts, of Shakespeare's *Hamlet.*

What all of these prequel texts and/or role expansions have in common, and yet where they also differ, is their focus on a single character: Gertrude for Wyman and Atwood, Claudius for Turing and Wain, and King Hamlet for MacKaye. By contrast, John Updike's 2000 novel *Gertrude and Claudius,* probably the best-known prequel to *Hamlet,* attempts to create a more balanced fictional world both in its presentation of the King Hamlet/Gertrude/Claudius triangle and in its allusions to the play and the play's two primary source texts. In the first third of the novel, the characters' names derive from Saxo; in the second, from Belleforest via the 1608 English translation; and in the third, from Shakespeare. However, the characters themselves are the same people throughout the three parts of Updike's text, and the name changes are given in-world explanations. For example, the change from Saxo's to Belleforest's names comes in part from the way Feng and Gerutha pronounce each other's names when speaking to each other privately: "she let the 'ng' linger in the air, so as almost to create a second syllable. Her own name too...was softened to 'Geruthe'" (Updike 76). The more drastic changes from the Danish names in Saxo and Belleforest to the Latinate names in Shakespeare, however, are for more public reasons of ceremony and royal dignity: "Fengon... had named himself Claudius at the coronation, and Corambis,[91] following his master into the imperial dignity of Latin, had taken the name Polonius" (Updike 164).

Updike's fictional world thus provides an interesting interpretation, even an inversion, of the counterpart relations described by Saul Kripke and by David Lewis, as well as of the descriptivist theory first proposed by Bertrand Russell. To reiterate, Kripke's theory of counterpart relations depends on names as rigid designators which necessarily *refer to* or *designate* the same entities in any world and never designate anything else; Russell's theory depends on "a standard cluster of descriptiv[e] attributes" (Norris 231) shared by counterparts; and Lewis's view is an intermediate position between these, arguing that neither names alone nor descriptors alone are sufficient to

---

[91] The seeming inconsistencies of the spellings of "Feng/Fengon," "Gerutha/Geruthe," and "Corambus/Corambis" in this section are intentional: Updike uses both spellings in the first two sections of his novel. Here I follow his choices of spelling of the characters' names.

identify counterparts, but that an entity's essential properties can and do include both names and descriptors. A reading of *Gertrude and Claudius* using a superficial interpretation of Kripke's theory of names and counterparts might regard Updike's text as composed of three counterpart worlds, each with its own set of characters, and each corresponding to its respective source text. In this respect, the novel seems to invite a descriptivist reading, in that, despite being referred to by three different sets of names drawn from the text's various sources, the characters are described throughout with the same sets of properties, and each component section of the novel provides its own advancing of the plot. However, as Updike's explanations for the name changes indicate, each of these readings is partially correct, and all of these readings co-exist, as what appear to be three counterpart worlds within the same text are meant to be one world, albeit influenced by three different source texts, with the same set of characters.

Updike acknowledges the interdependence of fictional worlds with each other and the actual world early in his text, when Gerutha and Corambus show their first real concern for young Amleth's behaviour. Corambus dismisses Amleth's fascination with the theatre, a characteristic that becomes prominent in the Shakespearean Hamlet, as an unhealthy interest in "this unholy travesty of theatrical performance, which, aping Creation, distracts men from last things and from first things as well" (Updike 42) – a commonly-voiced objection to drama and fiction in Shakespeare's time as well. He similarly ridicules Gerutha's love of "those immoral Gaulish romances, which would make idle, sterile adoration the main business of life" (Updike 45). Corambus's attitude toward fictional worlds has its counterpart in the equally dismissive stance both royal brothers take toward Hamlet's years of study at Wittenberg, where he has encountered multiple worlds and worldviews. At the beginning of the novel's second part, Horvendile complains that his son is "learning how to doubt – learning mockery and blasphemy when I'm trying to instill piety and order into a scheming, rebellious conglomeration of Danes" (Updike 80); and a year later, as the third part begins, Claudius too criticizes the "seditious doctrines – humanism, usury, market values, the monarchy as something less than the pure gift of God" (Updike 164) as distractions from the "reality" (Updike 164) of princely duty.

Like many other *Hamlet* adaptations that have attempted to provide a backstory to the events of the play, *Gertrude and Claudius* supposes that the title characters' relationship developed during Gertrude's marriage to King Hamlet, which left the queen unfulfilled. Indeed, Updike's Gerutha, knowing that her own mother had been forced into marrying "the son of her father's slayer" (8), is reluctant to enter a political marriage with Horwendil.

Corambus, who has come with Gerutha from her father's court, regards Horwendil as "an uncouth usurper" (32), remains in his service only for her sake, and even enables her relationship with Feng by offering the use of his own summer home (95-102) while her husband is away. Gerutha, meanwhile, is fascinated by Feng, partly because of the stories he tells her of his travels in Italy and Byzantium (e.g. Updike 49-50, 105-19, 126-28; cf. *Othello* I.iii. 128-70), and partly because of her realization that "Younger brothers...are like daughters in that no one takes them quite as seriously as they desire" (Updike 14).

Updike's revision of the Hamlet story shares with Wyman's version a profound sympathy towards Gertrude and the concerns of women in a male-dominated social circle. At the same time, Updike's Claudius is reminiscent of Turing's and Wain's in that he is presented, not as a one-dimensional villain, but as genuinely suffering for love of Gertrude (e.g. Updike 72) and finally driven to murder his brother after Horvendile has discovered their adultery and threatened him with banishment (Updike 139-50). However, where Wyman's Gertrude is defined as an archetypal mother whose main fault is caring too much, Updike's feels equally unfulfilled as mother and wife. Throughout the novel she remembers the painful experience of giving birth to Hamlet (Updike 33-35, 172; cf. *RIII* IV.iv. 166-75) and constantly takes his behaviour and moods as signs of being "an utter failure as a mother" (Updike 41), even relating that Hamlet's open disapproval of her remarriage makes her "feel dirty and ashamed and unworthy... shallow, stupid, and wicked" (Updike 165; cf. *Hystorie* 88). Similarly, where Turing's Claudius and Wain's Feng define themselves in opposition to their brothers' preoccupations with military might, Updike's Claudius defines himself with the compassion and concern he feels for Gertrude's unhappiness "in a mummifying royal propriety" (132) and the indignation both he and Gertrude feel when the King places the blame for the affair on her (Updike 145). Yet Gertrude's and Claudius's motives are not entirely selfish, for at the end of the novel, Claudius imagines a possible future in which nobody discovers his responsibility for his brother's murder, and Hamlet and Ophelia, with "the royal heirs lined up like ducklings" (Updike 210), ascend the throne peacefully. The reader is, of course, aware that Claudius's possible world does not become actual in Shakespeare's play or even any of the source texts.

Martha Tuck Rozett characterizes a central theme of *Hamlet* prequels as the challenge of living in the shadow of one's parent, as Wyman and MacKaye considered themselves to have done, and as Shakespeare's Hamlet often feels himself to be doing (e.g. *Hamlet* I.ii. 139-53). This theme is characteristic of *Hamlet* adaptations in general, which by their nature are doomed to be judged against the standard of their 'parent' text. However, in the case of *Hamlet* prequels, the relationship between the 'original' and the adaptations is ironic in that texts focusing on the parents have always, to some degree, remained in the shadow of a text focusing on the son.

He Has My Dying Voice: Horatio and Fortinbras as Main Characters

What happened after *Hamlet* is as much a mystery as what happened before, despite – or perhaps because of – the play's optimistic but rather abrupt ending. Only two characters, Horatio and Fortinbras, are left alive, and Shakespeare does not provide as much information on their characters as he has done for Hamlet and the royal family. Therefore, just as King Hamlet, Claudius, and Gertrude have provided inspiration for writers filling in the play's backstory, Horatio and Fortinbras have also provided inspiration for writers imagining the state of post-*Hamlet* Denmark.

As a counterpart to the protagonist, a potential threat from the outside, and the ultimate victor in the wake of the mass deaths at the play's end, Fortinbras is simultaneously one of the most significant minor characters and one of the most overlooked major characters in Shakespeare's *Hamlet*. Indeed, many productions of the play tend to reduce his role, if not ignore it completely, preferring to focus on Hamlet himself and, to a lesser extent, the main revenge plot. Dennis Kennedy notes in *Foreign Shakespeares* that placing primary emphasis on Hamlet sidesteps how the play ends "with a belligerent outsider taking over the Danish throne" (4). On the other hand, treatments of Fortinbras as a significant character often expand his position as a "belligerent outsider" and imagine him, not so much as the Hamlet that never was, but rather "as an oppressive ruler worse than Claudius" (Beyenburg 74).[92] It is this characterization of Fortinbras as successor to Claudius rather than to Hamlet that seems to have dominated his treatment in many post-Shakespearean sequels to the Hamlet story, while other sequels have struck a balance between Fortinbras as Claudius analogue and as Hamlet analogue, portraying him as an effective ruler who nevertheless does employ dubious methods. In seeking to expand the role of this minor yet significant character, Fortinbras-centered adaptations of *Hamlet* appear to share the common trait of interpreting the play's ending not as a hopeful new beginning, but seeing instead yet another link in the chain of violence and revenge.

---

[92] Two such examples in the play's production history are the Renaissance Theatre Company's 1988 production directed by Derek Jacobi, "who interpreted Fortinbras's final line as an order to execute Horatio and [the] attendant lords" (Beyenburg 74), and Kenneth Branagh's 1996 film, which ends in a similar, albeit less drastic, manner.

When comparing Shakespeare's play to Saxo Grammaticus's *Historiae Danicae,* we can find some justification for reading the succession from Hamlet to Fortinbras in this manner. The inspiration for Shakespeare's Fortinbras is Wiglek, a relation of Amleth's mother, who "harassed Amleth's mother with all manner of insolence and stripped her of her royal wealth, complaining that her son had usurped the kingdom of Jutland" (*HD* 78). Wiglek eventually defeats Amleth in battle and marries his widow, Queen Hermutrude of Scotland, in what seems to be a partial influence on the "o'erhasty marriage" (*Hamlet* II.ii. 57) of Feng/Claudius and Gerutha/ Gertrude. In fact, a more immediate source text for the play, François de Belleforest's *Histoires Tragiques,* makes the parallels between Wiglek and Feng, and thus between their Shakespearean counterparts Fortinbras and Claudius, more explicit, describing Amleth's rival and successor as "his uncle... having taken the royal treasure from his sister Geruthe" (*Hystorie* 121).

Shakespeare's play does attribute to Fortinbras the desire "to recover of us, by strong hand / And terms compulsatory, those foresaid lands / So by his father lost" (*Hamlet* I.i. 102-104) in battle against Denmark, but does not explicitly describe him as a relative of the Danish royal family. Fortinbras's "rights, of memory in this kingdom" (*Hamlet* V.ii. 389) stem primarily from the wish to avenge his father's defeat rather than from blood relation. Throughout the play, Fortinbras appears as a foil to Hamlet, first in the guards' supposition that the appearance of the Ghost is a sign of the danger Fortinbras poses to Denmark (*Hamlet* I.i. 95-107) rather than of the suspicious manner of King Hamlet's death (*Hamlet* I.v. 22-91). The parallels are made more explicit with the revelation that both Hamlet and Fortinbras have been denied the right to succession by their uncles (*Hamlet* I.ii. 27-38). Hamlet himself recognizes Fortinbras as both a counterpart and an example upon encountering the Norwegian captain in Act IV, scene iv, realizing that, whereas both seek to avenge their fathers, Hamlet delays action while Fortinbras, though on the surface "a delicate and tender prince /... with divine ambition puff'd / Makes mouths at the invisible event, / Exposing what is mortal and unsure / To all that fortune, death, and danger dare / Even for an egg-shell" (*Hamlet* IV.iv. 48-53). Indeed, it is perhaps admiration for Fortinbras's forthrightness in comparison to his own hesitation that leads Hamlet, at the end of his life, to give the Norwegian prince his "dying voice" (*Hamlet* V.ii. 356) as the new king. Fortinbras, for his part, shows some admiration and respect for Hamlet as well in his declaration that Hamlet "was likely, had he been put on, / To have prov'd most royal" (*Hamlet* V.ii. 397-98).

Post-Restoration productions of *Hamlet*, beginning in about 1676, tended to de-emphasize or omit the Norwegian subplot, both for time reasons and to focus more on Hamlet himself; as Margreta de Grazia notes, "Not until 1898 did Fortinbras return at the play's end to take over the Danish throne" (62). But it is in twentieth-century adaptations of the Hamlet story that Fortinbras truly begins to receive the sort of attention previously reserved for his Danish counterpart. He is a prominent character in Michael Innes's two contributions to *Three Tales of Hamlet*: the radio play *The Hawk and the Handsaw* and the essay "The Mysterious Affair at Elsinore," which, though written by the same author less than a year apart, come to virtually opposite conclusions about the Prince of Norway's character and motives. *The Hawk and the Handsaw* also employs Shakespeare's text not only as a source but also as a play-within-the-play, calling attention to the status of both Shakespeare's and Innes's plays as adaptations as well as to the interplay of multiple fictional worlds.

First produced in 1948, *The Hawk and the Handsaw*[93] begins forty years after the end of *Hamlet*, with a production of Shakespeare's play before Fortinbras and Horatio themselves, marked by "loud and prolonged applause, punctuated by cries of 'Long live the King!' and 'God save King Fortinbras!'" (*H&H* 30) whenever Fortinbras's name is mentioned. The reaction of both Fortinbras and the court to the play leads Horatio to comment on the use of drama as a means of remembering and glorifying important people and events in a nation's history, a theme surrounding many of Shakespeare's plays, including *Hamlet*:

> Would Plato, think you, have cast out these pestilent poets from his commonwealth, had he with the like subtlety considered the uses of them?... "That play's the thing," I said. "The ship of state sails thus, and there is needful... of the affection that the better sort in Denmark do bear King Fortinbras. And for that yon play's the thing!" (*H&H* 33-34)

However, Innes's use of Shakespeare's *Hamlet* as a reversal of the Mousetrap does not establish the post-Hamlet world as politically similar to that of Shakespeare's text, despite perhaps appearing to do so at first glance. There is no overarching suggestion of the play as propaganda, nor even just of praise to those in power – common objections that have been raised in criticism of, for example, Shakespeare's history plays. The play, in fact, inspires Fortinbras to learn the truth behind Hamlet's actions and the death

---

[93] Hereafter cited as *H&H*.

of the Danish royal family, "however it may be with the official historiographer" (*H&H* 41).

Fortinbras's curiosity about whether Hamlet was truly mad leads him to speak with Dr. Mungo, a Scottish physician who had previously treated "a sufferer... in the late reigning family...[who] would not minister to herself" (*H&H* 44) – an intertextual reference to Lady Macbeth that links the worlds of both plays. Dr. Mungo had also spoken to Hamlet several times between the death of King Hamlet (*H&H* 43-52) and the prince's voyage to England (*H&H* 53-71). Through his conversations with Hamlet, Dr. Mungo comes to believe that Hamlet had indeed imagined the Ghost, and even imagined the story of King Hamlet's murder from memories of reading *The Murder of Gonzago* (*H&H* 64). Mungo believes, furthermore, that Ophelia may have been the product of an affair between King Hamlet and Polonius's wife (*H&H* 66-68), which Hamlet had apparently witnessed. Dr. Mungo's story does not convince Fortinbras, who replies with questions of his own:

> You found Prince Hamlet in dejection and some doubt indeed... but yet whetting a dagger with good heart to use it. You left him... with a whole crop of doubts, as novel as deep, growing between him and any issue in action.... Had you not opened to him, perhaps, the vision of a climate too chill for the tree of the knowledge of good and evil to grow and bear in? (*H&H* 72)

A hypothesis much like Dr. Mungo's conclusion that "the ghost... had its origin not in any crime of Claudius's but in a mental aberration of his nephew Hamlet's" ("MA" 82), forms a key part of Innes's 1949 essay "The Mysterious Affair at Elsinore."[94] The essay is a tongue-in-cheek analysis of the Shakespearean play's ending, presented in the manner of a detective novel, a genre with which Innes had much experience.[95] However, the essay treats Fortinbras, as well as Horatio, in a far less sympathetic manner than the radio play did, a decision that Ruby Cohn characterizes as "symptomatic of a not uncommon modern distaste for Fortinbras" (180-81). While *The Hawk and the Handsaw* portrays Fortinbras and Horatio in a generally positive light, seeking answers and maintaining a healthy degree of skepticism about what they find, "The Mysterious Affair at Elsinore" "place[s] the blame" for the play's tragic end "squarely upon the shoulders of Prince Fortinbras of Norway" ("MA" 77) with Horatio as his accomplice.

---

[94] Hereafter cited as "MA."

[95] Innes also wrote the 1937 mystery novel *Hamlet, Revenge!,* which takes place at a production of Shakespeare's play.

Innes's narrator construes the orders in Fortinbras's closing speech (*Hamlet* V.ii. 395-403) as deliberate efforts to hide evidence, for "as we all know, the bodies must on no account be moved" ("MA" 77), and "the salvoes which Fortinbras caused to be fired off" ("MA" 79) would have hidden any sounds or smells that might provide clues to the multiple murders. Furthermore, since an important factor considered in the traditional detective story is which character would have most to gain from the crime, "we have only to ask ourselves... who would come to the throne if all these persons were liquidated?... the man who did come to the throne when they were!" ("MA" 86).

The narrator suggests that "Fortinbras's intent... was simply to embroil in mutual suspicion...all those who stood between him [i.e. Fortinbras] and the throne of Denmark" ("MA" 89), in a manner reminiscent of Richard III[96] or Macbeth. The narrator further implicates Horatio in the plot precisely because of Hamlet's request that Horatio "Report me and my cause aright / To the unsatisfied" (*Hamlet* V.ii. 339-40). If Horatio did become Fortinbras's "official historiographer" (*H&H* 41), it is possible, according to the narrator, that he would produce a treatment "hopelessly obscured beneath the devices of sensational fiction" ("MA" 82), designed to hide not only the involvement of Fortinbras, but also such details – found in Innes but not in Shakespeare – as Rosencrantz and Guildenstern being "Claudius's natural sons" ("MA" 86) and Ophelia having been secretly married to Hamlet.

Innes presumably did not intend for his theory of Fortinbras's involvement in the elimination of the Danish royal family to be taken seriously; however, a similar plot runs through Hunter Steele's 1987 prose retelling of the play, *Lord Hamlet's Castle*. From his first appearance in Steele's novel, Fortinbras is described with "Pugnacious determination in his mouth; ruthless ambition in his eye" (55), and the narrative makes it clear that even as the ambassadors announce that he "vows nevermore to scheme against your majesty" (70; cf. *Hamlet* II.ii. 70-71), he is indeed raising "troops and equipment" (70) for his planned invasion.

Steele's reason for establishing that "the precipitator [of King Hamlet's murder] was Young Fortinbras" (122) is similar to Innes's but adds to Innes's theory the observation that Claudius did not murder the king "until Old Hamlet was nearly dead of old age anyway" (122). Indeed, according to Steele, Claudius might not have done it at all had Fortinbras not suggested

---

[96] "The Mysterious Affair at Elsinore" is in some ways an anticipation of Josephine Tey's 1951 novel *The Daughter of Time*, a similar reversal of a Shakespearean fictional world – in this case *Richard III* – in the form of a detective story, and probably the best-known example of anti-Shakespearean revisionism (Murph 11, 118).

it. The revelation that not only was there no actual ghost, but "the Apparition on the clifftop was... staged by the Player King and his mercenary troupe" (Steele 238) at Fortinbras's request adds to this. Furthermore, the plot was actually a clandestine alliance between Claudius and Fortinbras under the guise of demands for the return of "disputed territories originally won by Old Hamlet from Old Fortinbras" (Steele 122), with Claudius's foppish servant, Osric, as the go-between. Unlike Innes, however, Steele does not make Horatio a co-conspirator, but does have him capitulate to Fortinbras, "whom his submissive temperament recognizes as the remaining dominant male" (236). Thus, "by telling most of the truth, and nothing but most of the truth" (238) to the people, Horatio becomes Fortinbras's "unwilling mouthpiece" (238) in convincing the public that Claudius, and not Fortinbras, was the real villain.

Yet the revelation of Fortinbras as "the metavillain, the superstrategist" (Steele 239) conceals another twist: Fortinbras proves a far better ruler than either Claudius or Hamlet could have been, and his forty-year reign is described in glowing, hyperbolic terms (Steele 239-40). In this way, Steele subverts the ending of Shakespeare's play, not by denying the restoration of peace and order, but by making that new order the product of, essentially, the benevolent tyranny of "the mastermind behind the murder of Old Hamlet [who] has duped, bought off, or seduced nearly everyone else" (Rozett 12).

Lee Blessing's 1991 play *Fortinbras* follows the examples of Innes and Steele in making Fortinbras into a morally suspect character, as well as in exploring the intersection of historical truth and politics. In both the characterization of Fortinbras and the exploration of political manoeuvring, Blessing's play and its fictional world reflect late-twentieth-century readings of Fortinbras as "an imperialist warmonger... everything [many readers] despised in the Vietnam era" (Rozett 18) and afterward. Like Innes's *The Hawk and the Handsaw,* Blessing's play incorporates passages from Shakespeare's text; but where Innes uses the Shakespearean text as an embedded fictional world, Blessing overlaps the beginning of his own fictional world with the end of Shakespeare's. He begins his play with Hamlet's request to Horatio "To tell my story" (Blessing 103; *Hamlet* V.ii. 349) and proceeds to the English ambassador's report of the death of Rosencrantz and Guildenstern (Blessing 104; *Hamlet* V.ii. 367-72) before Fortinbras's interruption with dialogue in modern English signals the humorous tone of this play and its difference from the Shakespearean fictional world. In a manner reminiscent of Innes's reference to the characteristic tropes of detective fiction ("MA" 77-79), Fortinbras not only moves the bodies but has the entire room washed, before requesting of

Horatio "a full report.... That's the only way I'm going to figure it out. Then maybe I can start to make up the truth" (Blessing 107).

It is this emphasis on the malleability of truth in a political context that makes Blessing's play a polemical rewrite, rather than merely a transposition or retelling, of Shakespeare's play; indeed, Blessing himself describes *Fortinbras* as "a loving liberty taken with Shakespeare's masterpiece – containing at the same time a dark, political undertone" (xi). However, unlike Innes's "The Mysterious Affair at Elsinore" and Steele's *Lord Hamlet's Castle,* Blessing's *Fortinbras* does not necessarily deal solely with the manipulation of historical facts to conceal wrongdoings by the current ruler, but also with the desire to present a more believable explanation for the succession crisis than a truth that seems highly improbable or unpleasant. In addressing both of these concerns, Fortinbras also alludes to a frequent criticism of Shakespeare's historical writing (see e.g. Murph 10-11, 18-23, 187-90):

> No one wants to hear how their whole royal family's incompetent.... We need a story that'll do something for us: explain the bodies, preserve the monarchy, give the people some kind of focus for their... anger, loss, whatever. And most of all, something that'll show people that everything that's happened up till now had to happen so that I could become king. (110)

The way Fortinbras achieves his goal is by claiming that the Danish court was infiltrated by "A Polish spy" (Blessing 110), thus providing a pretext for an invasion of Poland which he hopes will serve to "nourish our new nation on the very myth we've created" (Blessing 118). While Osric, in keeping with his sycophantic character in Shakespeare's play (*Hamlet* V.ii. 81-183), is quick to accept Fortinbras's story and urges Horatio to "try to get on board for once" (Blessing 115), Horatio becomes all the more determined to fulfill Hamlet's last wish and "tell the truth! To everyone I meet" (Blessing 115).

Blessing draws another parallel and contrast between his fictional world and Shakespeare's by having the ghosts of Polonius, Ophelia, Claudius, Gertrude, and Hamlet appear to Fortinbras, both to remind him and the audience of the mistakes they made in life, and to insist that he "tell the truth.... Without it, nothing can go forward – all is held back" (Blessing 135). The ghosts further question their representations not only in Blessing's play but in Shakespeare's as well, as Hamlet demands the proper presentation of "The mark I made in the world. The great lesson I have to teach" (Blessing 146), while Ophelia protests her marginalization by "Mr. Hamlet It's-All-About-Me the Dane... your point of view is clearly the most rewarding, the most complex. No wonder it has a special right to exist.... *I will not be marginal!*" (Blessing 147). She is also the only one of the ghosts who agrees with Fortinbras's desire to reimagine the history, insisting that the royal family should not "be remembered as a bunch of murderers, lecherers, liars, and fools" (Blessing 157). The play further symbolizes the mutability of truth and popular perception with a deliberate anachronism: where the other ghosts appear in the personas of actors on stage with the living characters, Hamlet spends the first half of the play as "an angry, brooding eye on [a] television screen whom an impatient and assertive Ophelia can 'silence' by turning off the sound" (Rozett 21; see Blessing 126).

Blessing's Fortinbras, like Steele's and both of Innes's, is ruled by ambition. However, unlike Steele's, who brings peace at a price, and Innes's, who is characterized either as a schemer ("MA") or mostly relatively harmless (*H&H*), Blessing's seeks to bring glory to his kingdom and be remembered as a counterpart to Alexander the Great (cf. *Hamlet* V.i. 197-216). This comparison is suggested by Horatio's description of Fortinbras's troops as "The combined Danish-Norwegian-Polish-Carpathian-Transylvanian-Anatolian-Trans-Caucasian-Persian-Afghan and Baluchistani forces" (160), regarded less as conquerors than as "heroes of liberation, ushering in peace, prosperity, enlightenment" (141). But, like the historical Alexander, Fortinbras is not invincible, and indeed reaches the limit of his power at "the banks of the Indus River" (160).

The end of Blessing's play further represents the danger of confusing a fictional world – in this case a political fiction – with the actual world, as Osric is imprisoned on a trumped-up charge of espionage and executed when Fortinbras's order to "Release [him] from his suffering" (Blessing 153; cf. *RII* V.iv. 2) is misunderstood, and Horatio avenges him by killing first Fortinbras and then himself, "in the Roman fashion" (Blessing 161), as a fulfillment of what Horatio thinks Hamlet should have done in the first place. Hamlet's desire to have his story told is also fulfilled, as the play ends with the guardsmen and two servant girls reading his lines from Shakespeare's play, "For in that sleep of death what dreams may come / When we have shuffled off this mortal coil" (Blessing 163; *Hamlet* III.i. 65-66).

Because Shakespeare did not develop Fortinbras to the same degree as Hamlet, leaving a gap in the play's fictional world, Fortinbras's character has allowed for many possibilities in derivative texts. On the one hand, Fortinbras's counterparts in Innes's, Steele's, and Blessing's fictional worlds may be seen as deliberate efforts to resist the idealized, if bittersweet, ending Shakespeare provided in his play. But on the other, reimagining Fortinbras as the sort of character who would not have been out of place in Claudius's court serves as a reminder that, while fiction can and does have neat endings, in the actual world history rarely ends so neatly.

In contrast to Fortinbras, whose presence in *Hamlet* adaptations comes precisely from his status as an enigma in the Shakespearean fictional world, Horatio is already a developed, if secondary, character in the play. His appeal to authors of adaptations comes in large part from the responsibility Hamlet places upon him at the end of the play, to ensure that the prince's story is properly told to Fortinbras and to the Danish people. Adaptations focusing on Horatio as a main character do often, as Innes and Blessing have done, present him in contrast to Fortinbras, especially through interpretations of what Horatio's duty to Hamlet may entail.

Horatio was not a significant character in the source texts for *Hamlet*; in fact, he shares an 'original' in Saxo's and Belleforest's histories with three other secondary characters: Laertes, Rosencrantz, and Guildenstern. All four of these Shakespearean characters ultimately derive, in varying degrees, from a single character in the histories: the "foster-brother of Amleth, who had not ceased to have regard to their common nurture" (*HD* 63) who serves only to warn Amleth of Feng's plot and then disappears from the narrative. The Shakespearean Horatio was also influenced by the character of the same name in Thomas Kyd's *The Spanish Tragedy*, but unlike his counterpart in Kyd, the Horatio of *Hamlet* survives the end of the play. As an intellectual, a skeptic, and a loyal friend to the protagonist, Horatio also serves as an emblem for a particular type of reader, and indeed, as Alethea Hayter suggests in the introduction to her 1972 novel *Horatio's Version*, "Perhaps... Shakespeare put Horatio into the play to stand for the audience" (10).

Hayter's novel was partly based on John Dover Wilson's *What Happens in Hamlet*, but was meant more as a fictional treatment than as a serious work of criticism. The novel combines entries from Horatio's diary with proceedings at Fortinbras's court as the new king leads an investigation into the circumstances behind the deaths of the entire Danish royal family at the end of Shakespeare's play. *Horatio's Version* is unusual among twentieth-century interpretations of Horatio and Fortinbras in that it does not portray Fortinbras as the villain, but merely as an impartial judge who does not wish to take sides (e.g. Hayter 81). It is, in fact, minor characters from the play such as Voltimand and Osric – the latter characterized as another Polonius (Hayter 40-42) – who are the principal antagonists in Hayter's story, and many times throughout the novel Horatio accuses them of conspiring against him and hiding evidence (e.g. Hayter 49-53). Like his counterpart in Blessing's play, Hayter's Horatio regards himself as "a mouthpiece for the truth" (21), even if such a role requires breaking his promise to Hamlet not to reveal anything about the Ghost (Hayter 76-79; cf. *Hamlet* I.v. 140-63).

Hayter's fictional world differs from Blessing's and Steele's, however, in that the belief of the court "that Prince Hamlet had killed Laertes and then the King with a dagger in an access of madness, and possibly had even poisoned the Queen too, and might finally have killed himself" (48) is not a deliberate fabrication on the part of the new king, but a combination of the initial impressions given by the royal family's final moments and the desire of the court officials "to protect the good name of [their] late respected master King Claudius" (Hayter 90). To an outside observer who does not know of Hamlet's encounter with the Ghost and his decision "To put an antic disposition on" (*Hamlet* I.v. 172), it may well have appeared that "Hamlet... could... have killed the other three [Claudius, Gertrude, and Laertes], and then committed suicide" (Hayter 20); and it could also appear that Horatio's testimony was designed to make Claudius look bad, as Blessing and Steele suggested of Fortinbras's official reports in their respective texts.

Hayter's Horatio shares with Blessing's and Innes's a desire to fulfill his promise to Hamlet "to tell [his] story" (*Hamlet* V.ii. 349); and like Blessing's and Innes's Horatios, he cannot easily convince the rest of the court that what he has told them of Hamlet is indeed the truth. He does present Claudius's original letter to the King of England calling for Hamlet's execution (Hayter 65-69; cf. *Hamlet* IV.iii. 58-68) as well as the alterations Hamlet made to the script for the Mousetrap play, to which the Player replies, "we never had a chance to pick up the local gossip, or we'd have refused to put in all those lines about second marriages and so on" (Hayter 56).

But it is in his private diary entries that Horatio reveals the most about Hamlet and his family, as well as himself. He speaks of the late King Hamlet as "splendid to look at... kind and gracious, but terrible when he was angry.... He was open and unsuspicious, too.... Nothing as clever as his son, though" (Hayter 27-28). Similarly, Horatio characterizes Ophelia as "just a puppet [who] said what they told her to say, and let herself be used as bait in a trap.... Perhaps she never really understood what was going on; she wasn't very intelligent" (Hayter 84). He believes, as does Gertrude's lady-in-waiting, that Ophelia's death was indeed an accident, and that "the suicide story was deliberately leaked to the public, in order to damage Prince Hamlet's reputation" (Hayter 95) because "Claudius wanted her dead, and was afraid of what she might let out" (Hayter 96).

However, the difficulty of convincing the court of the real motives behind Hamlet's actions leads Horatio to doubt himself, believing "I've failed in the one thing I could have done for him that he really wanted" (Hayter 71). It is this fear of failing Hamlet that leads Horatio to tell the court everything he remembers, including the appearance of the Ghost, and it does indeed prove the crucial evidence that "Horatio's version of the events has been shown to be the true one" (Hayter 101). The success of his testimony, however, does not mitigate the guilt he feels about having revealed what he was sworn to secrecy over, and so he decides to join a monastery to do penance for having broken his word to Hamlet. Of the fulfillment of Hamlet's final request, Horatio says:

> What Hamlet asked for is done, more or less. Does he know, wherever he is?... I never knew if he really, in his heart, cared about vengeance. Some of the time he did, but if he had really wanted it, why did he leave it so long? I sometimes thought that I could divine what was in his mind, but I was never sure. No one will ever be sure about that. (Hayter 106)

With this statement, Hayter's Horatio makes his strongest demonstration of his role in the text as the counterpart to the reader, for these are some of the very questions that scholars such as Wilson and writers of fiction such as Hayter have sought to answer.

The Horatio of Graham Holderness's 2002 novel *The Prince of Denmark* is burdened with more responsibility than the Horatios of Hayter's or even Shakespeare's texts, as he is charged not only with telling Hamlet's story but with fulfilling the final request of the dying Gertrude: "You must look to the boy.... Find the boy. He must be king" (5). The boy is Hamlet's son by Ophelia, born after her rescue from the river (Holderness 106-08) but raised in a monastery after she died giving birth to him. As a result, Holderness's Horatio finds his loyalties divided between the last surviving member of the Danish royal family and Fortinbras, who has put him in charge of the investigations into the mass deaths (cf. Innes, *H&H*; Blessing; Hayter). At first, Horatio feels reserved admiration for Fortinbras, "no young adventurer but a man of large intelligence, ruthless determination, and a passionate conviction of destiny" (Holderness 57), but he realizes that he must be wary of the new king as he seeks to honour Hamlet's and Gertrude's requests. During his search for Hamlet's son, Horatio finds more reasons to be cautious of Fortinbras, as the monks reveal that "the monastery of Helsingor... was sacked and burnt to the ground" (Holderness 145) by Fortinbras's men, and he also discovers a letter from Fortinbras to Laertes, revealing that the Prince of Norway was the one who provided the poison that killed Hamlet and his family, "for if we dispatch him, we do Claudius a service he will be bound to reward" (Holderness 188-89).

Holderness's novel is at once a prequel and a sequel to *Hamlet,* as well as an intertext to the play, alternating between the story of King Amled's victory against Fortenbrasse of Norway, Hamlet's ill-fated affair with Ophelia, and Horatio's search for Hamlet's son – named Sigurd after the legendary Norse hero "who [also] took revenge for the killing of his father" (190). The use of these multiple narrative threads, combined with excerpts from Norse and Anglo-Saxon histories and historical poetry, as well as dream

visions experienced by both Horatio and Sigurd, present the history of
Hamlet's Denmark as a succession of violence and revenge, with the
implication at first that the events of Shakespeare's text may soon repeat
themselves. However, though Sigurd finally does challenge Fortinbras, "the
man who had helped to murder his father, the prince who had stolen his
birthright" (Holderness 222), he realizes that the world of the Danish court
is not his world. Having been raised in quiet contemplation and the service
of the Christian God, in contrast to his people who still follow the old ways,
Sigurd allows Fortinbras to live and remain King of Denmark, preferring to
find his own path (Holderness 224-28). What becomes of any of the
characters is deliberately left a mystery. But with the contrast between
Hamlet, his father, and his son, Holderness displays a progression of attitudes
toward revenge: from the forthrightness of King Amled as representative of
the Norse worldview, to the hesitation of Hamlet, on the borderline between
the Norse and Christian worldviews, to the decision of Sigurd to show
forgiveness rather than seeking revenge at all, a decision that is considered
proper in the Christian worldview.

Revising Ophelia: Ophelia as a Main Character

Though he serves as a stand-in for the reader in the Shakespearean text as
well as in many derivative texts, Horatio has not received as much attention
as Ophelia, who is probably the most frequent subject of role expansions
from the text of *Hamlet*. Adaptations focusing on Ophelia use the familiar
character and plot from the play to examine changing views of gender
relations and to provide new and different approaches to a secondary
character who is generally, in both the world of the text and the world of the
reader, overshadowed by Hamlet himself. Authors' views of *Hamlet* in
general and Ophelia in particular have changed with and even influenced the
fluctuations of literary taste and perceptions of gender over time and across
cultures. Prequel texts focus on the development of Ophelia's character
through her relationships with Hamlet and her family, taking approaches
ranging from the romantic, idealized fictional world of Victorian juvenile
literature to the more realistic and historically informed world of the twenty-
first-century historical novel. More recent texts, informed by and in many
ways replying to the recent radical-feminist appropriation of Ophelia as a
symbol of the postmodern 'angry young woman,' tend to grant her more
agency, and often a happier ending, than she was allowed in the
Shakespearean 'original.'

It is useful to note that Ophelia does in fact have a greater presence in
Shakespeare's text than in the play's sources. Her counterpart in Saxo

Grammaticus's *Historiae Danicae* has no name and is identified only as Amleth/Hamlet's foster sister, whose "early rearing in common had brought them both into great intimacy" (*HD* 64). Indeed, her only purpose in the history is as a pawn in the political intrigue around her as well as a sex object for Amleth, and she is never mentioned again after Amleth's description of when and how "he had ravished the maid" (*HD* 64). It is Shakespeare who developed this marginal figure into a more complex counterpart to the protagonist, setting her up as a parallel character to Hamlet both in her role as thwarted love interest – rather than merely sex object as in Saxo – and in her fate, being driven to insanity and what, as the gravediggers suggest (*Hamlet* V.i. 1-29), may have been suicide, as a consequence of Hamlet's actions.

Yet, despite Shakespeare's expansion of the nameless foster sister in Saxo into the now-familiar figure, Ophelia, she still remains a peripheral character of whom relatively little is known as compared to Hamlet. As such she has become a source of inspiration for writers who create fictional works that further expand upon her role in the play to give her a past and a voice that were overlooked, or denied to her, in the Shakespearean text. Whether the resulting Ophelia-centric text is merely "revisionary" (Lanier 83) or "revisionist" (Osborne 125), all such works begin from the premise "that characters have a life beyond, and not dependent on, their drama...and that what we see of them is only part of a larger whole that exists outside the play" (Orgel, "Shakespeare Illustrated" 80). According to fictional-world theory, however, these retellings, or "transductions" (*Heterocosmica* 202), as Lubomír Doležel refers to them, do not reflect parts of a larger whole, as the psychological approach to characterization generally believes, but rather create distinct, though obviously related, counterparts to the character and her world.

One of the first widely-read expansions of Ophelia appears in the second volume of Mary Cowden Clarke's *The Girlhood of Shakespeare's Heroines,* first published in 1852. Clarke's book is a collection of short stories that describe the pre-play lives of Shakespeare's female characters, presenting her interpretations of the events in the characters' fictional lives that would have 'prepared' those characters for the events of the plays in which they appeared. Stephen Orgel notes that, while Clarke's presentations of Shakespearean women earned her a reputation "as a prototypical feminist" ("Shakespeare Illustrated" 81), her perception of both Elizabethan and Victorian gender roles is essentially a conservative one, as she "offers nothing to disturb her society's notions of what women are or should be" ("Shakespeare Illustrated" 81).

The title of Clarke's version of Ophelia's early life, "The Rose of Elsinore," plays upon the flower imagery that surrounds Ophelia in Shakespeare's text, and the story does indeed use much nature imagery in its account of Ophelia's childhood (e.g. Clarke 198-201). In the introduction to his online transcript of Clarke's text, Thomas Larque notes that in keeping with idealized Victorian views of young women in general and Ophelia in particular, the Ophelia of "The Rose of Elsinore" is "an innocent, who certainly had not had a sexual relationship with Hamlet" (*Shakespeare and His Critics*). Her knowledge of the bawdy songs she sings upon going mad (*Hamlet* IV.v. 23-26, 29-32, 36-40, 48-55, 58-66) comes from the peasant family with whom she spends her earliest years (Clarke 188-89, 217-18; cf. Wyman 244). Similarly, as a child she hears stories based on folktales and medieval romances, including the story of the owl and the baker's daughter (Clarke 217-18; cf. *Hamlet* IV.v. 42-44), told as an example of "the sin of uncharitableness" (Clarke 218). Ophelia's nurse Botilda, on being criticized by Polonius and his wife Aoudra for exposing her young charge to such "wickedness in words" (Clarke 189), defends herself by insisting that "I can't think they'd do mischief to any one that isn't set upon seeing more in 'em than's meant" (Clarke 189). This statement not only helps to establish Clarke's Ophelia as a relative innocent but also provides a reply to debates within the author's society of the 'appropriateness' of Shakespeare's texts themselves for young girls' reading, debates most notoriously exemplified by Thomas and Harriet Bowdler's 1807 'family-friendly' editions of the plays (Murphy, *Shakespeare in Print* 170).

In a reversal of the class differences between the Shakespearean Ophelia and Hamlet, the Ophelia of "The Rose of Elsinore" is the higher-class figure among her childhood social circle, which consists of Botilda's four children. The youngest, "Ulf the bear" (Clarke 198), dismissively refers to her as "little court-lady" (Clarke 189) and behaves toward her in a manner similar to Hamlet's during the prince's feigned madness: Ulf's behaviour "is capricious, and varies accordingly as he meets her alone, or with others" (Clarke 220). On the other hand, Ophelia develops a friendship with Botilda's only daughter Jutha, who serves as a counterpart to her not only as a companion and storyteller but also by sharing a similar fate: Jutha becomes depressed and dies after being rejected by a young nobleman (Clarke 219). It is Jutha's untimely death that prompts a change in Ophelia's character from the "innocent child" (Clarke 190) of the story's first half to Clarke's interpretation of her character in Shakespeare:

> The shock she had received was severe; and long left its effects upon her sensitive organization. Naturally gentle, she became timid. She shrank about, scared, and trembling; fearful of she hardly knew what, but feeling unassured, doubtful, full of a vague uneasiness and alarm. (Clarke 220)

Furthermore, Ophelia's parents become more protective of her once they return to the Danish court, wishing to provide her with "none but pleasant, healthful influences of person, scene, and circumstance" and fostering a strong bond of affection between her and Polonius (Clarke 226). But it is the relationship between Ophelia and Aoudra, not found in Shakespeare's text, that is the greater concern to Clarke, who speaks in glowing terms of the Victorian idealization of "Holy mother-love! Nearest semblance vouchsafed to mortals of Divine protection! Benignest human symbol of God's mercy to man!" (Clarke 225), even though we see relatively little of Ophelia and Aoudra's interaction in the story. Ophelia's strong connections to her parents do have a profound effect on her, as does her childhood experience of which she refuses to speak: she is described as "ever quiet, ever diffident, in her retiring gentleness and modesty; but serene, and happy" (Clarke 230).

Though she becomes close to her brother Laertes (Clarke 226-30), Ophelia also gains another companion similar to Jutha, another court lady named Thyra. In contrast to both Ophelia and Jutha, Thyra is described as "unrestricted in her proceedings, choosing her own associates, complete mistress of her conduct and herself" (Clarke 231) – the sort of behaviour of which Clarke's society generally disapproved in girls of that age. Indeed, Clarke uses Thyra, like Jutha before her, not only as a counterpart to Ophelia, but as an example by contrary to warn her readers to beware of libertines: "A gallant action, truly, to win the trust and love of a poor maid, and then requite her with destruction" (253). Both of Ophelia's childhood friends, Jutha and Thyra, meet their untimely ends through their associations with the same man: Eric of Kronstein, "the knight [on] the white horse" (Clarke 241) who refuses to acknowledge his betrayal of Jutha when Ophelia confronts him, and whose rejection of Thyra also drives her to suicide. Clarke underscores the connections between Ophelia and Thyra in her account of Ophelia's dream shortly after Thyra's death:

> I saw one approach, whose face I could not see, and whose figure I knew not. She was clothed in white, all hung about with weeds and wild flowers; and from among them stuck ends of straw, that the shadowy hands seemed to pluck and spurn at; and then the white figure moved on, impelled towards the water. I saw her glide on, floating upon its surface; I saw her dimly, among the silver-leaved branches of the drooping willow, as they waved around and above her, upbuoyed by her spreading white garments. (Clarke 255; cf. *Hamlet* IV.vii. 166-83)

This passage, a prose adaptation of the narrative passage in Shakespeare's play that describes Ophelia's death and shows influence from illustrations such as John Everett Millais's (see Young 340-41), foreshadows the corresponding moment in the play and creates dramatic irony. Though

Clarke's Ophelia remains unaware of it, the reader knows that Shakespeare's Ophelia comes to a similar end.

The unhappy affair between Eric and Thyra also serves as a counterpoint to an important state of affairs in the backstory of Shakespeare's play: the triangle of King Hamlet, Gertrude, and Claudius (Clarke 244-47). Like many other writers who have presented their versions of the events leading to King Hamlet's death, Clarke supposes that Claudius was in love with Gertrude and may have planned his brother's murder in order to eliminate both a romantic and a political rival. However, Gertrude's reaction to her brother-in-law's advances is vague: she protests Claudius's dishonour "of your brother, your king, my husband" (Clarke 247) as well as of herself. Yet, her insistence that the court ladies not know what is happening could be read as an indirect admission that she does indeed have feelings for Claudius, even though she knows it would be improper to act upon them. But, as Clarke reminds her readers, Gertrude could not be held entirely innocent in the matter because, according to the standards of the author's society, "The wife, who admits such thoughts, so judging, is already adulterate in spirit" (Clarke 261).

"The foul unwholesome weed of forbidden passion" (Clarke 260) between Claudius and Gertrude, in turn, forms a contrast to the "fair flower of love springing between [Hamlet and Ophelia]" (Clarke 260) that develops in part from mutual support upon the near-simultaneous deaths of Hamlet's father and Ophelia's mother. It is with the unhappy ends Jutha and Thyra meet after consorting with Eric of Kronstein, as well as the romantic triangle within the royal family, in mind that Clarke describes the attraction of Hamlet and Ophelia to each other in idealized terms reflecting the sort of relationship Victorian girl readers would expect, and be expected, to seek for themselves:

> His refined taste was attracted by her maiden beauty; his delicacy of feeling taught him to delight in her innocence, her retiring diffidence; his masculine intellect found repose in the contemplation of her artless mind: his manly soul dwelt with a kind of serene rapture on the sweet feminine softness of her nature.
>
> (Clarke 259-60)

The end of Clarke's story points back toward the tragic world of Shakespeare's play by acknowledging the affections between Ophelia and, on the one hand, Hamlet, and on the other, Laertes, and the inevitability of unhappy conclusions for both these relationships. Ophelia's final words, indeed the last words spoken in Clarke's text, to Laertes's request for her to write to him soon once he arrives in France, are the first words she speaks in Shakespeare's play: "Do you doubt that?" (Clarke 263; *Hamlet* I.iii. 4). These words also allude to Hamlet's first letter to her after learning the truth about his father's death (*Hamlet* II.ii. 116-19). Thus, as Clarke's story ends and her fictional world feeds back into Shakespeare's, the reader is reminded that the seemingly innocent Ophelia of this text will end up like the two unfortunate companions of her childhood, even if not entirely for the same reasons.

In the century and a half following the publication of *The Girlhood of Shakespeare's Heroines,* views of both actual and fictional women and the world(s) they inhabit have changed considerably. The sort of character Ophelia represented for writers such as Clarke, the long-suffering and largely passive replier to the turbulent world around her, was no longer held as an ideal for female readers. Instead of being read as an example of youthful innocence and the fragility thereof, Ophelia was increasingly seen as "a subservient and marginalized character... defined in terms that include the men around her... without whose influence she does not make a decision" (Hulbert 203). Works of psychology and sociology as well as literary criticism in the last years of the twentieth century and the beginning of the twenty-first, most influentially Mary Pipher's 1994 book *Reviving Ophelia,* have helped to reposition her in the popular imagination as an archetypal 'angry young woman' and a rallying figure for those whose mission is "to save teenage girls from the clutches of society" (Hulbert 210) – a statement not unlike Hamlet's diatribe against Gertrude, "Frailty, thy name is woman!" (*Hamlet* I.ii. 146), in its ironic assumption that young women cannot make up their own minds about how best to define their place in the world.

However, as Jennifer Hulbert points out, approaches such as Pipher's, while useful as reminders of the need for positive images and models of femininity, do often end up presenting one-dimensional views of the Shakespearean character, the modern young women to whom she is compared, and the societies of actual and fictional worlds alike. The concerns faced by the young women to whom Pipher's book and others like it are addressed are very different from those faced by women of Shakespeare's time or the time represented in the fictional world of *Hamlet.* For example, Ophelia's madness was more over "the loss of her father at the hands of a man she once thought loved her" (Hulbert 212) than over "her need to maintain appearances" (Hulbert 212), and not necessarily over what Pipher dismisses as "girl-poisoning culture"[97] (qtd. in Hulbert 215) that existed then or now. Similarly, "to define contemporary teenage girls as Ophelia" (Hulbert 218) also overlooks the fact that not all young women are miserable, and if they are, not only is it not always for the same reasons as Shakespeare's Ophelia,

---

[97] Pipher's often vitriolic indictments of contemporary society also bring to mind Gertrude's comment on the Player Queen: "The lady doth protest too much, methinks" (*Hamlet* III.ii. 230). For a summary of what Pipher means by "girl-poisoning culture," see Hulbert 209.

but not always for the same reasons as Pipher's actual-world case studies. As well, Ophelia is not necessarily a typical Shakespearean heroine, many of who show, by the standards of their time, a considerable degree of independence: "Imogen, Perdita, Miranda, and Marina [for example] never had to be revived" (Hulbert 218).

The challenge for Ophelia-centred adaptations of *Hamlet* in the wake of these approaches to actual- and fictional-world femininity is thus to move away from the relatively marginalized figure of the Shakespearean text while avoiding the risk of merely shifting the blame for that marginalization from "family and a lover" (Hulbert 217) to society as a whole. The predominant approach to recentering the text and its world around Ophelia in such works is to give her a more active role behind the scenes, suggesting that, like Hamlet himself, Ophelia is playing a part in a much greater scheme. Whether that scheme succeeds or fails, however, depends upon the individual decisions of each adaptation's author and the world he/she creates.

Jeremy Trafford's 2001 novel *Ophelia* is unusual among Ophelia-centric adaptations, both in being written by a male author and in, like Clarke's story, its implied retention of the Shakespearean tragic ending. The novel is also, in fact, an adaptation twice over, being a revised version of an earlier play entitled *Hamlet's Ghost*. Despite its title, Trafford's *Ophelia* does not focus solely on Ophelia herself; rather, it is a prequel to the Shakespearean text that presents Ophelia's relationships with Hamlet and Polonius as parallels to those between Hamlet and his father and between Gertrude, Claudius, and King Hamlet. The novel also introduces a counterpart character to Hamlet: Svendborg, the son of an officer in King Hamlet's army whom Claudius had executed on false charges (Trafford 11-13), and who spends much of the novel seeking revenge (e.g. Trafford 26-28) and pondering the differences between Christian and pagan views of revenge, justice, and mercy (e.g. Trafford 108-10; cf. *Hamlet* III.i. 55-87), thus following a course similar to yet different from Hamlet's in the play. Indeed, Svendborg takes a more direct approach to revenge than Hamlet does, though like Hamlet he does end up paying for it with his life (Trafford 215-16).

Trafford's Ophelia parallels her nameless counterpart in Saxo Grammaticus's history, but contrasts with Clarke's version, by having a full sexual relationship with Hamlet (Trafford 8-10), though the couple are forced to keep their relationship secret because of Hamlet's impending politically-motivated betrothal to a Swedish princess (Trafford 13). Midway through the novel, however, Hamlet insists to his father that "I really want to marry – but not someone I am not in love with" (Trafford 108), thus admitting his feelings about Ophelia to his father and Polonius. While Trafford's text does show the influence of interpretations such as Pipher's, which regard Ophelia as seeking the approval of her father and the other masculine/authority figures in her life, Hamlet engages in the same approval-seeking, in a manner recalling the oft-strained relations between Henry IV and Prince Hal in Shakespeare's second tetralogy (e.g. Trafford 23-25; cf. *1HIV* III.ii.). Indeed, Trafford's Hamlet seeks his father's approval much more than Ophelia seeks hers, as she often finds Polonius's attitude toward her dismissive and patronizing:

> He was often asking her to listen, as if he supposed she never did, when surely it was obvious she heard him far too deeply.... If only his fatherly devotion didn't take such unappealing forms at times – as in his absurd little lectures, his telling her what to do with such tedious insistence; as in doing all he could to keep her away from Hamlet, unbearably harping on the doubts she already had and diminishing the hopes the Prince himself so evasively had weakened. (Trafford 14)

Despite the displays of independence and even defiance by Trafford's Ophelia, these are not truly her predominant characteristics; rather, her most significant trait is compassion. The predominance of Ophelia's compassion is most powerfully illustrated in her protective attitude toward Svendborg after Claudius has him imprisoned (Trafford 129-36), which extends even to her helping to nurse him back to health following a poisoning attempt (Trafford 156-57). Like Hamlet, Svendborg develops not-entirely-unrequited romantic feelings for Ophelia, of which she wonders, "Is it wrong... to love two people – is that quite impossible? Is it mad of me?" (Trafford 207). Ophelia's conflicted feelings about Hamlet and Svendborg lead to a further complication when she discovers she is pregnant but does not know if the father is Hamlet or Svendborg, only to miscarry shortly after Hamlet angrily accuses her of being unfaithful (Trafford 227-28; cf. *Hamlet* III.i. 92-161). Trafford uses the triangle of Hamlet, Ophelia, and Svendborg as a counterpart to that of King Hamlet, Gertrude, and Claudius, suggesting – more explicitly than Clarke does – that Gertrude and Claudius were already having an affair before King Hamlet's death (Trafford 113): Gertrude because she felt unsatisfied in her own marriage, and Claudius because of the death of his previous wife.

Trafford's fictional world, like the characters who populate it, is also built on comparison and contrast, both within itself and intertextually with Shakespeare's play. To express it in Doležel's terms, the world of *Ophelia* places more emphasis on deontic modality – such as familial and social obligations – than on alethic modality – the presence of the supernatural – that marks the world of *Hamlet* (see *Heterocosmica* 114-23). Trafford does not entirely ignore the supernatural elements of the play, but rather explains them as manifestations of the characters' inner psychological worlds, "an illusion as precarious as a dream" (183). Hamlet, in fact, is not the only character in the novel to experience prophetic dreams alluding to the events of the play: Trafford's description of the death of King Hamlet (163-68) combines 'dream' with 'reality' to provide vivid glimpses into the minds of both the murderer and the victim at the moment of the murder. Similarly, Ophelia, like her counterpart in Clarke's story, has dreams of herself and Hamlet that foreshadow (for the characters) or recall (for the readers) their fates in the play (e.g. Trafford 229-30).

In its use of dreams as well as its third-person narrative, Trafford's novel is in many ways similar to Clarke's short story, despite the significant differences between the worlds of the Victorian girl's story and the postmodern historical novel. By contrast, Lisa Fiedler's 2002 novel *Dating Hamlet* is very much a recentering of the Shakespearean text around Ophelia, even to the extent that it makes her into a first-person narrator, in what Laurie Osborne describes as "the inverted, revisionist perspective of an individual character... [a] perspectival shift and investment in female agency" (125). Though not entirely a polemical revision in the sense that Doležel uses the term in *Heterocosmica, Dating Hamlet* can be called revisionist, or at least revisionary, because of its alterations to the plot and relationships between the characters, and its repositioning of "Ophelia's decisive narrative as more central than Hamlet's performances" (Osborne 125).

Dating Hamlet begins where Clarke's "The Rose of Elsinore" and Trafford's *Ophelia* leave off and Shakespeare's *Hamlet* begins: with the appearance of King Hamlet's ghost (Fiedler 7; cf. *Hamlet* I.i.). Fiedler's Ophelia is present, though unseen to Horatio and the guards, at the ghost's appearance, the first of many familiar incidents from the play in which she becomes not only spectator but active participant. She also has a loyal servant girl, Anne – her name an allusion to James I's Danish wife – who acts as a counterpart to Horatio, and who, like Ophelia herself, manages to be in the right places at the right times (e.g. Fiedler 98-102; cf. *Hamlet* III.iv.).

Fiedler's Hamlet and Ophelia have a more open and trusting relationship than in Shakespeare's play, though they are not as physically close as in Saxo's history or Trafford's novel. Hamlet confides to Ophelia as well as to Horatio, "I will show myself to be other than I am, appearing to suffer strange distemper. I shall put an antic disposition on" (Fiedler 45; cf. *Hamlet* I.v. 169-180). Thus, Ophelia is aware enough of the truth about Hamlet's behaviour to play along with him in order to fool Claudius and Polonius (Fiedler 74-80; cf. *Hamlet* III.i.), and even includes an "antic disposition" of her own. Even with the knowledge that Hamlet is not truly mad, however, she still finds some of his actions unnerving. For example, upon overhearing Hamlet's "To be or not to be" soliloquy, Ophelia comments:

> I have never heard such words as these from Hamlet. He speaks a truth, disguised by madness, and together they chill my blood. Has he thought upon this sin before?... And dare I confess it hath occurred to me? (Fiedler 75)

Fiedler's Ophelia has a reason of her own to fool Polonius: at roughly the same time that Hamlet learns the truth about his father's murder, she has a vision of her mother's ghost (Fiedler 66-70) revealing that Polonius is not her real father. She is, in fact, the daughter of the gravedigger who was once "a travelling player... come to Elsinore... to entertain the good King Hamlet's court" (Fiedler 84).

But it is the knowledge Ophelia had gained from her still-living mother that becomes the key to *Dating Hamlet*'s revisionary plot and conclusion. Ophelia's mother had taught her about medicinal plants, including a formula for a concoction reminiscent of but more potent than Friar Laurence's potion in *Romeo and Juliet*: a "perfume [that] is the beginning of a venom that... shall induce a sleep so full... that even the coroner himself would believe it death" (Fiedler 30; cf. *R&J* IV.i. 94-107), and used for similar purposes but with more successful results. The perfume allows Ophelia not only to fake her own death with the gravedigger's help (Fiedler 137-54), but also to insure the survival of Hamlet, Laertes, and Gertrude (Fiedler 174-81), as she had herself prepared, and knows an antidote for, the "unction of a mountebank" (*Hamlet* IV.vii. 141) that Laertes used on his sword. Fiedler makes the intertextual connection between *Romeo and Juliet, Hamlet,* and *Dating Hamlet* more explicit at the very end of her novel. Having left their kingdom in the capable hands of Fortinbras – here characterized in striking contrast to most post-Shakespearean adaptations – Ophelia and Hamlet decide that they will leave Denmark for Verona, and Hamlet mentions having met "at Wittenberg... an impetuous fellow from that place. His name, as I recall, was Romeo" (Fiedler 182-83).

While *Dating Hamlet* occupies a vague position between 'revisionary' and 'revisionist,' Rebecca Reisert's 2003 novel *Ophelia's Revenge* is very much 'revisionist,' not only in its focus on Ophelia as the main character and first-person narrator, but in its transformation of the Shakespearean fictional world's clearer demarcations of 'good' and 'evil' into a fictional world with very few redeeming characters whatsoever. Where *Dating Hamlet* "reworks *Hamlet* into a successful *Romeo and Juliet*" (Osborne 125) with an essentially optimistic worldview, *Ophelia's Revenge* is more reminiscent of *Macbeth* in its moral ambiguity and bittersweet resolution.

Reisert's "reworking [of] the 'truth' underlying familiar performances of *Hamlet*" (Osborne 125) does indeed grant Ophelia more agency than in Shakespeare's play, but in a very different way than Fiedler or Trafford. Reisert's Ophelia reveals herself in the novel's first sentence as the driving force behind the mass deaths at Elsinore: "By my sixteenth birthday, I'd murdered two kings, my father, my brother, a queen, a prince, and my husband" (Reisert 3). As in Fiedler's novel, Ophelia is the one who provides the poison for the fateful duel, insisting it is "protection for.... My brother Laertes and Lord Hamlet" (Reisert 398) and not realizing that it is in fact genuine. She also arranges for her childhood friend Ragnor to attack the ship taking Hamlet to England (Reisert 373-77) and pretends madness (Reisert 382-85) in hopes of protecting Hamlet from Claudius. But the greatest difference between *Ophelia's Revenge* and *Hamlet* and fellow counterpart texts is that Ophelia also first gave Claudius the idea and the means to kill King Hamlet (Reisert 234). She justifies this abettal by indicating that the King Hamlet of Reisert's fictional world, far from being the "Hyperion to a satyr" (*Hamlet* I.ii. 140) of the Shakespearean text, is himself a raging tyrant who disapproves of Hamlet (e.g. Reisert 200-04) and is abusive to Gertrude (Reisert 92-109). Furthermore, not only is Reisert's Hamlet truly mad (353-54), but he is in fact King Hamlet's younger son who lives in the shadow of his older brother Holger, even after the older prince's death from a fall off the castle walls (Reisert 197). Reisert's Hamlet shares with Trafford's a strong desire to seek his father's approval, even despite knowing little of his father's true nature, having spent most of his life abroad at school (303-04); and, as in Trafford's text, Reisert's Hamlet and Ophelia marry in secret to avoid the King's displeasure (292-300).

Reisert's Ophelia, like Clarke's, spends her childhood in a peasant village, learning both the trades and the stories of the people who surround her. She becomes especially fascinated by a book of mythology, adopting the figure of the Sphinx as her personal emblem, "the Flying Catgirl" (Reisert 7), and delighting the village children with improvised stories and plays in which "the Flying Catgirl faced a terrible enemy and overcame him through her courage and wit" (Reisert 8). Though Hamlet shares Ophelia's love of "stories with... twisting plots and tragic endings" (Reisert 175), Ophelia realizes that in order to win the favour of his family, she must make herself over into "the kind of woman with polished manners and polished edges.... Only in stories did kings marry hoydenish Flying Catgirls" (Reisert 182). Even so, the Flying Catgirl continues to remind Ophelia, and the reader, of the power of fictional worlds, such as those of literature and drama, to inspire action in the actual world.

Like Hamlet, and yet unlike him, Ophelia also follows the word of a ghost in her quest for revenge. In her case, it is the ghost of Yorick, who becomes her secret confidant and reveals to her that "Ghosts choose who can see them and who cannot" (Reisert 61). Yet Yorick too has an ulterior motive for appearing to Ophelia: he seeks to use her to gain revenge on Hamlet for the accident that led to his death (Reisert 497-502). In this way, Reisert addresses a concern Hamlet himself raises in the play, whether "The spirit that I have seen / May be a devil, and the devil hath power / T'assume a pleasing shape" (*Hamlet* II.ii. 598-600), but at the same time ironically denies Ophelia the agency the text seemed to have been granting her. Ophelia realizes, "All the while I thought I was controlling everything... all the time I myself had been Yorick's puppet" (Reisert 503). It is this realization that provokes Ophelia into her final decision not to marry Erik Strong Arm[98] – Reisert's counterpart to Fortinbras, and just as unpleasant as any of the other princes in her fictional world – but to escape to England where she and her son by Hamlet, "The child for whom I'd thrown away a kingdom and crown" (Reisert 519), can live out their lives in peace.

The Ophelia of Lisa Klein's 2006 novel *Ophelia* shares with Fiedler's and Reisert's a "herbal knowledge of near-poisons" (Osborne 125) as well as her own feigned madness alongside Hamlet's (Klein 176-209; cf. Fiedler 108-36, Reisert 409-22). She also narrates her story in the first person, and survives the end of the Shakespearean plot to start a new life – in this case, as a healer at a nunnery in France (Klein 230), thus ironically fulfilling Hamlet's admonition to her in III.i. 30 of the play. However, unlike Fiedler's Ophelia but like Reisert's, Klein's is left without Hamlet, who did indeed die in the duel (Klein 242; cf. *Hamlet* V.ii. 302-60). Hamlet and Ophelia in this text not only have a full sexual relationship, as in Trafford's and Reisert's versions, but also marry in secret on the very night that the ghost of King Hamlet first appears (Klein 114-16); at the end of the novel, Ophelia gives birth to Hamlet's son, whose "name is Hamlet, as was his father's, and he is a prince of Denmark" (Klein 302).

Klein's novel is both a sequel to and a retelling/role expansion of Shakespeare's play, told as a double-layered narrative with the events following the play told in the present tense, and the events that took place in the play[99] told in the past tense. Like Clarke's short story and Fiedler's and Reisert's novels, Klein's text not only recenters the narrative around the oft-

---

[98] The literal translation of the French name "Fortinbras" (cf. *HD* 60). His first name is Reisert's invention.

[99] Klein places the events of the play between May and November 1601, the approximate time frame at which it may have been first written and performed.

marginalized figure of Ophelia but also privileges the knowledge and social circles of women in a way that the male-dominated world of the play does not. Klein's novel devotes much attention to Ophelia's life as a lady-in-waiting to Gertrude and her relationships among the other court ladies, "with their bright plumage and twittering voices... like so many birds in a gilded cage" (28). Having grown up as "a motherless girl... [after] the Lady Frowendel died giving birth to [her]" (Klein 7), Ophelia finds various mother-figures among the court ladies, from Gertrude herself to the healers Elnora and Mechtild, who pass their "deep knowledge of medicine and herbs" (Klein 33) along to her, thus providing her with the means she needs to survive and flourish outside the Danish court. Unlike Reisert's Ophelia but like Fiedler's, Klein's Ophelia uses the healers' knowledge for the benefit of others, preferring to sustain and prolong life rather than to destroy it.

At the same time, Gertrude instills in Ophelia a love of literature, thus providing a commentary on the interdependence between actual and fictional worlds and between fictional worlds themselves, much the way Reisert's Ophelia had done with her "Flying Catgirl" stories in her youth. Both Gertrude and Ophelia enjoy reading medieval romances (cf. Updike 45), which the Queen justifies – in a moment of dramatic irony – by explaining, "This is fiction, Ophelia, not a true history. Often we love to read of deeds and desires we would not dare to perform ourselves. That is the pleasure of a tale like this" (Klein 43). Like Clarke before her, Klein uses the scenes of Ophelia's childhood reading to address the concerns often raised, in the story's time and afterward, of 'appropriate' reading for young girls; and, like Reisert, Klein illustrates the empowering effect of fictional texts upon their readers and disseminators. At the same time she also acknowledges her text's status as a fictional world created in part from the material of previous fictional worlds – be they medieval romances or Shakespearean plays.

It is through her love of reading that Klein's Ophelia, like Reisert's, also addresses the issue of gender inequality. In contrast to the romances she and Gertrude enjoy, and the philosophical lessons she learned of from Polonius and Laertes, she intensely dislikes "the conduct books... prescribed to teach me morals" (Klein 38) because of their narrow circumscription of female behaviour:

> They all said that I must be silent, chaste, and obedient, or else the world would be turned topsy-turvy from my wickedness. I scoffed at this, suspecting the writer had no knowledge of women and even less liking for them. (Klein 38)

Even in her later life at the convent of St. Emilion, Ophelia is made very much aware "of the insecure state of women, who must always abide the earthly authority of men" (Klein 253). For example, one of the nuns is a

Swedish princess who joined the convent in disgrace after nearly being raped by Fortinbras (Klein 315-17); and Ophelia herself must defend her honour on being accused by the convent's noble patron of "vile harlotry" (Klein 296) and witchcraft. Yet she does find in the convent a social circle as strong as any she had had at court, gaining in the figure of the prioress Mother Ermentrude[100] "a generous patron" (321) who allows her to remain at St. Emilion after the birth of her son.

Ophelia knows that "someday... [her] son must hear of the foul crimes of Denmark, the revenge unleashed there, and its foul ending...of his father's madness, his mother's grief, and their unfortunate love" (Klein 321-22). She also realizes that her son may even be called upon one day to avenge his father, as Hamlet did his. However, the ending of Klein's story is an optimistic one, as Ophelia establishes herself as a healer not only "to the complaints of the nuns, but country people and villagers" (Klein 320) nearby, and she even forms a relationship with her fellow survivor of the events at Elsinore, Horatio (Klein 328).

Whether adhering to the tragic resolution of Shakespeare's play, or allowing their Ophelias to reach a happier ending than Shakespeare provided for his, texts which focus on Ophelia as a main character combine the sympathy Shakespeare's character has traditionally elicited in generations of readers with concerns of "contemporary feminist ideology" (Osborne 125), in whatever form such ideology may take in the author's and reader's societies, to provide new perspectives from which to revisit the familiar fictional world. These 'revised,' 'revived,' 'revisionary,' and/or 'revisionist' Ophelias provide readers with glimpses and portraits "of what it means to be a woman in Western society" (Hulbert 214), both in Shakespeare's time and in the times of their respective authors and readers. These texts' references to the practices of storytelling, drama, and alchemy also serve as metaphors for the processes of both literary adaptation and social dialogue and critique, transforming the Shakespearean fictional world (cf. Doležel, *Heterocosmica* 206-22; Rozett 3-13) and taking their places alongside it while similarly seeking to transform the actual worlds in which they were written and are read.

Minor Characters in *Hamlet*, Major Characters in Adaptations

Though virtually all of the major characters in Shakespeare's *Hamlet* have become the focus of role expansions, this has not exhausted the possibilities

---

[100] The prioress shares a name with Amleth's second wife in Saxo's history (*HD* 75-76), though her name is also reminiscent of Shakespeare's Gertrude.

for alternative perspectives on the play and its world. As may be expected for a play of its length, *Hamlet* has a fairly large population for a fictional world: at least seventeen named characters in addition to several unnamed ones, as well as those who do not physically appear in the text itself but are spoken of by those who do. While many of the lesser characters in the play have generally remained in the background both in performance and literary study, they too have often inspired writers of adaptations. Texts that focus on the minor characters of *Hamlet* serve a dual purpose: they provide alternative views of a character who dominates the action of the source text and at the same time illustrate how the presence of that dominant character touches the lives of even the most insignificant inhabitants of the fictional world.

Elias Olan James's 1934 poem *Thieves of Mercy* stands out even among expansions of minor characters in that the protagonists of the poem are never seen on stage in the play itself, but are mentioned only in the letter Hamlet sends to Horatio (*Hamlet* IV.vi. 9-31). The poem is narrated by one of the pirates who attacked the ship that took Hamlet to England and tells of Hamlet's experiences on the voyage, leading up to his return to Denmark at the beginning of Act V of the play. In his introduction to the poem, James describes his reading of Hamlet's note to Horatio that "They have dealt with me like thieves of mercy; but they knew what they did: I am to do a good turn for them" (*Hamlet* IV.vi. 20-22) as follows:

> It is clear that [Hamlet] liked them. There is an undertone of zest, an eagerness for action, in him after his unplanned sabbatical. And why not? How refreshingly different the men of Mull from the schooled policy-servers of Denmark. And so Red Fergus and his people came into the story; had been waiting all the time to give Hamlet the understanding that is happiness. (vii)

James's poem is also, in its way, a counterpart text to the interlude in Saxo Grammaticus's *Historiae Danicae* describing Amleth's time in England, during which he impressed the English king, in both positive and negative ways, with a command of riddles (*HD* 67-69).

Thieves of Mercy is presented as a sequel to *Hamlet*, with the pirates telling their story in a Devonshire pub "six months after Fortinbras became king of Denmark" (James 1), though the story told in the poem takes place during Hamlet's voyage to England. Its narrator, Sir Peter Cruikshank, constantly compares the pirates' captain Red Fergus, "princely / By the left-hand side... /... / His mother, left-hand daughter to an earl" (James 1), to Hamlet, "a prince of the right hand" (James 2) who remained with them "for seven weeks" (James 2), thus presenting the captain and the prince, and by extension the pirate crew and the Danish court, as counterparts to each other. If, as James asserts, it truly is clear from Shakespeare's text that Hamlet liked the pirates, James's own text makes clear that the pirates too enjoyed having "had a prince in Mull" (2) and regretted having lost him to his tragic fate.

The most significant way in which the pirates contrast themselves and their world with Hamlet and his world is in their comparison, prompted by Hamlet himself, of their lives as "sheriffs of the sea" (James 2) who take what they want from anyone they encounter, to his life as a student at Wittenberg, "a scholar-place" (James 9) where students spend more time considering possible worlds "Of what might be if 'tother thing was or wasn't" (James 9) than the actual world in which they live (cf. *Hamlet* I.v. 166-67). Fergus's attitude toward Hamlet appears to be one of pity – as much pity as a pirate can be expected to show – as he agrees to allow Hamlet to stay on board their ship so that they can "teach him / That Denmark's not the world" (James 11), even as Peter himself argues that "a hawk / Is not a mourning dove. Our bird... / Should know he's prince – and act it" (James 11) while the other pirates dismiss Hamlet as "womanish" (James 13).

According to James, the "good turn" (*Hamlet* IV.vi. 22) Hamlet promised to the pirates for returning him to Denmark was "whatever blood there was to let /... / But no, he'd have all done in the high manner" (20). Though Peter credits himself with having taught Hamlet "a certain stroke... /... wherewith he paid his tricky foe" (James 21), he and his crewmates realize that the most important difference between themselves and the royal family is that, in their own way, the pirates are the honest ones: for not only do they not talk themselves out of their duty (James 20; cf. *Hamlet* III.i. 55-87), but they also fight fairly and "never poison swords" (James 21).

The final stanzas of James's poem reveal that Hamlet has also had an effect on the pirates. Fergus realizes that Hamlet's tragic flaw was "to see too well.... /... / All time's too little / For earth to breed the perfect joy his dream / Makes necessary" (James 21), while he and his men are realists. By contrast, the oldest of the crew, Davy Gam – who shares a name with a minor character in Shakespeare's *Henry V* – admits that Hamlet's presence has awakened a poetic sense in him, which he expresses in terms very similar to Hamlet's own last words:

> Maybe our prince
> Was but a sending, tuned to all of us.
> The dreams storm through us like a coloured wind.
> An unseen bird down in the hawthorne copse
> Keeps calling, sweet and clear; it always flies
> Before us, but we follow. The rest is silence.
>   (James 24; cf. *Hamlet* V.ii. 354-58)

As for Peter, the fact that he is the narrator of the poem demonstrates that, like Davy, he has discovered a poetic sense through his acquaintance with Hamlet. But, like Fergus, he remains a realist, more concerned with the harsh reality of his actual world than with musing on possible worlds, including – in a moment of dramatic irony – the possible worlds of Shakespearean scholarship,[101] which are often characterized by questions of what might have happened if Hamlet had made (or not made) the decisions that he did (or did not):

> You liked my yarn
> A *little*, you say; the better, *if* – your *if*s!
> We men of Mull, you think, had been the wiser
> *If* – ! Or the prince should this, or shouldn't that
> *If* – ! Masters, be lesson'd: cargoes, ships, and weather
> Be God's plain facts, the one commodity
> I deal in. Take your *if*s, a carrack-load,
> And go to – Wittenberg!
> (James 25; cf. *RIII* III.iv. 73-77)

In contrast to the pirates of James's poem, who never appear on stage in the play itself, the protagonist of Alan Gordon's 2004 novel *An Antic Disposition* does have a physical presence on stage, though only in the form of a skull. The fifth in Gordon's *Fool's Guild* series of medieval mystery novels, *An Antic Disposition* gives Yorick a backstory unexplored either by Shakespeare or by authors such as Percy MacKaye or Rebecca Reisert, both of whom had also included him as a significant if not entirely sympathetic character in, respectively, *The Mystery of Hamlet* and *Ophelia's Revenge*. In Gordon's text, Yorick is revealed as the young Hamlet's mentor and the ultimate inspiration for the prince's later decision "To put an antic disposition on" (I.v. 172) while seeking revenge for the death of his father.

The fool is a paradoxical character-type, simultaneously a marginal figure and a member of the royal court, who uses his/her position on the borderline as a means of drawing attention to the foolishness that exists in society as a whole. Through the use of comic inversion, the ancestor of the Bakhtinian concept of the carnivalesque, the fool seeks to remedy that foolishness by making people laugh at it. Yet, in another example of the paradoxes surrounding this character-type, as Theodore B. Leinwand notes, "The fool inverts what has been inverted already" (221), in order to reaffirm the status

---

[101] This is also an example of self-referential humour, as James was himself a Shakespearean scholar.

of his/her patron and the society in which they live, thus becoming both a provocative and a conservative figure at the same time.

The paradoxes of the fool are very much evident in *Hamlet,* which depicts a royal court that is, on the one hand, without a fool since the death of Yorick, either "three and twenty years" in the Folio version of the play (V.i. 173-74), or "this dozen yeare" in the First Quarto version (1195), prior to Hamlet's encounter with "Shakespeare's chosen Clown, the gravedigger, [who] unearths his bones" (Pignataro 74). On the other hand, the absence of an official court fool underscores the fact that "the state of Denmark" (I.iv. 90) is itself full of fools of many different types, from "the Clown Prince of Denmark" (Bell 103) himself, to the other members of the court, all the way down to the gravediggers who are described in the play's stage directions as clowns, in the senses both of rustics and of comic relief. Even the name of the play's protagonist, as previously noted, means "a fool" (Hansen 6), emblematic of his feigning madness in order to expose the true madness in his society. Indeed, it can well be said, as Robert H. Bell does, that "[i]n a court without a jester, Hamlet leaps into the breach" (103); and Hamlet's lament of the "cursed spite, / That ever I was born to set it right!" (I.v. 188-89) may refer to his taking on not only the role of avenger for his father, but also that of the satirist/commentator that was once held by Yorick.

All Shakespeare tells us of the relationship between Yorick and Hamlet is in the prince's elegy over the jester's skull in V.i., in which Hamlet refers to his long-dead childhood companion as "a fellow of infinite jest, of most excellent fancy" (V.i. 184-85). This scene serves to humanize Hamlet by granting him an affectionate remembrance of an important figure from his early life, as well as reminding him of the impermanence of life and the seriousness of his mission. However, it also creates a significant gap in the fictional world with the absence of Yorick as a living person, even as we identify the influences he may well have had on Hamlet, from the prince's skill with wordplay to his talent at pretending madness to the degree that characters and readers alike still continue to question his sanity.

It is this gap created by the absence of Yorick that Alan Gordon attempts to fill in *An Antic Disposition,* part of his medieval mystery series featuring the members of the Fools' Guild.[102] In part a retelling of Saxo Grammaticus's account of Amleth in *Historiae Danicae,* the main inspiration

---

[102] The *Fools' Guild* series contains other Shakespearean references as well. The third novel, *Thirteenth Night,* is a sequel to Shakespeare's *Twelfth Night;* and Touchstone of *As You Like It* makes a cameo appearance at the end of *An Antic Disposition.* Even the series' regular main characters, Theophilos and Claudia, are revealed to be counterparts of Shakespearean characters appearing in *An Antic Disposition* and *Thirteenth Night,* respectively.

for Shakespeare's play, Gordon's novel brings Yorick into the story as a major character and involves him in the intrigues of the court of Ørvendil and Fengi – the counterparts of Shakespeare's King Hamlet and Claudius – such that even his death and disappearance from both Gordon's and Shakespeare's fictional worlds is clouded in suspicion.

Gordon's Yorick is in fact an Englishman, Terence of York, who receives his more familiar name when the young Amleth mispronounces the name "York" with two syllables (A. Gordon 25-26). Yorick's origin thus alludes both to the historical position of York as the capital of the Scandinavian kingdom of Jorvik in the ninth and tenth centuries (B. Lewis and Ford) and to Shakespeare's gravedigger's comment that exile to England was a fitting fate for Hamlet because "there the men are as mad as he" (V.i. 154-55). He becomes Ørvendil's jester at the behest of the leader of the Fools' Guild, Father Gerald, who instructs him to "Deflate Ørvendil's ambitions. Teach him to be happy with his lot" (A. Gordon 18) and not pursue his desire to be king of all Denmark, rather than merely a lord of Slesvig, lest civil war break out.

As seems to be common with prequels to *Hamlet* (see e.g. MacKaye, Updike, Trafford, Reisert), the relationship between the young Amleth and his father is often a difficult one, as Ørvendil becomes jealous of the attention Amleth pays to Yorick: "He is surrounded by warriors, men of arms, great men. Yet he hides behind his mother's skirts and only comes out when some painted freak throws a ball to him. Is this the future king of Denmark?" (A. Gordon 27). However, though he never completely approves of Yorick teaching Amleth the ways of the jester rather than those of the warrior, he does realize that the English fool is a positive influence because he has "never heard Amleth laugh like that before" (A. Gordon 29), and thus allows him to stay. Yorick becomes close not only to Amleth, but to the prince's cousins Alfhild and Lother – who in Saxo's history are the nameless foster siblings of Amleth, and who in Shakespeare's play are the characters we know as Ophelia and Laertes – becoming an affectionate father-figure to them in contrast to their indifferent and often abusive father Gorm, whom Yorick ironically nicknamed "Appollonius" (A. Gordon 91) following the latter's long-winded speech at his wedding. Indeed, Lother learns many years later that Yorick was his real father (A. Gordon 323-24), and that revelation, more so than any knowledge of Fengi's plan to murder his older brother, may well have been the reason for Yorick's mysterious death: "Gorm knew Signe [his wife] had betrayed him, and Yorick's very existence would mock his every waking moment" (A. Gordon 324)

Though neither Saxo nor Shakespeare ever truly gives an explanation for Hamlet's pretending "an utter lack of wits" (*HD* 62) as the cover for his plan

of revenge, Gordon demonstrates that not only does Amleth use the lessons
he has learned from Yorick, but it was Yorick himself who suggested that he
act mad to draw attention away from his true intentions: "He [Fengi] fears
his brother's image. But he will not fear someone whose mind is addled....
It's an old trick, but it just may keep you alive" (A. Gordon 189). Amleth
and Lother also discover, with the help of their classmate Horace – the
counterpart to Shakespeare's Horatio – and the members of the Fools' Guild
whom they meet in Paris, the involvement of Gerutha in the deaths of
Ørvendil and Alfhild (A. Gordon 320-22), and Gorm in Yorick's (A. Gordon
323-24), the former in sharp contrast to the Shakespearean Ghost's refusal to
implicate Gertrude in his death (I.v. 84-87) and the ambiguous death of
Ophelia that may have been either accidental or self-inflicted (IV.vii. 163-91;
V.i. 1-29).

   In reconciling the endings of Shakespeare's play, in which the entire royal
family dies during the rigged duel between Hamlet and Laertes (V.ii.), and
Saxo's history, in which Amleth burns down the palace with his uncle's men
still in it (*HD* 70), Gordon has Amleth and Lother stage the duel using a
sleeping potion in place of the poison that was originally intended (A.
Gordon 291; cf. Fiedler; *R&J* IV.i. 94-107), another trick taught to them by
Yorick's fellow fools (A. Gordon 319). They then go on to destroy Fengi's
palace (A. Gordon 325-29) and, ultimately, live on under new names as
members of the Fools' Guild (A. Gordon 329). By granting his Amleth the
happy ending denied to Shakespeare's Hamlet, Gordon does restore some of
Saxo's 'original' story (cf. *HD* 70-78) to the familiar Shakespearean telling,
and also affirms the restorative power of humour on both an individual and
a societal level: even if the court of Ørvendil and Fengi – or Hamlet and
Claudius, for that matter – is destroyed by ambition and duplicity, the Fools'
Guild, and the potential of finding redemption in the midst of tragedy that it
represents, continues to endure.

   James's poem and Gordon's novel are distinct among role expansions of
minor *Hamlet* characters in their use of characters who are very much on the
periphery of the Shakespearean fictional world. The majority of such
adaptations draw upon characters who not only are physically present in the
Shakespearean world but have lines and positions in the plot. One such
example is Maurice Baring's short story "At the Court of King Claudius,"
which retells the presentation of the Mousetrap play from the perspective of
the actors who performed in it. In Shakespeare's play, the Players are
primarily figures who both represent and question the role of drama and the
dramatic world in the actual world. They are also a means for Shakespeare
to comment on the dramatic profession as it existed in his time (e.g. *Hamlet*
II.ii. 329-66; III.ii. 1-45). In Baring's story, they take on an additional role,

providing the commoner's perspective on the character of Hamlet as well as on events that are familiar to us from the play.

The Players in "At the Court of King Claudius" were fellow students at Wittenberg with Hamlet, "when he was as much our companion as our patron" (Baring 164). In contrast to Hamlet's usual idealized appearance and description, the First Player describes him as "older and more serious, and... more portly" (Baring 164) than in his days as a student. However, the most significant detail of the First Player's account of Hamlet is the recognition of the repressive environment in which the Prince exists, even though the Player is not fully aware of the reasons for Hamlet's behaviour:

> He is virtually a prisoner, for should he in any way transgress the fixed limits of the tradition and etiquette which govern this place, the courtiers... do not hesitate to say that he is deranged in his mind. (Baring 164)

The Player's ignorance of the fact that Hamlet is pretending to be mad for his own purposes, and so far has been successful at it, lends a sense of irony to the comment that "had he not had the misfortune to be born a Prince he would have been a player of first-rate excellence... his mind lives in the world of dream and holds office at the court of Art" (Baring 165-66).

The Player is at first surprised by Hamlet's request for *The Murder of Gonzago,* thinking it "a somewhat old-fashioned bit of fustian, chosen no doubt to suit the taste of the King and his courtiers" (Baring 164), and believing that the request for a tragedy is fitting because of the death of the former king (Baring 165). Indeed, upon being asked if there is "no offence in't" (III.ii. 232-33), the Players believe this to be an injunction against "all buffoonery of any kind" (Baring 165) out of respect for King Hamlet's memory. Reflecting upon the performance itself, the Players regard Hamlet's constant interruptions and remarks to the others as attempts to "elucidat[e] the passages which proved perplexing" (Baring 166). They also interpret Claudius's shocked reaction to the murder scene (III.ii. 265-70) as a sign, not that he is guilty of a similar crime, but that "he has no taste for letters" (Baring 166). To the Players, his reaction "signified that the play was tedious" (Baring 166), an interpretation very different from Hamlet's.

The Players' views of the characters other than Hamlet help to mark Baring's text as a humorous, if inadvertent on the characters' part, example of revisionism as well as of revisionary narrative, to borrow Douglas Lanier's term: the text is 'revisionary' in its use of a minor character's perspective, but 'revisionist' in its departure from generally-accepted views of the play's events. The Players' interpretation of Claudius as being offended by a play he did not like rather than being plagued by guilt is but one such contrast to the Shakespearean fictional world. The Players also have a rather

unsympathetic opinion of Ophelia, whom they dismiss as "an insipid minx...
likely to develop on the lines of her doddering old father" (165). To the
Players, Ophelia seems more interested in Osric – like themselves, a very
minor character – than in Hamlet, while it may be "Horatio who is in reality
plighted to her" (Baring 165). The only character besides Hamlet to whom
the Players show any noticeable degree of sympathy is Gertrude, mainly
because she "seemed much pleased, and... she has ever been fond of
spectacles and stage-playing" (Baring 166). But the strongest contrast
between the worlds of Baring's Players and of Shakespeare's *Hamlet* is the
role of the Mousetrap play itself. For Shakespeare, the play is a pivotal
moment, both as a means of advancing the plot and as an illustration of the
connections between fictional worlds; but for Baring, the play is just another
performance by a group of travelling actors who think nothing afterward
other than "Tomorrow we sail for Hamburg" (166).

For James, Gordon, and Baring, revisiting the events of *Hamlet* through the
eyes of peripheral characters has not changed those characters' status outside
of their respective fictional worlds *as* peripheral characters. By contrast, two
of the most famous of all role expansions of *Hamlet,* as well as of
Shakespearean adaptations in general, have succeeded in elevating minor
characters in the Shakespearean fictional world to the status of major
characters in their own right. These adaptations, written a century apart but
displaying much in common, are Sir William Gilbert's and Tom Stoppard's
plays about Rosencrantz and Guildenstern. Both Gilbert's *Rosencrantz and
Guildenstern* and Stoppard's *Rosencrantz and Guildenstern Are Dead*
reimagine the events of *Hamlet* through the eyes of minor characters while
simultaneously commenting upon the creation of their respective fictional
worlds from elements of the Shakespearean original. In both cases, these
plays also draw upon the theatrical conventions of their own times: Gilbert's
play is a parody and critique of Victorian approaches to Shakespearean
acting, and Stoppard picks up on devices from postmodern dramatic
movements such as Theatre of the Absurd (Cohn 211-18).

Gilbert's *Rosencrantz and Guildenstern* was first published in 1874 and
first performed in 1891. It is an example of Shakespearean burlesque, a genre
popular for much of the nineteenth century as a humorous commentary on
both Shakespeare's plays and the dramatic conventions surrounding them. As
Richard Schoch notes, these adaptations, as irreverent as they may seem on
the surface, "actively intervened to protect Shakespeare from his true
detractors" (4): actors and directors who showed, in the opinion of the
parodists, insufficient respect for the text of the plays by emphasizing style
over substance. Indeed, the crime Gilbert's Claudius is attempting to hide
from the court is not the murder of his brother, but having written a terrible

play which was laughed off the stage (Gilbert 77-78) – which Rosencrantz describes, echoing the Shakespearean Hamlet's description of Claudius himself, as "a thing of shreds and patches" (Gilbert 85; cf. *Hamlet* III.iv. 103).

Gilbert's Hamlet has no discernable reason for pretending madness and is seen by the court as depressed because of his "solitary tastes / And tendency to long soliloquy" (78). The character himself and what the other characters say about him exist primarily as Gilbert's commentaries on the many different actors who have played Hamlet and the many different interpretations scholars and directors have offered of his character:

> GUILDENSTERN. And what's he like?
> OPHELIA. Alike for no two seasons at a time.
> Sometimes he's tall – sometimes he's very short –
> Now with black hair – now with a flaxen wig –
> Sometimes an English accent – then a French –
> Then English with a strong provincial "burr" –
> Once an American, and once a Jew –
> But Danish never, take him how you will!
> And strange to say, whate'er his tongue may be,
> Whether he's dark or flaxen – English – French –
> Though we're in Denmark, AD ten-six-two –
> He always dresses as King James the First![103]
> GUILDENSTERN. Oh, he is surely mad!
> OPHELIA. Well, there again
> Opinion is divided. Some men hold
> That he's the sanest, far, of all sane men –
> Some that he's really sane, but shamming mad –
> Some that he's really mad, but shamming sane –
> Some that he will be mad, some that he *was* –
> Some that he couldn't be. But on the whole
> (As far as I can make out what they mean)
> The favourite theory's somewhat like this:
> Hamlet is idiotically sane
> With lucid intervals of lunacy.
>   (Gilbert 79-80)

Like his Shakespearean counterpart (*Hamlet* III.ii. 1-45), Gilbert's Hamlet also offers his opinions of what constitutes good and bad acting, criticizing both the Victorian taste for "pedantical bombast and windy obtrusive rhetorick" (Gilbert 86) and for overdone comedy which is "an impertinence

---

[103] See Chapter Two.

to your audience, for it seemeth to imply that they are unable to recognize a joke unless it be pointed out to them" (Gilbert 86).

Gilbert's play does not wholly follow Shakespeare's, confining itself to Act Three, scenes i and ii. *Rosencrantz and Guildenstern* makes use of Hamlet's most famous scene, the "To be or not to be" soliloquy (*Hamlet* III.i. 55-87), but here Rosencrantz and Guildenstern comically interrupt Hamlet's speech by attempting to answer all of his rhetorical questions and reciting portions of the speech alongside him, until he bitterly points out to them that "Three persons can't soliloquize at once!" (Gilbert 82). As well, in a reversal of the Shakespearean Mousetrap of Act III, scene ii, Gilbert's version is set up by Rosencrantz and Guildenstern as "a trap for Hamlet, not Claudius" (Robinson par. 7), for the play being performed is in fact Claudius's old shame; and the plan is not "to catch the conscience of the King" (*Hamlet* II.ii. 603) but to have Hamlet removed from the court so that Rosencrantz can be with his love, Ophelia. As in Shakespeare's play, Claudius reacts to the performance by having Hamlet banished to England (Gilbert 88-89; *Hamlet* III.iii., IV.iii.), a fitting fate because, with the prevalence of Shakespearean scholars in England, "men will rise or sink in good esteem / According as they worship him, or slight him!" (Gilbert 88).

As is evident from the play's closing sentiment, Gilbert's *Rosencrantz and Guildenstern* does not seek to undermine Hamlet as the focus of the play's world or of the myriads of literary criticism that surround it. By contrast, Tom Stoppard's *Rosencrantz and Guildenstern Are Dead*[104] is a displacement of the Shakespearean world as well as an expansion, as it makes minor characters into major ones and vice versa. However, though it is a *displacement* of the main character and his world, it is not meant as a *replacement* for the Shakespearean text, but a complementary text that stands beside and even within the original, as knowledge of *Hamlet* is essential for a proper appreciation of *Rosencrantz and Guildenstern Are Dead*. C.J. Gianakaris notes, however, that "Stoppard never intended to reshape *Hamlet*... [or] to clarify or enrich our understanding of *Hamlet*" (224) as is often the case with adaptations, but rather used Shakespeare's text as inspiration for a "witty commentary" (Cohn 217) on both metaphysics and metafiction.

The two textual worlds of *Hamlet* and *Rosencrantz and Guildenstern Are Dead* intersect yet remain distinct from each other, as symbolized in their use of language: direct quotations from *Hamlet* (e.g. *R&G* 35-37; *Hamlet* II.ii. 1-49) remain in Shakespeare's original words, while the remainder of the play is in Modern English prose. Stoppard uses his textual world to fill in gaps and blanks in Shakespeare's; events only narrated in *Hamlet*, such as

---

[104] Hereafter cited as *R&G*.

Ophelia's report to Polonius of her encounter with Hamlet in her room (*Hamlet* II.i. 71-97), are dramatized in *Rosencrantz and Guildenstern Are Dead* (*R&G* 34-35). Conversely, important events in Shakespeare's play, such as Hamlet's "To be or not to be" soliloquy, receive only passing mention in Stoppard's play, on the assumption that the audience is already familiar with these events and can fill in the details in their own minds. As in Gilbert's similar yet different treatment of the soliloquy/speech, Rosencrantz and Guildenstern speak to each other throughout Hamlet's soliloquy, but where Gilbert's Rosencrantz and Guildenstern undercut the seriousness – and iconic stature – of the moment by interrupting Hamlet, Stoppard's two protagonists never directly address Hamlet and indeed wonder how they will ever get a word in edgewise as "Hamlet enters...and pauses, weighing the pros and cons of making his quietus" (*R&G* 74). But Stoppard does not completely ignore the famous passage, giving a version of it to Rosencrantz and Guildenstern themselves as they reflect upon whether they can imagine themselves "as actually dead, lying in a box with a lid on it.... Eternity is a terrible thought. I mean, where's it going to end?" (*R&G* 70-71).

As a fictional world created through the processes of intertextuality, *Rosencrantz and Guildenstern Are Dead* is very much a metafictional text as well as a metaphysical one. Much of its humour, as well as its seriousness, comes from self-reflexivity, reminding the readers/audience of the plays' fictionality and the creative process. Like Baring, Stoppard makes the Players into significant characters, although for Stoppard they remain secondary characters. The Players recognize Rosencrantz and Guildenstern "as fellow artists" (*R&G* 23) and themselves as emblematic figures of the creative process in all its aspects – knowing the needs and wants of the readers/audience (*R&G* 32-33, 80-81), the willing suspension of disbelief (*R&G* 33-34, 84-85), and the gap between the fictional and actual worlds (*R&G* 83-84). Rosencrantz and Guildenstern themselves give voice to the different approaches to creating fictional worlds in their conversation with the Players about the types of fictional worlds each prefers:

> ROSENCRANTZ.... people want to be entertained – they don't come expecting sordid and gratuitous filth.
> PLAYER. You're wrong – they do! Murder, seduction, and incest – what do you want – *jokes?*
> ROSENCRANTZ. I want a good story, with a beginning, middle, and end.
> PLAYER. And you?
> GUILDENSTERN. I'd prefer art to mirror life, if it's all the same to you.
> PLAYER. It's all the same to me, sir.
>
> (*R&G* 80-81)

Whereas Guildenstern and, to a somewhat different degree, the Player, echo Hamlet's insistence that "the purpose of playing... is to hold... the mirror up to nature" (*Hamlet* III.ii. 20-22), Rosencrantz prefers the Neoclassical model of clearly defined fictional worlds governed by rules of unity and decorum.

The status of *Rosencrantz and Guildenstern Are Dead* as an adaptation of *Hamlet* also informs its views of fate and destiny, as shown in its use of the English ambassador's report to Horatio at the end of Shakespeare's play (*Hamlet* V.ii. 371; *R&G* 126) as the source of its title. Unlike Gilbert, who changes the familiar ending of the Shakespearean play for comic effect, Stoppard "freely creates the personalities of Rosencrantz and Guildenstern, but grants that their final destiny has been determined by Shakespeare" (Lenoff 46). The opening of the play, with the two protagonists flipping coins (*R&G* 1-17),[105] displays an ambivalent view of fate: on the one hand, the coin-flipping symbolizes the arbitrariness of fate and "the hazard of the die" (*RIII* V.iv. 10); but on the other, Rosencrantz's constantly calling "heads" suggests an attempt to manipulate destiny in a way that would cause "a weaker man...to re-examine his faith, if in nothing else at least in the law of probability" (*R&G* 12). Stoppard's use of fictional worlds to explore questions of free will and determinism recalls Leibniz's theories of the actual world as the 'best of all possible worlds' because it is the one that will produce the best possible outcome; this belief is most succinctly expressed by the Player's reminder to Rosencrantz and Guildenstern that "There's a design at work in all art – surely you must know that? Events must play themselves out to aesthetic, moral, and logical conclusion.... It is *written*" (*R&G* 79-80). The Player's statement leads into a rehearsal of the Mousetrap that is also a summary of *Hamlet* (*R&G* 80-83) and which foreshadows the protagonists' deaths at the end of both Shakespeare's and Stoppard's plays. The discovery that Hamlet has indeed altered the letter to the English king into an order for their execution leads Rosencrantz and Guildenstern to question their importance to their world(s):

> ROSENCRANTZ. They had it in for us, didn't they? Right from the beginning. Who'd have thought that we were so important?
> GUILDENSTERN. But why? Was it all for this? Who are we that so much should converge on our little deaths? Who are *we?*
> PLAYER. You are Rosencrantz and Guildenstern. That's enough. (*R&G* 122)

---

[105] Thanks to the popularity of Stoppard's play, this scene has become emblematic enough of Rosencrantz and Guildenstern that it has appeared or been referred to in productions of *Hamlet* itself.

The Player's statement, while an unsatisfactory explanation to Rosencrantz and Guildenstern themselves, reminds the reader/audience that, whether they are minor characters in Shakespeare's fictional world or major ones in Stoppard's, they are important for the work's success.

In elevating Rosencrantz and Guildenstern to major characters, Stoppard simultaneously, and perhaps inevitably, reduces Hamlet to a minor character who appears largely though not entirely as comic relief. Though we do hear him speak, all his lines are taken directly from the Shakespearean text; and when he does anything unique to Stoppard's text, it is almost always the sort of behaviour he would have been expected to display while pretending madness (e.g. *R&G* 111, 116). Away from the Danish court, Hamlet would presumably have no reason to continue acting mad; here, however, doing so "reduces [his] already diminished stature" (Cohn 214) and completes the role reversal between him and Rosencrantz and Guildenstern within Stoppard's fictional world.

In *Heterocosmica,* Doležel describes the relationship between a source text and an expansion of that text as one in which "The protoworld and the successor world are complementary... and the established structure is thus shifted" (207). The world of *Hamlet,* like those of many of Shakespeare's other plays, has traditionally been oriented around a single dominating character surrounded by many other lesser characters of varying degrees of importance, all of whom provide potential focus points for alternative fictional worlds. No matter which character a writer chooses as the protagonist for an expansion, the world embodied in the derivative text is simultaneously dependent on, and distinct from, that of the source text, challenging readers to make the connections between these various texts and their worlds in ways that enrich the source as well as the derivative texts. Role expansions of secondary characters from the text of *Hamlet* especially prove that "the state of Denmark" (*Hamlet* I.iv. 89) as Shakespeare presents it is large enough to accommodate the perspectives of more than just Hamlet himself, while in no way undermining his claim as the centre of attention in the Shakespearean world.

CHAPTER FIVE

HAMLET IN HIS POSTMODERN GUISES

> Good my lord, will you see the players
> well bestow'd? Do you hear, let them be well us'd,
> for they are the abstract and brief chronicles of the
> time. After your death you were better have a bad
> epitaph than their ill report while you live.
>
> (*Hamlet* II.ii. 522-26)

Texts that take postmodern approaches (see Hutcheon xiii) to Shakespeare's *Hamlet* provide new ways of approaching an old text by using the play as a basis from which to examine relationships between characters and texts alike. While translations and expansions can and do often use techniques that can be classified as postmodern, the term is more often applied to transpositions and displacements of the source text. This is because the techniques of transposition – transplanting the original characters and/or plot into a new setting in time and/or place – and displacement – changing an element of the source text in order to challenge that text and its world(s) – are commonly employed in a key feature of postmodernism: the challenging of the established literary tradition through the use of products of that tradition.

Transpositions of *Hamlet*

According to Doležel:
Transposition preserves the design and the main story of the protoworld but locates them in a different temporal or spatial setting. The protoworld and the successor world are parallel, but the rewrite tests the topicality of the canonical world by placing it in a new... historical, political, and cultural context (*Heterocosmica* 206)

Four examples of *Hamlet* transpositions – Hubert Aquin's *Neige Noire* (translated into English by Sheila Fischman as *Hamlet's Twin*), Ian Mark's *Heathrow Nights*, David Bergantino's *Hamlet II: Ophelia's Revenge*, and Ranulfo Concon's *Joker* – each use a complex narrative structure and update the plot of *Hamlet* (or elements thereof) to contemporary settings to demonstrate the play's relevance to contemporary readers and to ask questions about the nature of fictionality. All four of these novels use the plot and characters of *Hamlet* to mirror events in the lives of their protagonists: Aquin's novel considers the life of an actor playing Fortinbras in a filmed version of the play, narrates the circumstances surrounding the suspicious death of his wife, and dwells on his desire to produce an autobiographical film reflecting the text of the novel itself. Bergantino's book follows a college football star who is simultaneously a descendant and reincarnation of Hamlet, and who is haunted by the ghost of Ophelia; and Mark's and Ranulfo's novels both follow adolescent boys who use *Hamlet* to come to terms with the effects of the loss of their fathers – by death and divorce, respectively – and their mothers' remarriage. The narrative structures of each novel also link their respective fictional worlds to the world of *Hamlet* in non-linear fashion, making use of dreams, flashbacks and flash-forwards, and the visual/descriptive techniques of film scripts, to intertwine the worlds of Shakespeare's text and their own texts with the worlds of contemporary characters, authors, and readers.

Neige Noire was Aquin's final novel, published two years before his death,[106] and in many ways it represents what Pierre-Yves Mocquais calls in his annotated edition of the novel "la fascination... pour le personnage d'Hamlet, le mythe oedipien, et le personnage d'Oedipe lui-même" (xx) which dated back to Aquin's student years. The novel grew out of Aquin's 1970 translation of *Hamlet*, which was partly influenced by earlier translations by André Gide and Yves Bonnefoy (Mocquais xx; cf. Aquin 17-18; Fischman 15). Like the production described in the novel, Aquin's translation was prepared for "a ninety-minute television drama" (Fischman 7). In its reimagining and rewriting of *Hamlet, Neige Noire* also exemplifies the fashion in French-Canadian literature of the Quiet Revolution era for translations and adaptations – or both at once – of Shakespeare geared to the needs and interests of the Québécois reading public. Such works, as we have seen with Gurik's play, were often meant as simultaneous assertions of Québécois literature's distinctness from English-Canadian literature on the one hand – in the choice of language in which they were produced – and French literature as produced in France on the other – in the choice of non-French works as base texts.

The title chosen by Sheila Fischman for her English translation of *Neige Noire, Hamlet's Twin*, emphasizes Aquin's use of Shakespeare's text as a

---

[106] Patricia Smart notes that Aquin's "inability to continue writing after *Neige Noire* was certainly an important factor in his suicide" (169).

basis for his own, though perhaps more than the original novel does. It also adds further degrees of ambiguity to an already complex and multilayered text, as the protagonist, Nicolas Vanesse, appears to be more closely identified with Fortinbras – the role he plays in Aquin's 'film-within-the-film' – than with Hamlet himself. Yet, as we are reminded at the beginning of the novel, Fortinbras is a figurative twin to Hamlet in that both seek to avenge the deaths of their fathers, as does Laertes: the three characters are described as "Trois fils vengeurs, un seul victorieux: Fortinbras"[107] (Aquin 8). Within Aquin/Nicolas's interpretation of the play and its sources, however, Fortinbras and Hamlet are revealed to be literal twins as well: "Dans la version de Saxo Grammaticus, ce frère est appelé Amlethe, tandis que notre Hamlet est appelé Amlethus"[108] (Aquin 211). Aquin's digression on the history of Hamlet and Fortinbras thus provides a strong intertextual link between his fictional world and that of Shakespeare, as his explanation of what Fortinbras may have meant by his declaration of "some rights, of memory in this kingdom" (*Hamlet* V.ii. 389) provides a distinctive interpretation of the play's final scene, while Aquin's combining of Fortinbras and Hamlet into Nicolas invites the reader to reflect on Nicolas's role on screen within the fictional world and thus to confront this amalgamated character's significance in the novel. Aquin himself remarked upon how both Shakespearean characters informed his character, "Nicolas... donne des répliques de Hamlet mais il joue le rôle de Fortinbras... il n'a rien à voir avec ni Hamlet ni Fortinbras de toute façon" (560).[109] Yet, like both Hamlet and Fortinbras, Nicolas seeks, and eventually takes, revenge for perceived wrongs: in this case, the discovery that "the character who was introduced... as Sylvie Dubuque, and who changed her name to Sylvie Vanesse when she married Nicolas, is in reality Sylvie Lewandowski... lover and daughter of Michel Lewandowski" (Smart 175).

Aquin's novel does more than explore parallels between Hamlet and Fortinbras, however: the connections between Hamlet and Ophelia are equally important, and perhaps it can be said that within Aquin's fictional worlds, Ophelia can also be called 'Hamlet's twin.' Indeed, just as Hamlet and Fortinbras share a counterpart in the character of Nicolas, Ophelia has three counterparts in the world of *Neige Noire*: Sylvie Dubuque/Vanesse/Lewandowski, the ill-fated wife of Nicolas; Linda Noble, the actress who

---

[107] "Three vengeful sons; only one victorious: Fortinbras" (Fischman 8).

[108] "In the Saxo Grammaticus version this brother was called Amlethe, while our Hamlet is called Amlethus" (Fischman 157).

[109] Nicolas speaks the lines of Hamlet but he plays the role of Fortinbras... he has nothing in common with either Hamlet or Fortinbras in any way (translation mine).

plays Ophelia in Nicolas's production of *Hamlet* and is considered for the part of Sylvie in his screenplay (cf. Smart 175); and Eva Vos, the Norwegian friend of the Vanesses who enters into relationships with both Nicolas and Linda following Sylvie's death (cf. Iqbal 77). Of these three, Sylvie is probably the most obvious Ophelia-figure, as indicated not only by her untimely death but also by the hint of insanity in her family (Aquin 166; Fischman 125) and by her incestuous relationship with her father, Michel Lewandowski, whom Patricia Smart describes as "a Polonius... father-figure who remains off-stage and hidden... but who manipulates all the strings" (175). Conversely, Linda and Eva escape the fate of both Sylvie and the 'original' Ophelia after reading a draft of Nicolas's screenplay that reveals the truth about Sylvie's death (Aquin 248-68; Fischman 188-200), and their lesbian love scene at the end of the novel (Aquin 272-78; Fischman 202-08) may even be regarded as an anticipation of recent 'reclamations' of Ophelia as a symbol of female empowerment.

Aquin presents his examination of Hamlet and Fortinbras as literal and metaphorical twins, and Nicolas as a Hamlet-analogue, most prominently when Nicolas and Eva discuss the representation – or lack thereof – in his autobiographical screenplay of Sylvie's mysterious death while she and Nicolas were honeymooning in Norway. Eva's questions to Nicolas, after reading his notebook, anticipate the sorts of questions readers themselves may have on reading the novel:

> De mon point de vue, il ne manque pas seulement la scène du suicide de Sylvie au scénario... il y manque aussi l'explication à propos d'Hamlet, de Fortinbras et de leur signification dans le contexte du film.... Je me suis demandé si tu n'avais pas inséré cet élément à seul fin de mystifier le spectateur et si, en fin de compte, tu n'allais pas lui faire faux bond quand lui, précisément, attendra le mot de la fin. (Aquin 208)[110]

This passage confirms that, as Sherrill Grace notes, "the *Hamlet* sequences are misleading if used too literally as a key to the novel's signifying system" (92); *Neige Noire* is not a mere transposition of the Shakespearean text to the present-day world, "a closed one-on-one correspondence with *Hamlet*" (Smart 172). Indeed, Nicolas's and Eva's discussion of the significance of *Hamlet*

---

[110] "It seems to me that it's not just Sylvie's suicide scene that's missing from the screenplay... there's also a lack of explanation about Hamlet, Fortinbras, and their meaning in the context of the film.... I wondered if you hadn't inserted that element simply to mystify the viewer and if in the end you weren't going to let him down precisely when he's expecting the final word" (Fischman 155).

within both of the novel's fictional worlds – that of Nicolas's screenplay and that of the novel itself – comes as the centerpiece of a discussion of fictionality and literariness and their relationship to reality (Aquin 207-15; Fischman 154-60), a theme that permeates the entire novel and is profoundly illustrated by the screenplay form in which the novel is written.[111] Aquin combines his meditations on the character and role of Fortinbras, the metatheatrical/metafictional commentaries of the narrator/screenwriter, and the device of a play-within-a-play, the last so important to the text of *Hamlet*, to remind the readers of the complexity and incompleteness of the reading/writing/filming/viewing processes: "la fiction n'est pas un piège, c'est elle, plutôt, qui est piégée par une réalité qu'elle ne contenait pas et qui l'envahit hypocritement" (Aquin 159).[112]

The 'invasion' of fiction into reality, a key theme in Aquin's novel, is also prominently on display – albeit in a somewhat different manner – in Jan Mark's 2000 novel *Heathrow Nights*.[113] The protagonist of Mark's novel, Russell Jagger, uses *Hamlet* to address his father's death and his mother's remarriage, even to the point of nicknaming his new stepfather "Claudius," though only as "a private joke" (Mark 3) among his friends and himself. It is thus ironic, as Russell himself observes, that he and his friends are banned from a class field trip, thus leading them to spend the week of the field trip at Heathrow so their families will not know, for disrupting a performance of *Hamlet* on a previous class trip (Mark 8).

Throughout the novel, Russell describes the behaviour of himself, his mother, and his stepfather in terms of their respective counterparts in Shakespeare's play; for example, on the remarriage of Gertrude to Claudius, which suggests to him that of his own mother, he says:

> The Ghost says Claudius was the one who poured poison in his ear, or Hamlet thinks he does, but what was Claudius doing at Elsinore anyway? The King's brother, just hanging around making himself useful? He certainly made himself useful afterwards. "Here, little lady, lean on me."
> And she leaned. (Mark 69)

---

[111] Although *Neige Noire* is written as a screenplay, Aquin was more interested in exploring the literary qualities of the screenplay form as "un poème filmique" (573) than in making the film itself.

[112]"the fiction isn't a trap; it's the fiction that is trapped by a reality it didn't contain and which hypocritically invades it" (Fischman 120).

[113] A portion of this section was previously published in Chopoidalo and Syed, "Teaching *Hamlet* in 21st-Century Pakistan and Canada."

However, like Aquin's reimagining of the *Hamlet* plot, Mark's version is also not a simple transposition. First, there is nothing particularly suspicious about the remarriage except from Russell's perspective: his father died of a stroke (49), and the only reason his mother remarries is that "[s]he wants another baby... and she's afraid of leaving it too late" (173). It is Russell himself who reimagines his family situation as a counterpart to Hamlet's, both by analogy to a classmate who ran away from home when his parents were divorced (79-80) and because he had been accustomed to being "part of the running of the house, that what I wanted and thought mattered... which is why I'm certain that all the way from Wittenberg to Elsinore, Hamlet assumed he was going home to be King" (81).

Mark uses Russell's observations of the parallels, real or imagined, between Hamlet's life and his own as her commentary on the play and its relevance to the contemporary reader, often in comparison to other Shakespearean plays commonly read among students of Russell's age. Both *Hamlet* and *Romeo and Juliet*, for example, are presented in Russell's class as "meaningful and relevant and hip" (Mark 115) because of the ages and life experiences of the main characters, yet Russell himself finds *Hamlet* much easier to relate to, not only because of the perceived similarities to his family situation, but also because of his belief that "Romeo and Juliet... only fall in love because they haven't got anything else to do" (115). Mark/Russell also intertextually compares *Hamlet* and *Macbeth* by imagining what might have happened if characters from one play crossed over into the other: "Macbeth wouldn't have got very far if he'd been married to Gertrude.... And if Claudius had had Lady Macbeth to contend with he wouldn't have lasted five minutes... unless... she'd put him up to it in the first place" (69-70).

Mark's commentaries on *Hamlet* within the text of *Heathrow Nights* further imagine other divergent worlds from that of the original play by exploring other directions in which *Hamlet*'s plot might have gone (26, 82-83, 116, 156), while at the same time pondering other directions in which the lives of Russell, his family, and his classmates might have gone (78-81, 122, 155-57). Mark also gives glimpses of her ideas, expressed by both Russell and his stepfather Christopher, of a 'revisionist' approach to *Hamlet,* depicting the prince as "a weedy little runt with bi-focals" (179) who taunts Claudius with "crossword clues" (57). However, Mark's text itself also functions as a revision of *Hamlet*, not only through the embedded commentaries but also through the flashbacks describing Russell's father's death, his mother's remarriage, and his reactions to these events. At the beginning of the novel, Russell remembers that Christopher had said to him, "I'm not trying to replace your father" (4), and as the story progresses, we see the truth of Christopher's claim. Indeed, Mark's most vivid illustration of the differences between Russell and Hamlet is that Russell and Christopher finally do reach a common understanding through a discussion of the relationship between Hamlet and Claudius (176-80). Thus, *Heathrow Nights* can be read as a polemical/revisionist rewrite of *Hamlet* in a very different way from Aquin's: one that gives the story a happier ending, by positing no ill intentions in the family situation, reading the story as one of adjustment rather than of vengeance, and allowing the protagonist to live and grow.

In similar yet different ways to Mark's text, David Bergantino's 2003 novel *Hamlet II: Ophelia's Revenge* is a reworking of the *Hamlet* story on two levels. On the one hand, Bergantino's novel appears at first glance to be a straight transposition of the Shakespearean plot to a contemporary American setting, as its protagonist, Cameron Dean – a pun on "Hamlet the Dane" (*Hamlet* V.i. 258) – seeks to prove that his father, the dean of his university, was murdered by his aunt Claudia. However, at the same time, the novel is a sequel to Shakespeare's play, in that Cameron is a reincarnation of Hamlet: in his first encounter with his father's ghost, Cameron also has a vision of himself literally joined to Hamlet (Bergantino 13-15), whom his father describes as his "Siamese soul... sort of stuck in between, arrested before you could completely split off" (Bergantino 14). The parallels between Hamlet's and Cameron's lives as well as their being two different incarnations of the same entity are further said to be "the family curse" (Osborne 125), for which the only remedy is "Good old-fashioned vengeance" (Bergantino 17).

In Bergantino's fictional world, *Hamlet* is not fiction, but actual history; *Hamlet*'s veridicality is illustrated not only by Cameron being a reincarnation of Hamlet, but also by his being a distant descendant of the Danish nobility, which leads him to inherit the original Elsinore Castle on his twenty-first birthday (Bergantino 42). Furthermore, when developing his own 'Mousetrap' to "catch the conscience of" his aunt (*Hamlet* II.ii. 603), Cameron refers, not to Shakespeare's play, but to Edgar Allan Poe's *The Tell-Tale Heart* (Bergantino 40), as the inspiration for his plan. However, as Jennifer Hulbert and her co-authors note, "Shakespeare is... present in this world" (224) – as historian rather than playwright. Cameron's friends, the gay couple Rosenberg and Gyllenhal (obvious counterparts of Rosencrantz and Guildenstern), find a book in the castle library in which "Some guy named Shakespeare chronicled the history of the castle" (Bergantino 94), and thus also summarized, for both reader and characters, the events of the play. While these allusions could conceivably be read as a criticism of the reading habits of present-day American students (cf. Hulbert et al. 221-29), they are more immediately a means of establishing Bergantino's fictional world as separate from the reader's actual world by positing a different role for the source text and its author within that fictional world than in the reader's world.

However, *Hamlet II: Ophelia's Revenge* is not merely a transposition of the Shakespearean plot with a few twists, as the first third of the novel appears to suggest. Cameron's arrival at Elsinore triggers what is probably the greatest difference between Bergantino's novel and Shakespeare's play. Because Cameron is Hamlet's reincarnation, his presence awakens the ghost of Ophelia, who in this fictional world did not even receive the dignity of a formal burial, abbreviated or otherwise (cf. *Hamlet* V.i.), but had lain in a swamp beneath the castle for four centuries (Bergantino 71-74). However, unlike the ghosts of King Hamlet or of Mr. Dean, who cannot directly affect the physical world and must obtain revenge through their sons' actions, Ophelia's ghost can and does affect the world around her, having the ability to possess the bodies of young women and act through them. In this way, Bergantino's Ophelia is both a tongue-in-cheek reversal and a very literal interpretation of Pipher's image of Ophelia as the 'angry young woman,' the "oppressed teen who needs to be revived" (Hulbert et al. 223), as well as an inversion of the famously hesitant Hamlet himself.

Bergantino also follows the traditional tropes of the contemporary horror story in having his Ophelia prey upon beautiful and sexually active teenagers, with her particular target being on her present-day counterpart, Cameron's girlfriend, Sofia. Analogously to Cameron and Hamlet, Sofia is Bergantino's counterpart both to the Ophelia within her own fictional world and to the Shakespearean Ophelia. Not only are Sofia's and Ophelia's names somewhat phonetically similar as are Cameron's and Hamlet's, but the name *Sofia* means 'wisdom' (*Behind the Name*). Indeed, Bergantino does give Sofia the wisdom that Ophelia, in his interpretation, seems to have lacked in life, as illustrated in Sofia's partly successful attempt to reason with the ghost:

> I know times were different, but bad advice... is bad advice, and there's no need to go crazy over it.... If yours was such an inevitable, eternal love, then why did he treat you like that?... In short, Ophelia my love, get over him.... And while you're at it, get over yourself! (Bergantino 236)

Jennifer Hulbert and her collaborators read this statement as an evaluation of the Shakespearean text and its worldview "by a young woman who rejects them and what they stand for" (226) as well as a rebuttal to the place of honour *Hamlet* has traditionally held in academic circles: "transcend your time and context and situation and make yourself relevant to now or don't waste your time" (226). However, such a reading does not adequately consider that knowing the Shakespearean text is important to understanding

Bergantino's use of it. What Sofia rejects is not the entire Shakespearean world, nor even the view of women as passive sufferers of male indifference and worse, but rather a holdover from the world of Saxo: the valuing of revenge. Indeed, the futility of seeking revenge is dramatically illustrated by the fact that, between the ghost's rampage and Claudia's manipulation of Sofia's brother Larry into killing Cameron (Bergantino 216-42; cf. *Hamlet* V.ii.), all the characters die except for Cameron's best friend Harry, and Rosenberg and Gyllenhal – who use an ancient burial practice meant to protect against witches (Bergantino 223-26, 239-40) to insure that Ophelia's ghost will not rise again. But unlike Shakespeare's Horatio, Harry is unable to convince the local authorities of what really happened, and the whole scenario is finally "blamed... on a group of escaped mental patients" (Bergantino 239).

Like Aquin, Bergantino makes more explicit use of a modern-day genre – in this case, the horror story – than he does of the Shakespearean text, as exemplified in his tongue-in-cheek epigraph addressed "To William Shakespeare, who never went Hollywood." This statement is an acknowledgment that Shakespeare's plays were considered to be 'popular culture' in both senses of the term, 'written for the common people' and 'loved by many,' in his own time. The epigraph can even be read as a statement of hope (or despair, depending on the reader's position) that, perhaps, many of the literary and visual texts with which Bergantino's readership are familiar and which informed his own novel may someday transcend their own humble origins and be considered 'classic' works in their own right. Bergantino's "post-feminist *Hamlet* for a generation raised on horror films... and grrl power" (Hulbert et al. 226) also serves as a reminder to the reader that Shakespeare too transformed narratives already known to his audience into new and viable works using the literary tropes of his time, and Bergantino is carrying on that tradition in his own way.

In contrast to Aquin's and Mark's reworkings of the *Hamlet* story, and in some ways similar to Bergantino's, the 2006 novel *Joker,* by Filipino/Australian author Ranulfo Concon (who prefers to go by his first name), is in many ways a very close transposition of *Hamlet*; yet *Joker* is also a radical and polemically charged re-imagining of Shakespeare's play. The jacket description of the novel sums up, simply yet eloquently, Ranulfo's aims in transplanting the *Hamlet* story into twenty-first-century Australia: "It spits, snarls, screams, curses, and laughs at the world. It mocks leaders and followers. Restores our faith in love and security or drives us mad."

Like both Aquin's and Mark's texts, Ranulfo's work proceeds in non-linear fashion, incorporating narrative and descriptive passages, dialogues, flashbacks and flash-forwards, 'real' life and dream life, or what the protagonist Matt calls "visions, hallucinations, nightmares, epiphanies" (4). But where Aquin uses the screenplay format to expand on literary/ narrative/descriptive possibilities, and Mark uses a multilayered narrative to trace the convergence of past, present, and literary predecessors, Ranulfo uses the fragmented, chaotic structure of his novel to represent the fracturing of Matt's world and mental state after the divorce of his parents and the death of his friend Ray – Ranulfo's equivalent to both Horatio and the elder Hamlet. The "Joker" of the title is Matt's alter ego who appears to him in his dreams, representing Matt's transformation from "innocent and naive and caring... [to] angry and cynical and cruel" (20) after the loss of his best friend and the changes in his family.

Indeed, the most striking feature of Ranulfo's text is its cynicism, which reminds the reader that beneath the poetry of Shakespeare's text, Hamlet displays much the same self-doubt and uncertainty about the state of his world, "a prison...in which there are many confines, wards, and dungeons, Denmark being one of the worst" (*Hamlet* II.ii. 243-47), as Matt, who laments the loss of "Days of innocence when my family was one.... When I believed in love. When I believed in the future" (Ranulfo 43). The flashback sequences of Matt's life with Ray, his parents, and his girlfriend Leah, his life "like it used to be" (16), are described in idealized tones, evoking Matt's simultaneous desire for his world to return to the way he remembers it and dismissal of what he regards as naïveté in thinking such a world even existed in the first place. Even the novel's counterparts of Rosencrantz and Guildenstern, the free-spirited Roscoe and Guildo, despite identifying themselves with the 'old' Matt's optimism (72-73), "delight in talking about conspiracy theories... [that] somehow... make more sense than the stuff... from... schoolbooks" (60).

Nowhere is the cynicism of Ranulfo's fictional world more powerfully illustrated, however, than in Matt's analogue of Hamlet's Mousetrap play: a polemical, postcolonial rewrite of the musical *South Pacific* (103-25), put on by a group of unpopular students whom Matt calls "the Theatre of Truth... my dagger against lies" (104). While Matt justifies his revision of *South Pacific*, which is interrupted by the principal for being obscene, by insisting it is meant to "hold up a mirror to the obscenity of our society" (121; cf. *Hamlet* III.ii. 20-22), the revision serves an additional function in the world of author and reader, representing by analogy the relationship of the novel itself to *Hamlet*. It is in the aftermath of the play that Ranulfo explicitly mentions Shakespeare for the first time:

"Let me remind you that Hamlet dies in the end. He could have eventually become the king of Denmark, married Ophelia, lived happily ever after, but he threw it all away."
"But he accomplished meting out justice." (122)

Prior to this moment, Ranulfo's uses of *Hamlet* have been subtle allusions like character names and plot similarities, unlike Mark and Aquin, whose protagonists explicitly invoke Shakespearean counterparts in their efforts to make sense of their lives.

Yet, like Mark and, in a somewhat different way, Aquin, Ranulfo does not give his revision of *Hamlet* a tragic ending. Rather, after being caught up in an anti-capitalist protest in Sydney that turns violent (160-66), Matt wonders if militant rejection of the world as it is now is truly the right path for him. This incident illustrates the fragility of idealism as well as the wisdom in the principal's allusion to Shakespeare's tragic ending. On his return home, Matt imagines a series of possible future worlds for himself and the people he knows, some comic, some tragic, some pathetic, some optimistic, some cynical, before deciding that "Being human is about choices. Therefore I choose Love... Leah... Life... Good... Wisdom... Art. I choose Joker. His insanity keeps me sane" (192-93).

Neige Noire, Heathrow Nights, Hamlet II: Ophelia's Revenge, and *Joker* all illustrate Doležel's statement that an adaptation or revision of a previously existing text "enriches, expands the universe of fiction, without deleting the extant world; it takes its place alongside the canonical protoworld, and, hopefully, itself will enter the canon" (223). In the case of these four novels, there is certainly no intention of displacing *Hamlet*, as knowledge of Shakespeare's text is essential to understanding these works and realizing their authors' intentions. Mark's, Bergantino's, and Ranulfo's texts stand as useful supplementary and complementary texts to *Hamlet* in their authors' and characters' uses of the Shakespearean 'original' and each work's respective fictional worlds to enhance and explain each other, while Aquin's text breaks down barriers of both genre and language, simultaneously familiarizing the unfamiliar and defamiliarizing the familiar as postmodern texts generally set out to do.

Hamlet **and Humour**

Postmodern adaptations often share with their literary/dramatic forebears, the nineteenth-century genres of burlesque and travesty, the techniques of parody, satire, and pastiche, all of which help to create new texts and text-worlds that inspire readers/audiences to laugh with, and at, them and their sources. These types of adaptation generally fall into Doležel's category of polemical displacements, adaptations that seek to interrogate both the source text and the world(s) in which both the source text and the new text were produced and use that source text as their means of doing so. By cutting, moving, rearranging, updating, and/or colloquializing the source text, these works produce new fictional worlds literally from the material of the earlier one, and in doing so are able to critique the literary/dramatic conventions of

Elizabethan Britain as well as of their own times and places. These humorous adaptations of *Hamlet* function simultaneously as deconstructions of their literary genres and as playful reimaginings, attempts to lighten the mood of what is, in its original form, a dark tragedy.

We have already discussed Sir William Gilbert's *Rosencrantz and Guildenstern* as an example of Shakespearean burlesque, a genre that served as a humorous commentary both on the plays and on the "contemporary production methods" (Wells xiii) and literary and dramatic criticism that had grown up around them. This genre can be traced back to John Poole's *Hamlet Travestie*, published in 1810 and first performed the following year; in fact, "the *Hamlet Travestie* was his first play" (Wells xvi). Following its 1811 debut, it experienced numerous productions and revivals in both London and New York, some as late as 1870 (Wells xxi). The play launched a plethora of comic adaptations of *Hamlet* and other Shakespearean plays, generally marked by frequent use of puns, topical humour relating to actors and/or public figures of the parodists' time, and quite often resurrecting dead characters at the end of the play to join in a final dance, thus calling attention to the artificiality of the play and its world. However, because the parodies were presented, both for legal and aesthetic reasons, as separate plays in their own right that happened to be based on Shakespearean plays rather than productions of those plays, they differ from productions of more 'serious' alterations of the Shakespearean texts and function as counterpart texts and text worlds.

Poole acknowledges in the introduction to his play that "to derive entertainment from a burlesque, but more particularly to be enabled to decide whether it be ill or well executed, a familiar acquaintance with the original is indispensable" (6). Thus, despite the skepticism of more 'serious' scholars and critics of the time with regard to Shakespearean parody, these texts help to draw attention to the 'originals' even as they make fun of them.

Poole's play 'translates' and 'updates' the formal Shakespearean blank verse into colloquial language and rhyming couplets, much in the vein of music-hall performances and popular songs. Indeed, as became commonplace in later examples of Shakespearean burlesque and travesty, many of the important soliloquies and dialogues are set to the tunes of songs that would have been well known to Poole's immediate audience. As Stanley Wells points out, this was necessary because of the Theatre Monopolies Act, which restricted more conventional performances of Shakespearean plays only to certain theatres, and because of the accepted definition of "'illegitimate' dramatic entertainments" (xix) – that is, plays that could be performed at unpatented theatres – as containing songs and dances. One such occurrence of this convention is Poole's rendition of Hamlet's best-known lines, "To be or not to be" (*Hamlet* III.i. 55-87), set to the tune of the song "Here We Go Up, Up, Up":

When a man becomes tired of his life,
The question is, "to be or not to be"?
For before he dare finish the strife,
His reflections most serious ought to be.
When his troubles too numerous grow,
And he knows of no method to mend them,
Had he best bear them tamely, or no?
Or by stoutly opposing them end them?
Ri tol de rol, etc. (Poole 24)

Hamlet's infamous quarrel with Ophelia (III.i. 89-161) closely follows upon this, but the musical setting deflates the tension of the original scene and instead makes it comical:

Let me tell you, Miss Ophelia, your behaviour's very rude,
And your whims, and freaks, and fancies, ought in times to be subdued:
So if my advice will better you, to give it 'tis my duty:
Imprimis: – let your honesty discourse not with your beauty.
Won't you, won't you, won't you to a nunnery go? (Poole 26)

The 'modernized' and familiarized language and use of popular songs were not the only ways in which Poole's parody simultaneously updates and satirizes the 'original.' Hamlet's and Laertes's duel (*Hamlet* V.ii.), for instance, is presented as a boxing match (Poole 44, 49-53), with the poisoned drink being a mug of beer rather than a cup of wine; and instead of passing out flowers (*Hamlet* IV.v. 175-86), Ophelia brings vegetables with her (Poole 43) during her final scene.

Since a principal purpose of the Shakespearean parody was to act as a form of literary/dramatic criticism in a format more accessible to the layperson, Poole uses his version of Hamlet's advice to the actors (III.ii. 1-45) as a direct reference to several popular actors of his time, including three of the early nineteenth century's best-known Shakespearean actors, Robert Elliston, John Philip Kemble, and Henry Siddons:

But in speeches which, teeming in passion, require
All an E[lliston]'s spirit, a K[emble]'s own fire,
If you'd hope H[enry] S[iddons] to equal in fame,
You, like him, must be lifeless, insipid, and tame.[114]
(Poole 28; cf. Schoch 152)

---

[114] The names are indicated by initials in the printed text, but would presumably have been spoken out loud in the actual performance.

Rather than counselling the actors to avoid "inexplicable dumb-shows and noise" (*Hamlet* III.ii. 12), Poole's Hamlet encourages his troupe to imitate the actors to which he refers, as a means of attracting "the gods' approbation / In a horse-laugh" (Poole 28). In the same vein, the performance of the Mousetrap itself is done in the style of "a pantomimic ballet" (Poole 29) representing many of the usual excesses of contemporary acting, including "music, scenery, dresses, decorations" (Poole 29). This is, perhaps, one element that Poole's parody shares with its Shakespearean counterpart text, a comment by each respective playwright on the theatrical fashions of his time. Yet, the direct references in Poole's would be incomprehensible to later audiences and were thus either updated or omitted entirely in later productions (Schoch 52-53).

Unlike many later examples of the genre, and even later revivals of itself (see e.g. Schoch 48-56), Poole's *Hamlet Travestie* takes aim less at the excesses of nineteenth-century Shakespearean acting than at nineteenth-century and earlier Shakespearean textual criticism, with the paratext of the published version as much part of the joke as the main text of the play itself. Though in his preface, Poole apologizes for his "attempt to treat with levity the works of our Immortal Poet" (Poole 5), he justifies having done so by announcing his intention to satirize "Black-letter Critics and Coney-catching Commentators" (6), indicated by the use of the aforementioned font to print these words. The annotations, moreover, take the form of mock arguments between various Shakespearean editors of the eighteenth and nineteenth centuries such as Nicholas Rowe, Alexander Pope, Lewis Theobald, William Warburton, Samuel Johnson, George Steevens, and Edmond Malone (cf. Evans 32-34), alluding to such editorial controversies as Pope's criticism of Theobald in the 1728 edition of his poem *The Dunciad* (Evans 33). These annotations usually relate to the contemporary expressions and slang terms that Poole has introduced into his text, such as deciding upon the necessary punctuation for the phonetic representation of a trumpet sound (Poole 66), or literalizing the expression "Dash my wig" (Poole 52, 67) in Gertrude's last words in this play to indicate that "the Queen of Denmark wore a wig" (Poole 67), and then imagining a discussion amongst the various editors of exactly what that wig must have looked like, citing "one hundred and fourteen controversial tracts... expressly upon the subject" (67). Poole even has his fictionalized critics, as the actual ones were sometimes known to have done, directly attack each other in the notes; for example, Poole's Johnson accuses Pope of "not readily understanding [a] passage" and being "willing to plunge it still deeper into an abyss of unintelligibility" (Poole 61) or dismisses Warburton as "an unequal adversary... [whom] we disdain to punish, but we are bound to expose" (68).

Though the sorts of Shakespearean parodies produced by Poole at the beginning of the nineteenth century and Gilbert near its end were and are very much products of their time, comic counterparts of *Hamlet* and other Shakespearean plays have continued to be produced. As noted above, the purposes of these works have ranged from deconstructions of their literary/dramatic genres to playful reimaginings – very often both at the same time. The tradition received an interesting and often controversial update in Joseph Papp's 1968 production of *Hamlet* for the New York Shakespeare Festival Public Theater, which came to be known as the *"Naked" Hamlet*, not as any reference to nudity but as an allusion to Hamlet's declaration to Claudius, "You shall know I am set naked on your kingdom" (IV.vii. 43). Papp described his interpretation of *Hamlet* as "an expressionistic trip of the mind, a film in super-fast motion going through Hamlet's head" (7); in other words, a representation of the inner psychological world of the character of Hamlet as well as an unconventional counterpart fictional/dramatic world to that of the play. In contrast to the nineteenth-century tradition of Shakespearean burlesque, however, Papp's *"Naked" Hamlet* has been treated both as a production of the Shakespearean play, if a truncated and rearranged one, and as a separate work based on the 'original' play. Like Poole's *Hamlet Travestie,* Papp's *"Naked" Hamlet* retains the familiar tragic ending, but presents it in a humorous fashion, albeit a darker sort of humour than that of its Victorian ancestors. The target of Papp's satire is not so much Augustan literary criticism as in Poole's, or Victorian acting as in Gilbert's, but the social upheavals of 1960s America: his Hamlet the character and *Hamlet* the play are both examples of "a wounded name – survivor of wars, cataclysms, and catastrophes.... A testimony to the stubborn, relentless will to face life and create wonders in the shadow of annihilation" (27).

Like Poole's *Hamlet Travestie,* the *"Naked" Hamlet* uses its paratext – in this case, its stage directions – as part of its response to the Shakespearean fictional world and the actual world in which the play is read and performed. The stage directions, presented as direct addresses from the author to the director, indicate numerous possible approaches to the production, as "a modern-dress *Hamlet* emphasizing the severe military dictatorship that Claudius has ruthlessly imposed" (Papp 39), or a rock musical, or "an intellectual fiasco in which nobody knows what is happening" (Papp 40), or, as it happens, all of the above and more: "not only... *Hamlet,* but... a play about *Hamlet....* not only... a modern *Hamlet,* but a ridiculous *Hamlet*" (Papp 45, 46).

The *"Naked" Hamlet* further combines the 'original' Shakespearean language with modern colloquialisms, rather than completely translating the play into informal contemporary English or imitating the Elizabethan poetic style. Papp justifies this linguistic decision by noting that "Shakespeare's work had such moments for his original audience, and we are poorer because they are not always as funny for us" (48). But it is in the visual aspects of the play that Papp's *Hamlet* departs most strongly from the familiar world of Shakespeare's. His Hamlet first appears lying in a coffin, reading a copy of Shakespeare's play (Papp 41); Ophelia's mad scene is staged as a Broadway-style musical number (Papp 137-41); and the Ghost appears not as the imposing and dignified old King Hamlet but as "an old-time vaudevillian" dressed in "long underwear and a burned-out, battered, camouflaged army helmet" (Papp 55).

Another source of humour in Papp's *Hamlet* is its relentless breaking of the boundaries between the world of the play and that of the audience, with Hamlet and the other characters not only freely interacting with the audience but also periodically stepping out of their roles within the play. For example, when the guards notice that they have hung Claudius's portrait upside down (Papp 47-48), they briefly address each other by the actors' real names rather than by their characters' names; and Hamlet briefly takes on the roles of a peanut vendor (Papp 69-72) and a custodian (Papp 76-80), even blending those roles into his usual position in the play's world (e.g. Papp 145-46). At the moment at which Claudius realizes the reason for the Mousetrap (Papp 101-03), the entire play-world is disrupted as "Hamlet shoots Claudius. Everyone is startled" (Papp 103). The *"Naked" Hamlet* even revives, in more ways than one, one of the conventions of nineteenth-century Shakespearean burlesque by having all the characters perform a dance together at the end of the play after the mass deaths (Papp 156-57) – which are presented here as a game of Russian roulette rather than a rigged duel as in Shakespeare's text.

Papp's play is also what Douglas Lanier calls a "remotivated" (83) text, one that reassigns roles and motivations to various characters. For example, Hamlet does not leave Denmark for England, but instead speaks with his father's ghost in a dialogue based on his soliloquy in Shakespeare's IV.iv. on seeing Fortinbras – who does not appear in Papp's play – for the first time (32-66). He also appears in the role of the gravedigger (Papp 142-44), with the Ghost taking the role of the Shakespearean Hamlet in V.i., and kills Rossencraft and Gilderstone – Papp's names for Rosencrantz and Guildenstern, taken from the First Quarto text – himself before triumphantly announcing, "Rossencraft and Gilderstone are dead!" (Papp 136).[115]

The fragmented and chaotic nature of Papp's reimagining of *Hamlet* represents "Hamlet's new-found antic disposition in a production that is

---

[115] It may be useful here to note that Stoppard's *Rosencrantz and Guildenstern Are Dead* was first produced the same year as Papp's *"Naked" Hamlet.*

already antic at its very core" (Papp 69). It calls attention to the Shakespearean fictional world as a created entity, paradoxically demonstrating its simultaneous fragility and endurance. In the traditions of postmodernism and deconstruction, it shakes the fictional world to its foundations, yet at the same time demonstrates the resilience of the text and the text-world of *Hamlet* in still being recognizable even in a deliberately irreverent and iconoclastic production. The director's notes interspersed throughout the text as well as in the preface, in yet further examples of the fluidity of the worlds embodied in this text, demonstrate that the creation of the *"Naked" Hamlet*, out of numerous rehearsals and performances, itself serves as a testimony to the enduring appeal of the Shakespearean 'original.'

Hamlet, Thy Name is Woman: Gender and *Hamlet* Adaptations

As Doležel notes in *Heterocosmica*, "All postmodernist rewrites redesign, relocate, reevaluate the classic protoworld... motivated by political factors, in the wide, postmodernistic sense of 'politics'" (206). As we have seen in the previous chapter, adaptations which feature Gertrude and Ophelia as main characters have been motivated in varying degrees by the politics of gender, and specifically the desire to re-examine the historically male-dominated literary canon, and the similarly male-dominated world of *Hamlet* itself, from a feminine perspective. However, several adaptations of the play from the nineteenth century onward have taken a different approach to critiquing gender roles both in Shakespeare's society and their own, by envisioning female counterparts to Hamlet himself. This reimagining began on the nineteenth-century stage as well as in the visual arts and over the course of the century "became identified with the popular, the anti-traditional, and... the principle of social change" (Howard 36), as many of the actresses who chose to play Hamlet approached their performances as equalizing movements and were often themselves involved in the struggles for gender equality. Indeed, the popular perception of Hamlet owes as much, and perhaps more, to the women who played him as to the men who did: for not only did Eugène Delacroix's influential 1825-59 series of *Hamlet* illustrations feature an almost-androgynous Hamlet drawn from a female model (Young 215), but at the turn of the century, "The first Hamlet on film was... Sarah Bernhardt" (Howard 1), in a version of her celebrated London/Paris performances of the play.

With all their efforts toward establishing and popularizing the practice of gender-blind casting, however, these productions represented innovations in the actual world of actress and audience more than in the fictional world of the text of *Hamlet*: more 'woman as Hamlet' than 'Hamlet as woman.' Yet such performances did inspire writers to create fictional worlds with more definite female counterparts to Hamlet; among the earliest of these was Mary Elizabeth Braddon's 1863 novel *Eleanor's Victory,* one of the first English detective novels to feature a woman protagonist. Braddon had briefly been an actress before establishing herself as a writer (O'Toole xi), and many of her books, including *Eleanor's Victory,* frequently allude to Shakespeare and other English dramatists. Though the novel makes only one direct reference to Shakespeare's *Hamlet* (Braddon 340), it can be considered a transposition of the play because of the similarities in plot.

Like Hamlet, Braddon's protagonist Eleanor Vane Monckton seeks to avenge her father's death and prove the identity of the man who wronged him. Tony Howard notes that one of Braddon's purposes in *Eleanor's Victory* was to show "that a young Victorian woman can experience Hamlet's sufferings... [and] that she will feel them more appallingly, because she is denied Hamlet's hopes of redress" (71). On the other hand, the novel also demonstrates that a young Victorian woman, if given the opportunity, can reach the sort of happy ending denied to Hamlet, and that this success comes in part from the very values and qualities a male-dominated society generally overlooks or underestimates.

Both Hamlet and Eleanor delay their acts of revenge, but for very different reasons. Where Hamlet's delay stems largely from his character, Eleanor's is imposed upon her first by her need to "go out into the world" (15) and earn her keep as a governess and then by her marriage to a jealous husband who mistakenly believes her to be in love with the man she suspects of ruining her father (e.g. 186-89). Throughout the novel she continuously reminds herself that honouring her father's last request must come before even her own happiness, and thus, when she does accept Gilbert's marriage proposal, she has a brief flash of memory very similar to King Hamlet's ghost appearing in Gertrude's bedroom: "the image of her father arose angry and reproachful, as if to say to her, 'Have you so little memory of my wrongs and my sorrows that you can shrink from any means of avenging me?'" (Braddon 179; cf. *Hamlet* III.iv. 106-14).

Although Eleanor recognizes that "whether it is unwomanly or Christian-like... it is henceforward the purpose of my life, and that it is stronger than myself" (Braddon 71) to fulfill her father's dying wish, she does not, as Hamlet does, overtly seek an eye-for-an-eye revenge. Her goal is to honour the pact her father made with his old friend M. de Crespigny that "If either died a bachelor, he was to leave his fortune to the other" (Braddon 23). The pact, in its way, is a counterpart to the promise made between the kings of Denmark and Norway in Saxo Grammaticus' *Historiae Danicae* "that the conqueror shall give funeral rites to the conquered" (*HD* 61). It was because of this pact that M. de Crespigny's great-nephew, Launcelot Darrell, arranged the scheme that led to Mr. Vane's death. Like Claudius in Shakespeare's play, Launcelot finds that he cannot enjoy the fruits of his labour: he insists that "Heaven knows I never wished him ill, much less meant him any harm" (256) and is constantly reminded of the depths to which he had been willing to sink for the sake of an inheritance. Unlike his Shakespearean counterpart, however, Launcelot is sincere in his feelings of guilt and does genuinely repent of his deeds (Braddon 379-81). But it is Launcelot's mother who is the most successful in convincing Eleanor to show him mercy, insisting not only that the scheme had ultimately been her idea, but also that "If you are pitiless... now, God will be pitiless to you" (Braddon 380).

Braddon uses her novel not only "as a feminist social critique" (Howard 73) informed by the Shakespearean text and the conventions of melodrama and sensational fiction, but also as an exploration of the fictional worlds – and worldviews – embodied in Shakespeare's play and the above-mentioned nineteenth-century genres. Her Horatio-figure, Richard Thornton, a scene painter for a London theatre and Eleanor's childhood friend, expresses much of the text's metafictionality. Although Richard is Eleanor's ally and confidant in her mission, he does recognize that the sort of revenge Hamlet craved and Eleanor seeks is possible only in works of fiction, and thus draws attention to the status of Braddon's text as a fictional world:

> Life is not a three-volume novel or a five-act play, you know, Nelly. The sudden meetings and strange coincidences common in novels are not very general in our everyday existence....For Heaven's sake, then, abandon all thought of an impossible revenge!... If the melodramatic revenge of the stage is not practicable in real life, we know at least... that wicked deeds do not go unpunished. (Braddon 95)

Richard's comment on fictional worlds creates dramatic irony even as it asks whether art imitates life, vice versa, or both. Yet, in keeping with the genre of the sensational novel, Eleanor does encounter the very sorts of "sudden meetings and strange coincidences" about which Richard had attempted to warn her, and which do eventually lead her toward the 'victory' prophesied in the novel's title.

By granting Eleanor her victory, Braddon simultaneously re-evaluates the revenge narrative and repositions its heroine in contrast to both the fictional and actual worlds. Her text's most significant break with the tradition of the revenge narrative is that, while revenge narratives and plays such as *Hamlet* generally produce Pyrrhic victories marred by the death of the avenger as well as of innocent bystanders, "Eleanor's victory was a proper womanly conquest, and not a stern classical vengeance" (Braddon 383). Even

Launcelot is treated kindly, being allowed to establish an honest profession as an artist "to redeem himself from the disgrace that had fallen upon him" (Braddon 382). However, the happy ending of Braddon's novel is itself a bittersweet victory, reminding the reader that in the actual world of nineteenth-century Britain, "a Victorian woman in her teens" (Howard 70) in Eleanor's situation would most likely be forced into a low-paying or degrading profession, or at the very least "[a] limited [life] of domesticity and dependence upon others" (O'Toole xiii).

Though in the character of Eleanor, Braddon created a capable and endearing counterpart to Hamlet and a model for subsequent heroines in detective fiction, it was not until the publication of Edward Payson Vining's *The Mystery of Hamlet: A New Solution to an Old Problem* in 1881 that the idea of Hamlet's being a woman, in a more obvious manner than Braddon's, would truly take root. Originally meant to "account for...hints of repressed homosexuality that Victorians were reluctant to bring out of the closet" (Rothwell and Melzer 57), Vining's theory provided, for its time, an innovative approach to comparing and contrasting Elizabethan and Victorian views of gender, especially as those views related to questions of inheritance and succession. Based on Hamlet's references throughout the play to behaviours stereotypically considered feminine, his treatment of both Gertrude and Ophelia, and his affections for Horatio, Vining concluded that "the charms of Hamlet's mind are essentially feminine in their nature" (46-47). Similarly, examining the discrepancy between Hamlet's youthful appearance and the gravedigger's comment that the prince is in fact thirty years old (*Hamlet* V.i. 161-62) leads to the supposition that "Hamlet's bodily characteristics seem to be as feminine as his mind" (77). While Vining does hedge his bets by pointing out, "It is not claimed... that Shakespeare ever fully intended to represent Hamlet as a woman" (59), the possibility certainly exists in this reading that the Prince of Denmark might in fact have been a princess, raised as a boy both to avoid disappointing his/her father and to ensure the continuation of the royal line (Vining 81-83), and "trapped in that fiction" (Howard 21) as a result.

How seriously Vining intended his reading of *Hamlet* to be taken is uncertain; indeed, the introduction to *The Mystery of Hamlet* includes an acknowledgement that readers may "smile with disdain or laugh with ridicule" (6) at its conclusions. However, in addition to explaining possible homosexual undertones in the relationship of Hamlet and Horatio, Vining's theory also accounts for "men's attempt[s] to deny their femininity" (Howard 23) in a very literal sense. Intentionally or not, *The Mystery of Hamlet* "was, in its time, swiftly dismissed... as obvious quackery masquerading in the guise of serious criticism" (vi), as the American film historian Douglas Brode observes in the introduction to his 2004 novel *Sweet Prince,* which takes Vining's reading of *Hamlet* as its basis.

Brode's novel, which has the intriguing subtitle *The Passion of Hamlet,* plays upon the ambiguities and double entendres of Vining's theory, wavering between 'gay Hamlet' and 'female Hamlet' for the majority of the text until firmly coming down on one side of the equation. Unlike Braddon's novel, Brode's is not a transposition of the Hamlet plot into a modern setting, but is a reimagining of the Shakespearean text in "an historically accurate portrait of northern Europe at that moment in time when...Hamlet actually lived" (Brode vii), albeit with a few touches of humorous anachronism for the benefit of the modern reader (e.g. Brode 185; 216-17). In addition, in much the same way that Braddon used the characteristic tropes of revenge tragedy and detective fiction to draw attention to her text's status as a counterpart world to that of *Hamlet,* Brode constructs his world out of numerous, often ironic, intertextual references to virtually all of Shakespeare's plays in order to fashion dialogue and interpolated scenes for his characters.

The Hamlet of Brode's *Sweet Prince* begins the story as Amuleth, a variant of the name Saxo Grammaticus gives him, a twenty-one year-old student at Wittenberg who is very much inspired by his education to become "a beloved leader, forsaking past prejudices, dragging Denmark... into a progressive future" (Brode 17). As a student he is fascinated by the interconnection of scholarship and skepticism, as exemplified in his comparison of the Norse, Christian, and scientific worldviews, which leads him to conclude that every generation "first created, then inhabited a universe tailored to their specific needs" and changes in worldviews are "not so much a rejection... as the restatement of identical concepts in alternate terms" (Brode 64). His change of name halfway through the novel, from the Saxo-esque "Amuleth" to the Shakespearean "Hamlet," is in fact meant as a nod toward modernity as well as a restoration of his father's name in defiance of his uncle (Brode 121). At the same time, his fellow students regard him as a "delicate dreamer... nicknamed 'Artist' by friends...[and] notoriously unseducible" (Brode 17-18). But the reasons for Amuleth's indifference toward women only become apparent when, shortly before leaving Wittenberg for Elsinore upon the death of his father, he confesses to Fortinbras, "I have a woman's longings!" (Brode 82).

Brode follows Vining's suggestions that "If Hamlet be considered as in love with Horatio, his treatment of Ophelia is easily explained as caused by jealousy" (Vining 69) and by "the bitterness of one woman against the failings of the other" (Vining 57), which may also partly explain his treatment of Gertrude. To build upon this line of argument, Brode's Horatio begins the story very much in love with Ophelia (108-09) and becomes uncomfortable at the affectionate behaviour Amuleth often displays toward him (e.g. Brode 111). Similarly, when around Gertrude Hamlet behaves so as to indicate to the court and the reader that she has been keeping secrets about him; his most prominent such demonstration comes when he arrives at a banquet "in a flowing cream-coloured gown of fine imported silk" (Brode 180) and warns Claudius that Gertrude "has deceived my father, and may thee" (Brode 181).

It is not until Hamlet's confrontation with Gertrude following the Mousetrap play (Brode 195-98; *Hamlet* III.iv.) that the truth about Brode's "sweet prince" is finally revealed, as then "it was time for these two, mother and child, to confront... the desperate ploy assumed so long ago, a single false statement... which had forced Hamlet to live a lie during every waking hour of every single day for each of the past 21 years" (Brode 198). Gertrude had decided to pass her newborn daughter off as a "son [who] suffered from a rare condition, a tenderness of flesh requiring careful attention from its mother" (Brode 203) out of fear of her husband's potential defeat in battle, in the knowledge that "the only son of a defeated king could not be summarily executed, though any... worthless daughter might" (Brode 202).

The revelation of Hamlet's 'true' gender not only signals the greatest difference between Brode's protagonist and his/her Shakespearean counterpart, but also marks a shift in the fictional world itself, from tragedy to tragicomedy. The final duel (*Hamlet* V.ii.; Brode 260-79) does indeed end, as in Shakespeare's play, with the death of the Prince of Denmark. However, for Brode this is true only in a symbolic sense, for this is the moment at which Hamlet is fully revealed to everyone as "a modern incarnation of the Amazon women of ancient myth, feminine yet formidable, beautiful and deadly" (Brode 263-64). At the same time, however, yet another secret about Brode's Hamlet comes to light, as the dying Claudius confesses that he, not King Hamblet (as he is called in Brode's text), was her true father (278-79).

The end of *Sweet Prince* reflects Brode's view of his fictional world as "a kind of darkly romantic fairy tale for grown-ups" (viii), with Hamlet and Horatio ascending the throne of Denmark and Ophelia alive and married to Fortinbras, who becomes Hamlet's political ally. Furthermore, the new queen's establishing a "new order of things – scientific, social, religious, and personal" (Brode 289), described in rather idealized terms, serves as an ironic acknowledgment of the actual world in which Shakespeare lived and wrote. Brode's Hamlet thus becomes – as many of Shakespeare's female characters often are – a counterpart to Elizabeth I, as well as to her successor James I, who had been a formative influence on the Shakespearean Hamlet.

Braddon's and Brode's female Hamlets share positive resolutions to their respective plotlines, succeeding as women in situations in which their male counterpart in the Shakespearean fictional world did not. By contrast, the protagonist of Allison Williams's 2001 play *Hamlette* combines the 'woman-as-Hamlet' of the gender-blind modern stage with the 'Hamlet-as-woman' of texts such as Braddon's or Brode's to serve as a humorous, and cynical, commentary both on gender roles in the actual world and on the Shakespearean fictional world and its influences. Though the treatment of Shakespeare's text is humorous and irreverent, Williams's Hamlette "uses Shakespeare's words to genuinely express her problem" (3). The play is also more self-consciously metatheatrical than Braddon's and Brode's novels, reproducing in parodic fashion the multiple-world structure of Shakespeare's play while commenting upon various dramatic conventions of both Shakespeare's time and Williams's time.

Williams's play is written for five actors, one of whom (the Ghost/Polonius) is definitely male and one of whom (Hamlette) is definitely female; indeed, Williams specifically insists that "Hamlette absolutely may not be played by a man in drag" (3). Like Brode's Hamlet, Williams's Hamlette is a woman filling a male role, both on stage and in her society, as indicated by the other characters' constantly referring to her as "Hamlet, Prince of Denmark," with her insistence on the correct form "*Hamlette, Princess* of Denmark" answered with a dismissive "Whatever!" (A. Williams 5). Both the Ghost and Horatio also make use of various stereotypes of male-female interaction when speaking to Hamlette, with the Ghost approaching her as an overprotective father (A. Williams 11) and Horatio remarking of Hamlette's pretended madness, "Where will we find an antic disposition in your size, and the right colour?" (A. Williams 12).

Williams does not provide the same detailed explanation for Hamlette's cross-gendered status as Vining and Brode do. Unlike Brode's Hamlet, who is believed by all to be a man for the first two-thirds of the novel, Williams's Hamlette is very obviously a woman but is treated as a man and speaks bitterly of the reasons why:

> QUEEN. What do little girls do?
> HAMLETTE. They get married.... And they act as social figureheads in backward Central European kingdoms.... And due to the overbearing patriarchal system their husbands are endowed with any property they leave, forcing women into a lifetime of financial dependency, petty household concerns, and an early death from excessive childbearing.
> QUEEN. And what do little boys do?
> HAMLETTE. Inherit lands, money, and titles granted to them solely because of an accident of genetics.

QUEEN. And that's why sometimes Mother History needs a little help. (A. Williams 7-8)

Williams also undercuts the idealized view of the Elizabethan period that appears in works such as Brode's with Horatio's equally detailed explanation of why he refuses to acknowledge Hamlette as a woman:

But Shakespeare and the place of women in British society during the Renaissance despite the presence of a powerful Queen who pretended to be a virgin to manipulate her people and the succession to the Danish throne is patrilinear so you couldn't inherit and besides if you're a girl we can't be friends because there will be sexual tension and things will chaaaaaange... and girls are scary! (A. Williams 9)

"The place of women in British society... despite the presence of a powerful Queen" is, of course, a common subject both for Shakespeare and for Victorian writers such as Braddon. Williams, however, uses the discrepancy between the Queen as empowered woman and the general disempowerment of Elizabethan women as a way to question not only Shakespeare's views of women but also the idealized image of Elizabeth I. Williams chooses to see Elizabeth's efforts to maintain relatively peaceful diplomatic relations by refusing to marry as nothing more than 'Tudor propaganda' – a dismissal that has been applied to much of Shakespeare's writing as well.

Many of the other characters in Williams's play also question their own representation, either openly or indirectly. For example, Laertes refers to himself as "son of Polonius, brother of Ophelia, plot device of Shakespeare" (A. Williams 12), while Polonius expresses a desire to be a character in a very different type of play: "I said, 'Willy, scrap that Hamlet play. Too long, too wordy, too many deaths. Write "Polonius, King of the High Seas"!'" (A. Williams 12). Claudius is represented not directly by an actor but by a puppet voiced by Gertrude (A. Williams 8).

Williams's mixing of genres and representational strategies goes beyond characterization, as *Hamlette* uses various popular-culture tropes and allusions to create both humour and dramatic criticism. For example, the Mousetrap is performed in the style of a game show (14-15), and Horatio narrates the final duel in the manner of a sports announcer (18-20). In this way Williams shares with Brode an ironic use of elements familiar to the reader to simultaneously create and deconstruct a fictional world or series of worlds. But unlike Brode and Braddon, she does not allow her Hamlette a happy ending nor even the sort of dignity granted to the Shakespearean Hamlet. Following his famous elegy "Good night, sweet prince, / And flights of angels sing thee to thy rest" (*Hamlet* V.ii. 359-60; A. Williams 20), Horatio rather unceremoniously drops Hamlette, and when he once again refers to her as "Prince Hamlet," she "makes a last effort and stabs Horatio" (A. Williams 20) for refusing to call her by her proper name.

Whether in the form of a transposition with little overt reference yet many subtle similarities to its prototext, such as Braddon's, a semi-serious work of literary criticism, such as Vining's, or a humorous polemical rewrite of the source text such as Williams's or Brode's, woman-centered reinterpretations of *Hamlet* serve as reminders of the powerful appeal of the Shakespearean text to readers of all genders, as well as how an obviously male-dominated text can be made to serve the needs of the female reader, writer, or performer. All of these texts do highlight the inherent paradox in appropriating a male voice as a means of female empowerment, and each text approaches this paradox in a distinct fashion. These texts also throw light upon the progression of gender relations between Shakespeare's time and the times in which they were produced, while simultaneously pondering whether true gender equality, in the actual or fictional worlds, has been achieved or indeed is even possible.

Hamlet and Possible-Worlds Fantasy[116]

Whereas textual worlds such as Braddon's, Brode's, or Williams's focus on and hope to influence issues present in the actual world, texts which take a fantastic approach to the world of *Hamlet* use the possible-world(s) model itself as a device with which to explore the concept of fictionality and the construction of fictional worlds, to show that there are indeed "more things in heaven and earth... / Than are dreamt of in your philosophy" (*Hamlet* I.v. 166-67). At first glance, Lars Walker's 2003 novel *Blood and Judgment* and Jasper Fforde's 2004 novel *Something Rotten* appear to be 'merely' postmodernist rewrites of Shakespeare's *Hamlet*, expansions of the play's fictional world and those of its sources, as well as four hundred years' worth of critical speculation, in the form of popular fantasies (cf. Doležel, *Heterocosmica* 207). However, these novels' explorations of the Shakespearean fictional world and/or those of its sources as seen from the perspective of yet another world, that of each respective novel, go beyond the usual interfictionality present in postmodern rewrites to incorporate many of the principles of possible-worlds theory, especially the belief that, as David Lewis has famously stated, "there are possible worlds other than the one we

---

[116] A portion of this section was previously published in Chopoidalo and Syed, "Teaching *Hamlet* in 21st-Century Pakistan and Canada."

happen to inhabit... [and] entities that might be called 'ways things could have been'" ("Possible Worlds" 182).

Although Lewis's theory maintains the separateness of these possible worlds from the actual world (*Plurality* 80), Walker presents a fictional universe typical of many works of fantasy and science fiction, in which "transworld causality... [and] transworld travel" (D. Lewis, *Plurality* 80) can and does happen, taking his characters out of their textual actual world and into the fictional worlds of *Hamlet* and *Historiae Danicae*. Like other authors of adaptations, though more explicitly than many, Walker uses this interconnection of possible/fictional worlds to explore – and provide wry commentary on – many of the questions that scholars have had about Shakespeare's play, and to demonstrate "the power of great literature" (Walker 289) literally to create its own worlds, not just in the minds of its readers, but elsewhere in the universe as well. Indeed, Walker's use of the possible-worlds model is strongly hinted at many times throughout the novel's expository chapters. For example, in the very earliest pages, the protagonist, Will Sverdrup, comments on his school principal's decision to dress like the students rather than like a teacher, to which the principal replies: "The students'll never listen to you unless you get into their world" (Walker 6).

There are three worlds presented in *Blood and Judgment*: two actual worlds and one fictional world. The first actual world is a small college town in present-day Minnesota, which at first seems to follow "the principle of minimal departure; that is, while reading a text and reconstructing a storyworld from it, the reader assumes the minimal possible departure from the actual world unless such a departure is specified or strongly indicated by the text" (Palmer 35). In the novel's first chapter, the first hint that the textual actual world is different from the reader's actual world is that all but one of the students in Will's class have the same first names, Jason and Kimberly. The one student who does have a different name, Eric, is introduced as the typical antisocial school bully but is later revealed to be a hybrid of human being and magical entity – a detail that is introduced in the second chapter, when we are told of "his long tongue... with little suckers along its length" (Walker 35).

The second world, sixth-century Denmark, is really both an actual world and a literary world: it is the world of Saxo Grammaticus's Amleth, whom Walker calls by the Welsh-influenced name Amlodd. To Amlodd, the world of ancient Denmark is the actual world; but to Will, as to the reader, it is a fictional world. The textual/fictional worlds of Will and Amlodd, actual at the level of the text, and the actual world in which the literary work was created diverge with the appearance of magical entities: in this case, a talking raven, which in Norse mythology was "the guide... to the next world" (Walker 18), as well as more human-like beings known as the Old Ones, who exist in the space-time between all possible worlds and "know the ways between the worlds" (Walker 144) – including the worlds of both Amlodd and Will.

The third fictional world is that of *Hamlet*, into which Will and his amateur theatre group are transported: this world is presented, not as a third actual world, but as "an alternative world, the fictional world of Shakespeare's play" (Doležel, *Heterocosmica* 16). As a fictional world, it is shaped by the imaginations of its author and readers, initially appearing as a formless, undefined environment but becoming clearer and more recognizable as the story progresses, "drawing images from our minds – our imaginations of what Elsinore was like" (Walker 126-27) and thus appearing to the actors in the design of their production of the play. The world of *Hamlet* is presented as the embodiment of a purely fictional world rather than as another textual actual world because it is part of the Old Ones' experiment concerning the nature of fictional worlds, which strives to discover why works of fiction, especially tragedies, exert such a hold on the human imagination, even in a time when tragic heroes such as the ones of fiction are in short supply. One Old One who is a member of Will's theatre group, and the ghost of a disgraced priest that haunts the theatre where the group performs, explain the nature of possible worlds as follows:

> The stories told among men have a reality of their own. Surely you've all felt that there is a sense in which Don Quixote and Sherlock Holmes exist in their own rights, more than other fictional characters but less than real people – than most people at least.... Some characters and stories...only the greatest ones, and only the ones which hold and compel human belief, can become the bases of universes in their own right. (Walker 96-97)

The fictional worlds of *Blood and Judgment* generally follow Doležel's definition of alethically dyadic, or mythological, worlds in which "[t]he inhabitants of the supernatural domain have access into the natural domain, but for the humans the supernatural domain is, as a rule, off-limits" (*Heterocosmica* 129). In both Will's and Amlodd's worlds, the Old Ones can appear in recognizably human or animal forms or in monstrous forms such as the one Eric favours, with "torso and legs... like a lizard's or like a dinosaur's... [with] suckered tentacles of various lengths" (Walker 158); they can also navigate the space-time between possible worlds and even bring people and objects from one possible world into another. The only limitation to the Old Ones' power is that they are unable to experience emotions such as love or pain (Walker 146-49) except vicariously through ordinary humans. By contrast, although the actors can define and reshape the world of the play through their imaginations, ordinary humans are unable to travel between the possible worlds without supernatural assistance, becoming trapped "in the labyrinth of worlds" (Walker 260) if they attempt to do so.

Will and his fellow actors are drawn into the fictional world by the appearance of a supposed copy of Thomas Kyd's lost source play for *Hamlet* (Walker 32-36; cf. Bullough VII. 15-20), which turns out to be exactly the same as Shakespeare's Second Quarto text – the earliest recognizable printed version of the play – and thereby throws the true authorship of the play we know as Shakespeare's into question. Is the book merely Shakespeare's text mislabelled as Kyd's, as Will believes; or was Kyd's text in fact mislabelled as Shakespeare's, as Will's former thesis supervisor believes? According to Doležel, the creation of an alternative version of a text, including the discovery of new historical evidence that may potentially alter the status of the original text, "does not invalidate or eradicate the canonical protoworld" but instead "enriches, expands, the world of fiction, without deleting the extant world" (*Heterocosmica* 223). However, the introduction of the *Hamlet* source text into Will's actual world by the ghost and the Old Ones disrupts the balance of the play's world, thus creating a "vacuum of a world collapsing" (Walker 128) that draws in the actors. The book's appearance also – in part through the actions of Will/Amlodd – results in the creation of yet another possible world, one in which Shakespeare does not even exist, and "instead of Shakespeare the great playwright, there is another master – one named Thomas Kyd – who wrote the great historical play of *Hamlet*" (Walker 259). When Will escapes the world of the play at the end of the novel, he finds that the book no longer exists in his 'actual' world, "gone as if it had never been there" (Walker 310); the book was presumably sent back to the possible world from which it came.

The fictional worlds of *Blood and Judgment* also allow Walker to explore questions of free will and determinism. Because the worlds of *Hamlet* and Amlodd are those of fictional works, they are controlled by the plots of those works; as Randy, the actor who is also an Old One, explains to the group, "There's nothing more powerful than a story in any universe, except perhaps for the High One Himself" (Walker 184). Once in the storyworld, each member of the theatre group takes on the role of the character he/she is playing in the actual-world production of the play, even to the point of dying in the same way as the corresponding character, while – except for Will – still retaining his/her original mind. The ghost who has brought the actors to the play's world advises them that if they are to escape the fates of their characters, they must "break the play... refuse to follow the script, and so frustrate whatever Old One has brought [them] here" (Walker 98) – though, aside from Will, only the director and the actors playing Claudius, Gertrude, and Horatio do survive their experiences in the play's world. Similarly, as Will finds himself living out the life of Amlodd/Hamlet, he notices that the events described by Saxo Grammaticus and, to a lesser extent, Shakespeare are happening to him as he remembers from reading them: he even repeats Amlodd's riddles from Saxo's history (e.g. Walker 137-40; cf. *HD* 63-64) as well as many of the lines of Shakespeare's Hamlet (e.g. Walker 138; cf. *Hamlet* III.i. 82-84). Though as both an actor and a scholar, Will cannot resist giving the proper answers when he knows them, he still wonders if "he was living out the story without intending to... Was he being compelled by some force? He felt no compulsion – he was only acting naturally" (Walker 139).

It is not just the plots of plays or historical narratives that define the fictional worlds of Walker's novel, however, but also the belief systems of the people within these worlds. In possible-worlds theory, the only traits that must be shared by all possible worlds are the basic laws of logic (Doležel, *Heterocosmica* 19; cf. Girle 181-90), and therefore, dominant belief systems can vary from one possible world to another: while within the world of *Hamlet,* the actors realize, "This universe is being built. In this universe, we can make our own rules" (Walker 181). Indeed, this realization proves an important principle for the actors' survival in the storyworld. For example, Peter, the actor playing Polonius, being deeply religious, refuses to accept either the sixth-century Danish attitude toward revenge or the discovery that Eric, already a magical being in the first place, has reimagined himself as the god of the storyworld (Walker 179-92). Peter's rigidity proves fatal when, like Polonius, he is killed by Amlodd – though while at prayer and thus in a context more similar to Hamlet's missed opportunity to kill Claudius (*Hamlet* III.iii. 35-98) than to Polonius's death in the play (*Hamlet* III.iv. 21-33).

The question of dominant belief systems in these worlds plays upon an important characteristic of both fictional and real minds: that of cognitive dissonance, the co-existence of two incompatible belief systems in the same mind, when "we believe one thing in our heads, and another in our hearts.... But we try to believe in both of them at once" (Walker 13). Cognitive dissonance, however, is not truly an exception to the rule of non-contradiction that states that within any one possible world, a statement and its converse cannot both be true. In his lecture to his students, Will defines cognitive dissonance as a key feature in understanding the popularity of revenge tragedies in Shakespeare's time: "Elizabethans... were nominal Christians, but they set aside Christian teaching when it came to avenging the murder of a family member.... Take revenge and the Protestants will call you a sinner. Don't take it and your friends will call you a coward" (40). Even the novel's title, taken from Hamlet's praise of Horatio after meeting the actors, signals the prominence of both cognitive dissonance and balance within the fictional mind:

> As one in suff'ring all that suffers nothing,
> A man that Fortune's buffets and rewards
> Hast ta'en with equal thanks; and blest are those
> Whose blood and judgment are so well co-meddled,
> That they are not a pipe for Fortune's finger
> To sound what stop she pleases. (III.ii. 66-71)

Walker uses the phrase "blood and judgment" not in the sense of the balance of emotion and reason as Shakespeare uses it in this passage, but to symbolize the difference between physical and spiritual needs: "Blood and judgment, flesh and spirit, God and man, death and resurrection" (391). It is only upon recognizing and acknowledging his own spiritual needs, which he has long denied, that Will is able to find his way out of Amlodd's world and into Hamlet's, and thereby transfer himself and Amlodd back into their own bodies.

The exchange of minds and bodies between Will and Amlodd is not only an important factor in the plot of *Blood and Judgment*, but also the most prominent mechanism it uses to explore the counterpart theory of possible worlds, which holds that, although each entity exists in only one possible world, different versions of the same entity can exist in more than one possible world (D. Lewis, "CT" 111-12), even to the point that "among the possible worlds... there are those in which you play the role that I play in this one and in which I play the role that you play in this one" (Chisholm 83). Walker therefore presents Will and Amlodd as counterparts to each other, as Amlodd and Hamlet are fictional counterparts in the writings of Saxo and Shakespeare, but literalizes the counterpart relation as Chisholm describes it by transferring each mind into the other's body. In the manner common to fantastic fictional worlds, there is no concrete explanation given for the exchange other than the messenger-raven's advice to Amlodd on avenging the murder of his father: "You lack the art to feign madness. But you are lucky. I know where to get a feigning mind" (Walker 64). However, the ghost later reveals to Will that the exchange with Amlodd was part of his (the ghost's) plan to change history, independent of the Old Ones' experiment in fictional world-making. The ghost explains that by putting Will in Amlodd's place and trapping Amlodd in Will's body and Will-as-Amlodd in the realm of the Old Ones – the seemingly-inescapable space between all possible worlds – he has "reshaped history to fit Shakespeare's pattern"

(Walker 259), in the process creating the possible world in which Shakespeare did not write *Hamlet*.

For most of the story – with one significant exception to be discussed later – the narrator refers to the characters of Will and Amlodd according to which mind is in which body: the person the actors recognize as Will is referred to by the narrator as "Amlodd," whereas the person known in Denmark as Amlodd is referred to by the narrator as "Will." From this narrative convention, meant to differentiate the two characters by convenience, the reader gains the initial impression that characterization is here defined by the mind rather than by the body; however, while in Amlodd's body, Will finds himself doing things he would never otherwise have done in his own world but which are commonplace for Amlodd. His experiences lead him to realize that, since coming to this possible world:

> He was no longer Will Sverdrup. He had Will's knowledge and memories, but he wore Amlodd's body, and the body has its own memory. He wondered what it was that made a person a person. It didn't seem to be the mind alone, or the body alone. (Walker 249)

Just as he learns that all people have physical and spiritual needs that must be balanced, Will learns through the experience of not just playing but *being* Hamlet that both mind and body contribute to the whole person: that "nothing is 'either-or', only 'both-and'" (Walker 268), and that he can no longer think of himself as the same person that he was before he came to Amlodd's world.

The exception to the narrator's strict distinction between Will and Amlodd occurs in Chapter XV, in which the protagonist is referred to as "Amlodd" throughout, although it is still Will in Amlodd's body, as we know from the brief dream Will/Amlodd has of the ghost that has brought him to this possible world (Walker 219). The narrative voice of this chapter is also different from the rest of the novel: where the majority of the novel uses an omniscient third-person narrator, Chapter XV is written as a 'lost chapter' of Saxo Grammaticus's history, told in a narrative voice combining that of a medieval storyteller with that of a contemporary anecdote. It begins: "I will tell you the tale of Amlodd the Dane, son of Orvendil... the tale of what he did while he raided in Britain.... I have the tale from my father, who heard it from Amlodd himself" (Walker 213).

The chapter appears to be a takeoff from Saxo's history, in which, when explaining why he refused the British king's feast, Amlodd guesses that the food came from "a field, covered with the ancient bones of slaughtered men, and still bearing plainly all the signs of ancient carnage" (*HD* 68; cf. Walker 249), as well as from Belleforest's digression on the prevalence of magic and superstition in Amlodd's time: "for that in those days, the north parts of the world, living as then under Satan's laws, were full of enchanters" (*Hystorie* 103). Walker combines all these details in his account of how "Amlodd Orvendilsson broke the power of the Britons" (239) by summoning a demon, in revenge for the killing of a woman he had befriended. This chapter, aside from filling in gaps in Saxo's text and creating an interfictional connection between Saxo and Walker, also foreshadows two significant events later on in the novel. The first is Will's fulfilling of Saxo's plot and exacting revenge on Amlodd's uncle by burning down his hall after finding Amlodd's beloved Katla dead (Walker 251-58; cf. *HD* 69-73). The second is the ghost's revelation to Will that one of the Britons killed by the demon Will/Amlodd unleashed was an ancestor of Shakespeare, in an event that "altered the past" (Walker 259), or more accurately, that created the possible world from which the Kyd book came, for as Rod Girle notes, "each different [possible] world is actually generated from some world" (153).

The co-existence and interaction of possible worlds in *Blood and Judgment* does more than merely provide the novel's plot: it also symbolizes the status of the novel itself as an interfictional rewrite of both Shakespeare's play and Saxo Grammaticus's history. Indeed, the novel is derived more from Saxo than directly from Shakespeare, as Walker's reference to the tragic hero by the Welsh/Danish name *Amlodd*, rather than by his more familiar English name, indicates. Amlodd's physical appearance is also more reminiscent of the hero of a Norse saga than of a Shakespearean play: he is described as having "red-gold hair and beard, and grey eyes... middling-tall, but wide in the shoulders, with chest so massive as to look unhealthful" (Walker 62). The only appearance of Shakespeare's Hamlet, as opposed to Amlodd, in Walker's novel occurs in its penultimate chapter when, just before he returns to his world, Will sees "a fair-haired man with a small beard, dressed in black [who] looked a little like Kenneth Branagh, a little like Richard Burton, a little like Laurence Olivier and John Gielgud, a little like John Barrymore and a little like Edwin Booth" (Walker 306) and presumably more besides – in short, like a composite of every actor who has played Hamlet over the centuries. Hamlet's composite appearance symbolizes the endurance of the play's world even after the introduction of both the book from its possible world and the actors from the 'real' world. Of course, we must remember that this Hamlet is not, in fact, Shakespeare's, nor is Amlodd truly Saxo Grammaticus's character. Rather, both are Walker's interpretations of Shakespeare's and Saxo's characters; or, in terms of possible-worlds theory, Walker's Will-Amlodd-Hamlet triad are counterparts of the Hamlet and Amlodd/Amleth in Shakespeare's and Saxo's fictional worlds, within "a new, alternative fictional world" (Doležel, *Heterocosmica* 206) or set of fictional worlds.

The other characters common to Saxo, Shakespeare, and Walker also show intertextual similarities and differences: they are referred to by variations of the names they have in *Historiae Danicae* – for example, Feng and Gerda are Walker's versions of the characters called Claudius and Gertrude by Shakespeare – but they sometimes quote from Shakespeare's play, though far less than Will/Amlodd does. Others who were developed by Shakespeare but unnamed and marginal in Saxo are given new and different backstories by Walker.

For example, the originals of Shakespeare's Ophelia, Rosencrantz, and Guildenstern have no names in Saxo's history, where they are referred to as, respectively, Amlodd's foster sister whose "early rearing in common had brought [them] into great intimacy" (*HD* 64) and "Two retainers of Feng" (*HD* 67) who do know that the original letter they were given was "an implement of destruction to another" (*HD* 67; cf. *Hamlet* V.ii. 1-62). In *Blood and Judgment,* Walker develops these characters more fully, drawing on their familiar versions in Shakespeare's play but retaining their roles from Saxo's history. The nameless foster sister in *Historiae Danicae* becomes Katla, Amlodd's mad half-sister with whom Will does fall in love and whose murder by Feng's men – an incident unique to Walker – makes Will realize for the first time "how one could want to kill someone who had killed someone he loved" (Walker 252). Meanwhile, the nameless courtiers of Saxo and the not-entirely-willing accomplices/comic relief of Shakespeare are combined into "Hrolf and Gudbrand... the standard Abbott and Costello pair, only blond and not funny" (Walker 195).

Other similar intertextual references, both to other Shakespearean plays and to other literary works, abound in Walker's novel. For example, in casting her company's production, the director decides that Randy is less suited to playing Hamlet than to playing other Shakespearean characters such as "Richard III or Ariel or Puck" (Walker 5). The status of one character as an evil genius and the others as mischievous magical beings provides clues to Randy's true nature. Similarly, the female Old One whom Will meets reveals that her people are descendants of Cain (Walker 147-48), like the monsters in *Beowulf*, which Malone had suggested as a possible analogue for Saxo's version of the Hamlet story. As well, the visions Will sees of future possible worlds, in which lost souls are punished for their sins in life by eternally repeating their mistakes (Walker 269-76), are reminiscent of portions of Dante's *Inferno*. Even Will's name is intertextual; his first name is an obvious allusion to William Shakespeare, and his last name establishes his sharing Danish/Norwegian ancestry with the characters of the play.

For Walker, even critical speculation on *Hamlet* falls into the category of
intertexts. By making his protagonist an actor and English professor who is,
at the beginning of the novel, both playing Hamlet and teaching a
Shakespeare class but who ends up becoming "in fact who [he has] only
feigned to be" (Walker 86), Walker uses the character(s) of Will/
Amlodd/Hamlet to provide his own answers to some of the questions scholars
have had about the play. This approach is also a distinct variation on the
practice of postmodern rewriting, which generally "questions and 'corrects'
the established, inherited literary canon" (Doležel, *Heterocosmica* 206), often
according to a specific political or ideological framework. Within Walker's
novel, the 'typical' postmodern re-evaluation of literary works is embodied
in Will's thesis supervisor Del, a former Shakespearean scholar who now
rejects all the "dead white males" (Walker 44) of English literary tradition
and welcomes the existence of the mysterious book as proof that *"Hamlet* is
just a bad play by Kyd... misattributed to Shakespeare, or even stolen by him
to meet a deadline" (Walker 44) – and who becomes the first member of
Will's group to die in the storyworld. It is not Walker's purpose to "dethrone
this whole Shakespeare religion" (44) by disrupting the playwright's most
famous work, and thus within the novel he makes an example of one who
does wish to do so. Instead, Walker uses Will's experience living out
Amlodd/Hamlet's life to answer, within the possible worlds of this text, at
least three oft-debated questions: Was Hamlet mad or merely pretending?
Why did he wait to kill Claudius? And why did Horatio stay behind in
Denmark when Hamlet went to England?

In his commentary on Saxo's *Historiae Danicae*, Bullough notes that the
story of Amleth was but one variation of "a common type of revenge-story
in which the hero feigns insanity or stupidity to save his life and gain an
opportunity for a coup" (VII. 6; cf. Hansen 16); and Saxo does indeed say
that Amleth "chose to feign dullness, and pretend an utter lack of wits. This
cunning course not only concealed his intelligence but ensured his safety"
(*HD* 62). However, in making the murder of Katla the final impetus for
Will/Amlodd's taking revenge, Walker implies the answer to the first
question; he notes that her death would have left Amlodd alone in the world,
and "Nobody lived by themselves in this time, save madmen and prisoners.
Hamlet had been mad after all" (258). On the second question, Walker shows
that, in his lectures, Will posits the conflicting Elizabethan attitudes toward
revenge as "the reason for Hamlet's famous hesitation" (291); however, in
this fictional world, the reason is that it is not really Hamlet who hesitates,
but Will in Hamlet's body, and had it indeed been Amlodd, then Katla might
have lived. Walker's answer to the third question relates not to the
Will/Amlodd mind-body switch but to the presence of the actors in the

storyworld: when Sean, the actor playing Claudius, becomes overwhelmed by his character and begins acting like a real king, the other actors realize that they have to make him remember who he truly is. Therefore, we can see that it may well be true that "Horatio stayed on in Denmark after Hamlet had gone.... to plot against the tyrant. He was a revolutionary" (Walker 208).

Jasper Fforde's *Something Rotten,* the fourth in his series of novels featuring Thursday Next and her 'literary detective' agency Jurisfiction, takes a similar yet opposite approach to Walker's novel in its exploration of the character of Hamlet and the world of *Hamlet.* Where Walker brought his characters out of their actual world and into the fictional worlds of Shakespeare's play and Saxo's history, Fforde brings his Hamlet out of the Shakespearean fictional world and into the 'actual' world of an alternative-historical Britain in which time travel, travel between fictional worlds, and even travel between 'fiction' and 'reality' are so commonplace that they are overseen by specific organizations such as Jurisfiction, which are not unlike many British government offices in the reader's actual world (cf. Fforde 81). Indeed, the work of literary detectives like Thursday is necessary in Fforde's fictional universe, for not only can people and events in the actual world affect fictional worlds, but characters and events in fictional worlds can affect the actual world as well. Thus, what in the reader's actual world would merely be literary criticism is, in the textual actual world, literally a matter of life and death.

Fforde's Hamlet leaves his fictional world for "the Outland" – the name literary characters in Fforde's novel have for its 'actual' world – precisely because of his reputation among readers and scholars: he was "concerned over reports that he was being misrepresented as something of a 'ditherer'....This was unusual in that fictional characters are rarely troubled by public perception, but Hamlet would worry about having nothing to worry about if he had nothing to worry about" (Fforde 21). As Gilbert does in *Rosencrantz and Guildenstern* and Walker does in *Blood and Judgment,* Fforde uses the presence of Hamlet in his fictional world(s) as a wry comment on the many different interpretations of Hamlet – and indeed, of literary characters in general – that have been proposed over the centuries (e.g. Fforde 155-56, 234-35). While in Thursday's world, Fforde's Hamlet encounters numerous performances and interpretations of the play, including "sixteen different film adaptations... two plays... three comic books and... a wireless [radio] adaptation" (234), only to realize that "[e]very single one of them is different" (234). As a result, Hamlet decides to settle which is the 'true' representation of his character by becoming more active and decisive than in his previous portrayals. The 'new' Hamlet becomes a key player in Thursday's attempt to stop a character from an obscure self-published romance novel from taking over 'actual'-world Britain under the guise of stirring up anti-Danish prejudice but then expresses a desire to bring his newly-found decisiveness back into his own textual world (Fforde 320-21).

As an adaptation itself, albeit a loose adaptation founded on "a thoroughly postmodern metaphysics of literary reality" (Osborne 131), *Something Rotten* addresses the questions of how a new adaptation and/or interpretation of an existing text affects the reception – or even the existence – of that 'original' text. The effect that Hamlet would have on his fictional world as a 'man of action' rather than as a "ditherer" (Fforde 21) is one of those questions.

Contrary to Doležel's assertion that an adaptation does not destroy the existing fictional world but rather expands it, adaptations and reinterpretations in Fforde's fictional world(s) have drastic effects on the textual worlds that inspired them. For example, the success of Stoppard's *Rosencrantz and Guildenstern Are Dead* prompts other characters in the Shakespearean fictional world to demand their own stories. Thus, Ophelia, Laertes, and Polonius each revise the world of *Hamlet* to their own liking, transforming the familiar world of *Hamlet* into, successively and respectively, *"The Tragedy of the Fair Ophelia, Driven Mad by the Callous Hamlet, Prince of Denmark.... The Tragedy of the Noble Laertes, Who Avenges His Sister the Fair Ophelia, Driven Mad by the Callous and Murderous Hamlet, Prince of Denmark.... [and] The Tragedy of the Very Witty and Not Remotely Boring Polonius, Father of the Noble Laertes, Who Avenges His Fair Sister Ophelia, Driven Mad by the Callous, Murderous, and Outrageously Disrespectful Hamlet, Prince of Denmark"* (Fforde 112-13). In a satire of both literary crossovers and corporate mergers, Fforde imagines fictional worlds joining together "to increase the collective narrative advantage of their own mundane plotlines" (162), with *Hamlet* and *The Merry Wives of Windsor,* for example, blending into the hybrid fictional world of *The Merry Wives of Elsinore*, which "features Gertrude being chased around the castle by Falstaff while being outwitted by Mistress Page, Ford, and Ophelia" (162). Rather than creating alternative worlds to their 'originals' and taking their place beside them in the fictional universe, however, all of these revisions, repositionings, and combinations of fictional worlds and characters could, if not reverted to their 'original' states, cause "the play as we know it... [to] cease to exist" (Fforde 163). Even so, the destruction of literary works is not always considered a bad thing, as illustrated in Fforde's take on *King Lear* as the result of the merging of two supposedly inferior protoworlds, *"The Daughters of Lear* and *The Sons of Gloucester"* (162).

The multiplicity of interpretations of *Hamlet* is also symbolized in *Something Rotten* in a plot by "the novel's corporate villain" (Osborne 131) to clone Shakespeare himself (Fforde 177) and use the clones, each called by a variant spelling of the playwright's name, to rewrite the 'original' Shakespeare's plays into "scraps of old plays cobbled together to give new meaning" (Fforde 299). However, one of the clones becomes the key to restoring the merged fictional worlds to their 'original' state in which "one [is] enigmatic, the other a spin-off" (Fforde 380), thus allowing Hamlet to return to the 'proper' version of his fictional world. Although his experience in the 'actual' world has temporarily inspired him to take a more active role and thus help Thursday save both her actual world and the various fictional worlds, Hamlet realizes that his status as a complex character is precisely what has kept him in the popular imagination for so long:

> My play is popular because my failings are your failings, my indecision the indecision of you all. We all know what has to be done; it's just that sometimes we don't know how to get there. Acting without thought doesn't really help in the long run. I might dither for a while, but at least I make the right decision in the end: I bear my troubles, and take arms against them. (Fforde 380)

Thus, Hamlet decides to return to his own world, now restored to the way he and readers remember it, but considers accepting Thursday's offer to become "the Jurisfiction agent for all of Shakespeare's works" (Fforde 381) to protect his world and those of his fellow Shakespearean characters. In this way, Fforde's Hamlet is able to remain the familiar figure of the Shakespearean text(s) in his own world and still use what he has learned from his experience in the 'actual' world.

The recastings of *Hamlet,* its source texts, Shakespearean criticism, and possible-worlds theory alike into the fantasy genre in *Blood and Judgment* and *Something Rotten* are ingenious manners of keeping the material interesting even for non-specialists, for whom dry academic volumes on either *Hamlet* or possible-worlds theory, the sorts of books that Walker or Fforde might have written in other possible worlds, would not hold interest. It is not necessary to know all the prototexts in order to appreciate the use Walker and Fforde have made of them – indeed, whereas most university-age readers are already familiar with *Hamlet* and the other texts that make up Fforde's fictional universe, Saxo's *Historiae Danicae* is known primarily to only a small subgroup of Shakespearean scholars. However, a reader familiar with the play and its original source texts is able to appreciate more fully how, just as Shakespeare transformed what was essentially "a Clever Jack fairy tale, and a bad one... [which] even on its own terms... doesn't hold together" (Walker 10) into one of the greatest works of English literature, Walker and Fforde transform the play, its source texts, other literary texts, and theories of possible worlds into clever mixtures of fantasy, literary criticism, and scientific/philosophical speculation. Walker's and Fforde's use of possible-worlds theory to explore textual questions from *Hamlet* has the additional advantage of accommodating the vast array of critical opinions the play has provoked: rather than adhering to a rigid, dogmatic view of Hamlet's character or the play's plot, a reader could perhaps claim that, without going beyond what is actually present in the text, every answer a scholar provides to these questions may well be true in some possible world.

The Abstracts and Brief Chronicles of the Time: *Hamlet* Retold in Juvenile Fiction

As noted earlier in this study, retellings are adaptations that combine elements of Doležel's two supercategories of translation and transduction. Within the tradition of Shakespearean adaptation, the most common retellings are those aimed at younger readers, generally meant as "abstracts and brief chronicles" (*Hamlet* II.ii. 524-25) of the plays and their worlds, in ways reflecting both the adaptors' admiration for Shakespeare and their beliefs about 'appropriate' subject matter and presentation for young readers. In recreating the Shakespearean fictional world(s) in simplified form, these adaptations walk a precarious borderline between retaining as much of the original text's world as possible and infusing it with the concerns of the adaptors' worlds, both actual and textual.

Like much of the popular image of Hamlet himself as we know him today, the practice of retelling Shakespeare for young readers was an outgrowth of the Romantic period. One of the earliest such versions of *Hamlet* appeared in Jean-Baptiste Perrin's *Contes Moraux Amusants et Instructifs*, published in 1783, while Charles and Mary Lamb's well-known and influential *Tales from Shakespeare,* itself in part a fictionalization of Charles Lamb's literary criticism, first appeared in 1807.[117] Erica Hateley notes that the Romantic period marked the codification and intersection of two particular literary/social ideals, that of "Shakespeare [as]... the figure of ideal authorship, [and] the child [as]... the figure of ideal readership as a result of discursive connections between innocence and the natural" (24); and it was these views of Shakespeare and young readers that shaped much of the tradition of retelling for students. Retellings of this time, such as those of Perrin and the Lambs, were also influenced by the belief (which endures to this day) that young readers had profoundly different needs than older

---

[117] Ironically, the Lambs' prose retellings appeared the same year as another brother/sister team's reworking of Shakespeare for young readers, Thomas and Harriet Bowdler's much-maligned, yet popular, *Family Shakespeare* edition (see Richmond 15-16, Hateley 32-35, Murphy 170).

readers, primarily the need, as perceived by adult society, for examples of the types of behaviours and attitudes expected of children, and eventually of adults, in that society.

The very title of Perrin's French "tradaptations" (to again use Michel Garneau's term) of Shakespeare for his students suggests the desire to use Shakespeare's plays as exemplary models and educational tools. The collection in its original printing is entitled *Contes Moraux Amusants et Instructifs à l'Usage de la Jeunesse Tirés des Tragédies de Shakespeare,* or *Moral Tales, Amusing and Instructive, for the Use of Youth, Taken from Shakespeare's Tragedies.* There is, however, an ambiguity in the title *Contes Moraux,* which, though taken by many readers and translators to mean "morality tales" (Prince 4), could also indicate "manners or mores" (Prince 11, n. 6); and indeed, as Kathryn Prince points out, "Perrin was a French tutor... not a moralist" (5). The main educational aims of Perrin's stories, therefore, were not so much to teach morals to their readers as to help English-speaking readers learn French by reading translated adaptations of familiar stories/plays, or to help French-speaking readers become familiar with Shakespeare. Perrin addressed the book primarily to French readers wishing to learn more about English literature, as indicated in its preface:

> Si on n'avait écrit ces Contes Moraux que pour la nation Anglaise, une longue préface aurait été superflue; mais, comme il est probable, que ce livre passera par les mains des étrangers, on a jugé à propos d'entrer dans un plus long détail, pour mieux faire connaître le poète favori des Anglais....
> En les traduisant on a cru rendre service à des étrangers, qui ne le connaissent que par réputation. Chez les Anglais, il est regardé comme le premier des poètes tragiques. Toutes les fautes de cet auteur sont contrebalancées par les deux plus grandes excellences, qu'un poète tragique puisse posséder, sa peinture vive et diversifiée des caractères, son expression forte et naturelle des passions. (Perrin vii-viii)[118]

Perrin's retelling of *Hamlet* rearranges the Shakespearean text in places, beginning not with the first sighting of the Ghost (I.i.) but with Hamlet's

---

[118] If we had written these Moral Tales only for the English nation, a long preface would have been superfluous; but, since it is probable that this book will pass into the hands of strangers [i.e. foreigners], we judged it proper to enter into longer detail, to better get to know the favourite poet of the English....

In translating them [the plays] we thought to serve the strangers who know him only by reputation. Among the English, he is regarded as the first of the tragic poets. All of this author's faults are counterbalanced by the two best excellences that a tragic poet can possess, his vivid portraits and diversity of characters, his strong and natural expression of the passions. (All translations of Perrin are mine, and all spelling has been modernized where possible.)

brooding over his father's death (Perrin 3-5; *Hamlet* I.ii. 1-159) and Horatio's report to Hamlet about what he and the guards had seen (Perrin 5-7; *Hamlet* I.ii. 160-257). In contrast to later retellings such as those of the Lambs, whose nearly dialogue-free renditions often give the impression of "abstracts" (II.ii. 524) of the play, Perrin's is essentially an abridgment, interspersing soliloquies and dialogues from the play with brief narrative passages.

The *Contes Moraux* dispense entirely with poetic rhythm in favour of semantic accuracy, rendering the Shakespearean dialogue into French prose while retaining as much of the meaning(s) of the words as possible. At least two of Hamlet's major soliloquies, "O that this too too sallied flesh would melt" (I.ii. 129-59) and "To be or not to be" (III.i. 55-87), are included, though with some small omissions. In the former case (Perrin 4-5), Hamlet does not comment on Gertrude's "most wicked speed, to post / With such dexterity to incestuous sheets" (I.ii. 156-57), presumably for reasons of decorum, while the latter (Perrin 13-14) leaves out Hamlet's address to "the fair Ophelia" (III.i. 88), as it is incorporated into the brief narrative passage that follows:

> Hamlet fut interrompu dans ses réflexions par l'arrivée d'Ophélie, qui était amoureuse de lui, malgré ce que son frère Laërtes lui avait dit, pour la dissuader de ne pas entretenir une passion pour le jeune Prince (Perrin 14).[119]

The passage alluded to here, in I.iii. 1-52, as well as Polonius's advice to both his children elsewhere in this scene (I.iii. 55-135), thus appear only in passing in Perrin's narrative, rendering the "moral" aspect of his title ironic in that the overt moralizing present in the Shakespearean text is reduced to a bare minimum, when acknowledged at all, in Perrin's. But whereas Perrin omits or minimizes Shakespeare's examples of parents and/or elder siblings advising younger family members, Hamlet's admonishments to his mother (Perrin 18-20; *Hamlet* III.iv. 7-102, 156-96) are reproduced in dialogue form, directly translated from the play, albeit with some abridgment as the intended purpose and readership of the text suggest. For example, Perrin's Hamlet merely warns Gertrude "n'allez pas au lit de mon oncle" (20), and does not provide a litany of Claudius's behaviours toward her (*Hamlet* III.iv. 182-96) out of respect for the sensibilities of younger readers; however, as a result, he also does not admit to her that he is "But mad in craft" (*Hamlet* III.iv. 188). Unlike the Lambs, who felt the need to intrude upon their fictional

---

[119] Hamlet was interrupted in these reflections by the arrival of Ophelia, who was in love with him, despite what her brother Laertes had said to her to dissuade her from entertaining a passion for the young Prince.

world with a note to the reader that "though the faults of parents are to be tenderly treated by their children, yet in the case of great crimes the son may have leave to speak even to his own mother with some harshness" (Lamb and Lamb 337), Perrin sees no reason to break the boundary between fictional and actual worlds at this point, even "to rescue Shakespeare... from promoting domestic disorder" (Gearhart 53).

Like many of her counterparts in other *Hamlet* adaptations, Perrin's Gertrude is not entirely innocent, while his Claudius comes to realize the truth about Hamlet's madness in a different manner than in the play. Perrin notes that "[l]e Roi et la Reine, à qui les écarts de Hamlet n'étaient pas inconnus, appréhendaient que le jeune Prince n'eût quelque soupçon de leur crime, et qu'il ne songeait à une vengeance éclatatante"[120] (9). Furthermore, it is upon overhearing Hamlet's outburst toward Ophelia, rather than seeing the Mousetrap – which Perrin does not mention in his text – that Claudius, "troublé par ses remords, donna un libre cours à ses plaintes et à ses lamentations"[121] (Perrin 17; cf. *Hamlet* III.iii. 36-72).

The omission of the Mousetrap is but one of the ways in which the action of Perrin's narrative/dialogues differs from Shakespeare's play. As was common with many contemporary adaptations of *Hamlet* in English as well as in other languages, the Fortinbras subplot is ignored, thus removing the hopeful resolution of the Shakespearean text in order to focus on the loss of the Danish royal family including Hamlet. However, Perrin also leaves out Ophelia's madness and death, instead having her disappear from the story with no explanation. Thus, Laertes's indignation at Hamlet is not only because of the death of his father, but to avenge the honour of his sister "qu'il avait négligée, méprisée, et insultée"[122] (Perrin 21). Similarly, Hamlet does not give an elegy to Yorick (*Hamlet* V.i. 184-95) nor send Rosencrantz and Guildenstern to their deaths in England (*Hamlet* V.ii. 371); and rather than entrusting Horatio "To tell [his] story" (*Hamlet* V.ii. 349), "n'eut que le temps de dire à son ami Horatio, 'Oh! Je suis mort!'"[123] (Perrin 24).

Whether Perrin had much influence on Shakespearean adaptation in either the English-speaking or the French-speaking world is uncertain. Kathryn Prince notes that his position as a French tutor to the British aristocracy provided two strikes against him during and after the French Revolution: "After 1789, the idea of a Frenchman teaching morality to the British was as

---

[120] The King and the Queen, to whom the antics of Hamlet were not unknown, were concerned that the young Prince should not have any suspicion of their crime, and that he should not dream of some swift vengeance.

[121] Troubled by his remorse, gave free reign to his complaints and his lamentations.

[122] Whom he [Hamlet] had neglected, badmouthed, and insulted.

[123] Had only enough time to say to his friend Horatio, "Oh! I am dead!"

absurd as the notion that a tutor to foreign lords and ladies could introduce anything wholesome to the French *citoyens*" (6). Even so, the *Contes Moraux* are useful documents in the history of Shakespearean adaptation in general and retelling for juvenile readers in particular, being among the earliest known examples of the latter.

The tradition that may well have begun with Perrin and was popularized by the Lambs has continued to bear much fruit in the centuries that have followed. While critics such as Stephannie Gearhart have questioned the idea of retelling Shakespeare for younger readers both on the usual grounds of whether "murder, revenge, adultery, [and] suicide" (44) are appropriate subjects for juvenile fiction, and in the belief that familiarizing students with Shakespeare is better done "through direct contact with the poet's texts themselves" (45), generations of writers who "loved Shakespeare and wanted to share their passion" (M. Williams, "Bravo" 31) continued to produce their own counterpart texts and text worlds to the simultaneously familiar and mysterious 'original.' But where many nineteenth- and early-twentieth-century adaptations have tended to re-present the plays as Perrin and the Lambs did, as gentle yet essentially conservative moral tales, those produced in the latter half of the twentieth century and afterward have used their fictional worlds to challenge established preconceptions as much as or more than they uphold them, including the preconception of Shakespeare as a culturally entrenched writer whose relevance to present-day readers may not be immediately recognizable or may even be intimidating.

Marcia Williams comments on her own adaptations of Shakespeare for elementary-school-age readers, "Unless we keep reimagining Shakespeare for a new audience, his works will be inaccessible to vast numbers of every new generation, and they will become the property of an academic elite" ("Bravo" 31). Erica Hateley, on the other hand, regards Shakespearean adaptation as a "circulation of cultural capital" (13) which helps to perpetuate that very "academic elite" even as it familiarizes students to the text and vice versa. Stephannie Gearhart, meanwhile, likens the plethora of retellings for student readers to their counterparts in non-fiction, the innumerable critical books and essays that *Hamlet* and the rest of Shakespeare's works have provoked, for with both, the reader "will get different stories and then perhaps begin to wonder which one is correct" (60). There is some truth in all of these assertions, and these are all important reasons for both the production and consumption of Shakespearean retellings. What seem on the surface to be merely "abstracts and brief chronicles" of Shakespeare's time, that of the adaptor, and that of the adaptor's readership serve useful purposes as examples of literary analysis in the more pleasing form of a fictional narrative, while simultaneously following in Shakespeare's own footsteps as ways of keeping familiar stories alive in the public imagination.

Thus far, the worlds of *Hamlet* we have explored have been largely literary worlds, represented in the forms of histories, plays, fiction, essays, and poetry. However, as a play, the world of *Hamlet* represents an intersection of literary and visual elements. As well, non-dramatic literary texts themselves evoke visual representations in the minds of their readers. It is with all of this in mind that the final set of adaptations to be discussed in this study involves the interplay of literature and visual art.

CHAPTER SIX

HAMLET IN ART:
VISUAL AND LITERARY POSSIBILITIES

> Look here upon this picture, and on this,
> The counterfeit presentment of two brothers.
> See what a grace was seated on this brow:
> Hyperion's curls, the front of Jove himself,
> An eye like Mars, to threaten and command,
> A station like the herald Mercury
> New lighted on a heaven-kissing hill,
> A combination and a form indeed,
> Where every god did seem to set his seal
> To give the world assurance of a man.
>
> (*Hamlet* III.iv. 53-62)

Hamlet's invocation to Gertrude of the portraits of her two husbands demonstrates a similarity between visual and literary representations in the ability of both to evoke possible worlds in the minds of their creators and observers. Adaptations of dramatic works such as *Hamlet* into visual artworks, much like productions of the plays themselves, involve recreating the work on the literary and the visual levels, allowing the artist/adaptor to reproduce and represent the play's world in ways that printed words alone cannot. These artistic works in turn may well influence other interpretations and productions of the play as the visual work and the world it represents take their places in the popular imaginations of readers and directors. Artistic works have also been important documents in tracing the play's production history: in the days before sound recordings and film, portraits of actors and drawings of scenes from the play were the best ways in which readers/audiences, directors, and drama historians could obtain permanent records of specific productions. Whether portraits of actors in the roles of particular characters or artists' impressions of the world(s) embodied in the play text, many visual works produced in the Romantic period and afterward, such as Eugène Delacroix's well-known paintings and prints of *Hamlet,* influenced future generations' visual, dramatic, and even literary conceptions of Shakespeare's fictional worlds. Even today, illustrated editions of Shakespeare's plays, ranging from texts accompanied by reproductions of artworks such as Delacroix's to full-blown graphic novels, play important roles in the communication and appreciation of this great body of dramatic literature, whether for students encountering the play for the first time or longtime admirers of either Shakespeare's works or visual representations of literature.[124]

Illustrations of Shakespeare's plays have most probably existed since the first productions of the plays themselves, although very few contemporary illustrations survive, and the earliest complete illustrated edition of the plays appeared at the beginning of the eighteenth century (Young 17). The first known *Hamlet* illustration, appearing in Nicholas Rowe's 1709 edition of the plays, was François Boitard's and Elisha Kirkall's engraving of Hamlet's conversation with Gertrude (III.iv.). The engraving shows the characters in eighteenth-century dress and posed as a tableau, as though taken from the artists' observation of a contemporary production (Young 18-20). It was the mid-eighteenth century that saw the first major flowerings of Shakespearean art, as exemplified in David Garrick's Stratford Jubilee of 1769 (Young 44-47) and in Josiah Boydell's ambitious Shakespeare Gallery project that began in 1786 only to end in financial disaster in 1805 (Young 53-58). The artists who participated in the Boydell Gallery sought to transcend the reliance of Shakespearean artists on relatively simple actor-portraits or performance illustrations and instead portray the characters and events of the play in their own worlds rather than merely as representations on stage – an aim reflected in the use of the term "history painting" for these works (Young 373). As such, while portraits and tableaux were prominently featured, many of these illustrations also incorporate landscapes and architectural studies – though more often those of eighteenth-century England than of the times and places in which the plays are meant to take place.

Despite the objection of critics such as Charles Lamb – who, as noted in the previous chapter, had himself adapted Shakespeare's plays into prose – that illustrations could never do justice to the experience of reading the plays, Shakespearean illustration continued to flourish in the nineteenth century, influenced by the Romantic period's developments in both art and literary criticism. *Hamlet,* and especially the characters of Hamlet and Ophelia, made the strongest impression on the Romantics, who saw Hamlet as a character with "a noble but paralyzed nature...a thinker and philosopher unable to take the action required of the traditional hero because of his deeply ingrained

---

[124] For a detailed discussion of the history of *Hamlet* illustrations prior to the twentieth century, see Alan R. Young's *Hamlet and the Visual Arts, 1709-1900.*

sensibilities" (Young 75) and Ophelia "as an innocent victim, both of Hamlet and the corrupt court in which she finds herself" (Young 77). The play thus became a focal point for a symbiosis of literature, drama, and art that saw illustrations and portraits that did not draw directly from the theatre but rather from the fictional world of the play as imagined by the artists. Many productions of the play further used these illustrations as inspiration, both in design and in dramaturgy.

The most prominent Shakespearean illustrator of the Romantic period was the French painter Eugène Delacroix,[125] whom Malcolm C. Salaman describes as "the head and front of the Romantic movement in French painting" (38). Delacroix's series of paintings and lithographs based on the play, made between 1825 and 1859, reflect his "lifelong obsession with *Hamlet*" (Greene 509); it was the Shakespearean play for which he produced the most illustrations, including an early self-portrait in which he depicts himself as Hamlet (Young 251-52; Joannides 130-31). While Delacroix's illustrations were in part influenced by productions of the play, including the celebrated 1827 Paris production featuring Charles Kemble and Harriet Smithson (Young 108), his treatments of the play transcend the more-or-less stagebound works of earlier *Hamlet* illustrators to provide glimpses into a vivid world defined as much by the illustrations as by Shakespeare's texts themselves.

Delacroix's illustrations followed the dramatic tradition of his day by portraying Hamlet as a young man dressed in black. This design element not only reflects the brooding and melancholy nature of the character, "more readily associated with late Romantic France than with Elizabethan England" (Greene 512), but also provides emphasis: in both the paintings and the lithographs, the dark-clad Hamlet is generally shown against backgrounds of lighter colours or shades. The characters are usually in typically 'Elizabethan' dress with some medieval overtones, also in keeping with dramatic traditions of the time which tended more to a semblance of historical accuracy than the contemporary, and often overdone, designs of most eighteenth-century productions. The character of Hamlet himself appears to range within the illustrations from a "slight, neurasthenic" (Joannides 141) figure in the 1834-35 works "to a more virile, forceful type...[whose] emphasis on hesitancy disappears" (Joannides 141) in the final seven lithographs done in 1843. But even though Delacroix's representations of Hamlet do show the prince's potential for action, especially in the depiction of Hamlet's first sighting of the ghost (*Hamlet* I.iv. 38-86) and the death of Polonius (*Hamlet* III.iv. 21-

---

[125] Delacroix's illustrations can be seen at *Shakespeare Illustrated*, http://www. english.emory.edu/classes/Shakespeare_Illustrated/dh.html.

33), it is the portraits of Hamlet in the graveyard with Yorick's skull (*Hamlet* V.i. 184-95) that helped to pave the way for later illustrators, actors, and directors to establish this moment as the iconic representation of the character. Delacroix's positioning of the characters against open backgrounds, with dark clouds or sunset colours in the sky, also moves the characters out of their indoor environments, whether the royal court within the play or the theatre in the actual world.

Interestingly, however, Delacroix's Hamlet, though intended as youthful in contrast to the older and bearded Horatio, often displays features and mannerisms that seem feminine, in part because Delacroix used a female model, Marguerite Heydinger Pierret (Howard 14; Young 215), for some of his illustrations. These representations thus foreshadow the vogue at the end of the nineteenth century for actresses playing Hamlet, as exemplified by Sarah Bernhardt's famous 1899 performances in London and Paris, as well – perhaps – as much later adaptations of the play such as Allison Williams's *Hamlette* and Douglas Brode's *Sweet Prince*, which, as we have already seen, do imagine Hamlet as a woman.

Delacroix provides a much more vivid and, by the standards of his time, explicit, representation of femininity in his portrayals of the death of Ophelia (*Hamlet* IV.vii. 163-91). His three versions of Ophelia drowning in the stream, done between 1838 and 1853, combine portraiture with landscape to provide memorable images of "a near-naked and soon-to-be drowned Ophelia within a natural setting" (Young 338). His depictions also emphasize the action of the drowning, in contrast to the now-famous image produced by his British contemporary, John Everett Millais, in 1852[126] (Young 340-41). Paul Joannides characterizes Delacroix's blending of Ophelia's body and dress with the water as a "pictorial technique [that] unites flesh and clothing with water, as if drowning were metamorphosis" (144). The picture also uses a technique of emphasis through contrast of colours/shades similar to the one Delacroix used in his Hamlet portraits: here, the light colours of Ophelia illuminate her against the darker background of water and trees.

While Delacroix did not produce his *Hamlet* illustrations specifically to accompany printed texts of Shakespeare's play, they were later used for that purpose, beginning with the publication of the lithographs in 1863 by Paul Meurice (Young 109), collaborator with Alexandre Dumas on an influential French translation of the play. To this day the Delacroix illustrations are

---

[126] Millais's portrait of Ophelia can be seen on the Tate Gallery website, http://www.tate.org.uk/art/artworks/millais-ophelia-n01506.

frequently reprinted in editions of *Hamlet*[127] and still exert a significant influence on representations of the title character and his world.

Illustrations often figure prominently in editions of Shakespeare's plays meant for student readers, in hopes that visual representations of the characters and events of the play will make the text less intimidating to a student encountering the play for the first time. It is for the most part this readership that comprises the main audience of a fairly recent development in the history of Shakespearean art and adaptation: the comic-strip or graphic-novel adaptation, begun in 1941 with the launch of *Classics Illustrated* by publishers Albert L. Kantner, Raymond Haas, and Meyer Levy (Jensen, "Part I" 82; Wetmore 174-80) as a means not only of making Shakespeare and other famous writers more accessible to younger readers, but also of defending the comic-book format against disapproving critics who did not regard it as a legitimate art form. The quality of early examples of Shakespearean graphic novels was generally uneven, but from the 1990s onward, many striking examples of this form of adaptation have appeared. Though often aimed at "textbook adopters and students who want to avoid reading a play" (Jensen, "Part I" 81), these versions demonstrate a vast range of approaches to the text, from homages to more 'traditional' Shakespearean artists such as Delacroix and his contemporaries, to whimsical reimaginings of the plays and their world(s), to alternate-universe retellings of the plays. By directly taking on, using, and playing with Shakespeare's language as well as with the visual/narrative conventions of the graphic novel, these adaptations also go beyond the earlier illustrations that merely created visual equivalents of the language of the texts.

The British writer/artist Marcia Williams treats *Hamlet* in her 1998 book known as *Mr. William Shakespeare's Plays* in the British edition and *Tales from Shakespeare* (recalling Charles and Mary Lamb) in the American edition, the first of her two collections of brief but entertaining Shakespearean comic strips aimed at upper-elementary-school-age readers.[128] Williams's retelling of *Hamlet* abridges the play to only four pages and thirty panels plus marginalia but presents it in a three-layered narrative that creates a sophisticated multiple-worlds structure in its fanciful representation of what a contemporary performance of the play might have been like. The three narrative layers in Williams's adaptation are the play itself, represented by actors performing the play and speaking Shakespeare's

---

[127] For example, the Paddington Press edition of 1976, the first edition to reproduce Delacroix's illustrations with an English text of the play.

[128] Williams has also adapted other famous literary works, including Homer's *Iliad* and Chaucer's *Canterbury Tales,* in a similar format.

words; a prose narrative in modern English, for the convenience of the reader; and the comments of the audience watching the production, shown in the margins of each page. While critics such as Michael P. Jensen have characterized Williams's multiple visual/narrative layers as "cluttered" ("Part III" 66), the amount of detail present in these layers depicts a dynamic relationship between her two textual worlds – the world of the play itself and the world of its audience – and the actual world of the reader.

Williams's unabashedly cartoony style is a stark contrast to the realism of Delacroix, although both artists do share common elements. Like Delacroix, Williams uses colours, light, and shadow to create emphasis: her Hamlet is the only character in the play who dresses in black; and even in scenes rendered in shades of grey such as the appearance of the ghost or Hamlet's funeral, the contrast between Hamlet's light hair and dark clothing emphasizes him. However, in contrast to the Romantic concentration on Hamlet's brooding introspection, Williams focuses on Hamlet's feigned madness – even illustrating his calling Polonius a "fishmonger" (*Hamlet* II.ii. 174; M. Williams 5) by having him dump a basket of fish on the old man's head – and takes visual cues from Saxo Grammaticus's *Historiae Danicae* by showing Hamlet sitting among the fireplace ashes during his "To be or not to be" soliloquy and being followed around by the palace watchdogs.

In the book's marginalia, Williams notes that the behaviour of audience members in Shakespeare's time was often noisy and frequently rude by modern standards, and she does reflect this aspect of Shakespearean playgoing in the borders of each page. Like the narration, the audience members' comments are in modern English, which draws attention to the contrast between the play's world and the worlds of both the audience and the reader, though in somewhat different ways for each. The use of modern English both illustrates the division between the play and the reader and makes the comments directly accessible to the reader, in contrast to the quotations from the original play, which are mediated by the narration. On the other hand, in showing the division between the two textual worlds of play and audience, Williams has the audience members direct comments toward the actors – for example, one man says "Good thinking, Hammy!" (6) in reply to Hamlet's decision to put on the Mousetrap play; while another remarks, "He hasn't got the courage" (6) upon the reappearance of the ghost in Gertrude's bedroom. These sorts of marginal comments underscore the difference between the worlds of play and audience by reminding the reader that "the here and now of the playworld acknowledges no other place and time than Denmark's" (Hill 135); in other words, the advice from the audience has no effect on the predetermined world of the play.

Still other marginalia draw the reader's attention to the actual-world history of Shakespeare's time. For example, one audience member wonders whether Shakespeare deserved a knighthood for writing the play, only to remember that "the queen only knights explorers" (M. Williams 8) – a reminder to the present-day reader that while Elizabeth I did not usually grant knighthoods to writers, Elizabeth II has done so many times. Another spectator says, on seeing Fortinbras's cannons, "I hope those guns don't set fire to the theatre" (M. Williams 8), a reference to the destruction of the original Globe Theatre in 1613, during the first production of *Henry VIII*. This comment functions not only as a historical reference but also as the dramatic irony of the reader's actual world informing the playgoers' fictional world, given its placement in an adaptation of *Hamlet,* a play that was probably first produced twelve or thirteen years before the historical incident occurred.

Though their approaches to the text and illustrations are very different, Delacroix and Williams do share the common goal of representing and re-presenting Shakespeare's fictional world in visual form, with relatively minimal intrusion of their actual worlds. Other Shakespearean illustrators have followed the lead of directors of 'modernized' productions of the play by creating alternative fictional worlds in which Shakespeare's text is preserved but the visual elements are those of the artist/director's world. This is the approach that artist Emma Vieceli and editor Richard Appignanesi take in their 2007 adaptation of *Hamlet* as part of the *Manga Shakespeare* series,[129] which combines Shakespeare's original text with the art style of Japanese comic books to create a cross-cultural hybrid world.

Vieceli and Appignanesi's adaptation of *Hamlet* is set in a cyberpunk-influenced future world in which "global climate change has devastated the Earth [and] this is now a cyberworld in constant dread of war" (*MSH* i). Vieceli's choice of costume designs for the characters represents the hybrid nature of this text, blending traditional Elizabethan/Jacobean and Romantic designs (sometimes vaguely reminiscent of Delacroix's) with elements generally associated with anime and manga and with the cyberpunk genre, such as the facial expressions and hairstyles she gives her characters, and the use of cybernetic enhancements and implants, which are demonstrated throughout the text. The colour scheme of Vieceli's Hamlet is black and white, playing off the traditional colour scheme of Hamlet while emphasizing his status as existing between the royal court and the outside world – and between the more 'traditional' Shakespearean fictional world and the new counterpart world embodied in the *Manga Shakespeare* text.

---

[129] Hereafter cited as *MSH*.

Vieceli's Hamlet is not as prominently set apart, in terms of design, from his environment as Delacroix's and Williams's are, although the shadings of his costume are generally darker than those of the other characters. Because manga are usually printed in black and white, the artist depends on light and shadow to create mood and emphasis, in a manner somewhat analogous to yet very different from Delacroix's use of similar techniques in his uncoloured lithograph series. The amount of detail present in Vieceli's drawings also varies to show emotions, with panels ranging from those that use only a few lines to convey the mood of the scene to those that are more intricately detailed. An example of both such cases is Vieceli's depiction of the ghost telling Hamlet of the manner of his death (*MSH* 38-39): the first page shows Claudius in black and King Hamlet in white to underscore the contrast between them while the second page, representing Hamlet's reaction to the ghost's story, mixes high-contrast shading with the movement of Hamlet's hair and clothing. Conversely, Vieceli represents Hamlet at the graveyard (*MSH* 162) in the opposite manner to Delacroix: she uses cartoonish 'chibi' (small) figures (cf. *MSH* 56-57), sound effects, and word balloons with bubbly edges to undercut the seriousness of the passage and instead play it up as a moment of comic relief.

Though Appignanesi's text streamlines the Shakespearean 'original' to fit within the format of a graphic novel, the modernization of the text's fictional world comes almost entirely from Vieceli's imagery. The supernatural elements of Shakespeare's original play exist side-by-side with wonders of very different kinds, such as "implements of war" (*MSH* 8) very reminiscent of the actual world of the late twentieth and early twenty-first centuries, or communication via holograms, as illustrated by Polonius's advice to Laertes (*MSH* 42), and even in the setting of Hamlet's "The play's the thing" soliloquy in a virtual-reality room (*MSH* 72). However, despite her use of futuristic means of communication throughout the book, Vieceli chooses a more recognizably 'traditional Shakespearean' manner to depict the Mousetrap play (*MSH* 96-101) and makes no significant update to the final duel (*MSH* 178-89).

At first glance Vieceli and Appignanesi's 'updated' *Hamlet* may seem to be little more than an attempt to 'disguise' *Hamlet* as a work of popular culture, to dress the play up for students who would sooner read cyberpunk than Shakespeare. However, such cynicism about this text – not to mention about its dramatic 'cousins,' updated stage productions – overlooks how the mixture of Elizabethan English text and twenty-first-century Japanese comic art (albeit by a British artist) simultaneously enriches and ennobles both the play and the artwork. On the one hand, Vieceli, like Williams and Delacroix before her, responds visually to Shakespeare's play in the artistic sensibility of her time and place, demonstrating the flexibility of the text in its ability to be adapted into such a far-ranging rendition. On the other hand, this book shows the viability of the graphic novel as a means of keeping Shakespeare fresh and exciting for new generations of readers, just as Delacroix's paintings reimagined Shakespeare for the Romantic period and Williams's comic strips made his texts accessible to younger readers who may well encounter Vieceli and Appignanesi's adaptation – and eventually the 'original' in whichever form(s) that may take – as their education progresses.

CONCLUSION

> O God, Horatio, what a wounded name,
> Things standing thus unknown, shall I leave behind me!
> If thou didst ever hold me in thy heart,
> Absent thee from felicity a while,
> And in this harsh world draw thy breath in pain
> To tell my story.
>
> (*Hamlet* V.ii. 344-49)

What do all of these adaptations suggest about Shakespeare's *Hamlet,* and what does the play suggest about its literary/artistic descendants? How different is Shakespeare's handling of his source texts from later writers' handlings of the play? Are taxonomies of adaptation such as those of Doležel and Lanier useful methods of approaching these texts, or do they oversimplify the texts' purposes and appeals?

Tracing the development of Shakespeare's *Hamlet* from its historical and literary sources demonstrates the various techniques of adaptation outlined by Doležel and Lanier. The play creates a complex fictional world with many characters and viewpoints yet still unified by a dominant character, from the worlds and characters represented in the various source texts. In so doing, Shakespeare's play displays characteristics of all three of Doležel's types of transduction: transposition, expansion, and displacement. It transposes the story as told by Saxo Grammaticus and later retold by Belleforest from the sixth century to the sixteenth, and its setting, though clearly identified as Denmark, is equally informed by both England and Scotland. It expands the nameless and relatively insignificant secondary characters of the histories into full-blown characters with distinct names, personalities, and stories, which in turn helps to make those characters attractive to authors of later adaptations. As well, it displaces the source texts and their worlds through its reflections on changing worldviews and in its use of the conventions of the Elizabethan/Jacobean revenge tragedy, resulting in changes to the plot; it can also be said to have displaced the source texts in a more literal fashion, by taking their place in the popular imagination.

The status of *Hamlet* as all of these types of adaptation shows that attempting to pigeonhole adaptations as "translation," "expansion," "transposition," *or* "displacement," without recognizing the potential mutual inclusiveness of those types, is not always a satisfactory method of analyzing such works. Indeed, even though classifications such as those formulated by Doležel and Lanier do have their value in accounting for the different approaches to adaptation that writers and artists choose to employ, it is probably more useful to think of these classifications as parts of a continuum, rather than as distinct categories into which works can be summarily placed. Regarding adaptations and the adaptation process as a continuum also helps readers appreciate more fully how writers of Shakespearean adaptations emulate the playwright himself in reimagining familiar stories for their own purposes and those of their intended readers/audiences. In turn, reading *Hamlet* and its adaptations in this manner can provide a useful counterbalance to the centuries of cultural baggage that Shakespeare and his plays have accumulated. Doležel's statement, "The game is no longer exciting, and it is time to invent a new one" (*Heterocosmica* 226), though on the surface a dismissal of adaptation as making new worlds of old ones, is in part a reminder that the study and appreciation of adaptations should not result in losing track of the source texts. Rather, the source texts should be examined and enjoyed alongside the adaptations, to show how each affects and is affected by the existence of the others.

Adaptation has, in fact, been a significant reason why Shakespeare is one of the best-known and most appreciated writers in history. Contrary to Ben Jonson's oft-quoted statement in the introduction to the First Folio that Shakespeare "was not of an age, but for all time" (66), the prevalence of Shakespearean adaptations has helped to show that he was, more properly, simultaneously "of an age" and "for all time." Whether reintroducing Shakespeare's work to new generations of readers, disputing with or even rejecting his portrayals of certain characters and/or events, or illustrating one author's speculation on details about a play and its sources that have baffled generations of literary scholars, or all of these at once, the authors of Shakespearean adaptations attempt to bring the texts out of Shakespeare's time and place and into their own, while at the same time demonstrating the transcendent appeal of the Shakespearean texts to readers and audiences in other times and places. Meanwhile, the derived texts are as much products of their authors' times and places as the Shakespearean prototexts are of his.

The presence, multiplicity, and persistence of Shakespearean adaptation in all its forms vividly illustrates Marjorie Garber's thesis that "Shakespeare makes modern culture and modern culture makes Shakespeare" (xiii). That is, each new generation must rediscover Shakespeare for itself and reimagine his works for its own purposes, and this reimagining has as much effect on the actual world of the reader as it does on the fictional world embodied in the text: "the purpose of playing is to hold 'the mirror up to nature'.... But the metadrama of modernity... holds nature up to a mirror, and it believes the mirror" (Garber 230). In other words, though analysis of literary/dramatic/ artistic works has not, and perhaps should not, completely moved away from the Aristotelian model of art as a reflection of the actual world, these works have increasingly become valued not only for their ability to describe and show the actual world, but also – if not more – for their ability to create and embody distinct worlds in themselves. Yet these fictional worlds, while separate from the actual world, do reflect aspects of the actual world that produced them even as they remain independent of it, and it is this simultaneous separateness and reciprocation between source text and derivative text, and the worlds they represent, that makes the works fascinating to see, hear, and/or read.

Nonetheless, adaptation is still a controversial means of access to Shakespeare and his fictional worlds. Commentators from George Eliot (qtd. in Schoch 20) to Richard Burt have worried that adaptations may cause readers to forget the 'originals' and may even go so far as to claim that readers who require any sort of mediation to appreciate Shakespeare are inherently unsophisticated (Burt 1-28; cf. Schoch 20-21).[130] Meanwhile, postmodern readers and literary critics such as Martha Tuck Rozett or Jennifer Hulbert appear to be taking the opposite approach, believing that adaptation, especially of a polemical variety, is the best, or possibly only, way in which readers can or even should approach canonical writers (see e.g. Hulbert et al. 226). Between these two extremes, there are as many opinions on the purposes and viability of adaptations as there are adaptations themselves. It is useful to remember, however, that each production of the play, no matter how 'faithful' and/or 'transgressive' to readers' mental images of the textual world, is an adaptation in itself: "we want to see *your* Hamlet and *his* Hamlet and *her* Hamlet; to embody the role is to reinvent it" (Coppa 236); just as the play we call *Hamlet* is composed of three different print texts, so is the archetype of Hamlet composed of innumerable productions and readings, often vastly different from each other.

In his dying speech, Hamlet expresses concern over the "wounded name" (V.ii. 344) he leaves behind and requests Horatio "To tell [his] story" (V.ii.

---

[130] Schoch seems more accepting of the adaptation process and its results than Burt, at least in the two works cited here. Burt seems to fall more squarely on the side of 'textual purism,' even to dismissing modernized adaptations of the plays as "inane or just plain stupid... precisely a dumbed-down Shakespeare" (xiii, 4). On the other hand, Schoch regards adaptations, especially of the humorous/satirical variety, as legitimate forms of interpretation in an accessible and enjoyable format.

349) so that it will not be forgotten and so that his successor will know the truth behind his death and that of his family. The authors of Shakespearean adaptations can be said to act as the Horatio-figures to Shakespeare himself, keeping the story of Hamlet and *Hamlet* alive in the public consciousness. These writers, actors, directors, and artists also follow in Shakespeare's own footsteps, "tell[ing] the same story again, but differently" (Coppa 236), as he did in transforming his historical and literary sources into the *Tragedy of Hamlet*.

There are far more adaptations of *Hamlet,* and indeed of all of Shakespeare's plays, than can be discussed in a single volume. But no matter what form these adaptations take, which character is their focus, or from which sociocultural milieu they are produced, what they all have in common is their status as "infinite alternate universes" (Coppa 236) into which the familiar characters and situations of Shakespeare's play as well as of its lesser-known source texts can be and have been made to fit. All of them serve as tributes, be they reverent or mocking or somewhere in between, to the position that Shakespeare and *Hamlet* have held in literary/dramatic/artistic history for over four hundred years and will without a doubt continue to hold for future generations. Though the last words of the Shakespearean Hamlet are "The rest is silence" (V.ii. 359), the Hamlet story in whichever form it is presented insures that the world of *Hamlet* will, presumably, never be silenced.

WORKS CITED

Primary Sources

Aquin, Hubert. *Neige Noire*. 1975. Edited by Pierre-Yves Mocquais. Bibliothèque Québécoise, 1997.

Atwood, Margaret. "Gertrude Talks Back." 1983. *Hamlet: With Related Readings,* edited by Dom Saliani, Chris Ferguson, and Tim Scott, International Thompson 1997, pp. 167-68.

Baring, Maurice. "At the Court of King Claudius." 1910. *Hamlet: With Related Readings,* edited by Dom Saliani, Chris Ferguson, and Tim Scott, International Thompson, 1997, pp. 164-66.

Belleforest, François de. "Avec quelle ruse Amleth, qui depuis fut Roy de Dannemarch, vengea le mort de son père Horwendille, occis par Fengon son frère, et autre occurrence de son histoire." *Le Cinquième Tome d'Histoires Tragiques.* J. Hulpeau, 1572, pp. 149-91.

Bergantino, David. *Hamlet II: Ophelia's Revenge.* Pocket Star, 2003.

Bertram, Paul, and Bernice W. Kliman, editors. *The Three-Text Hamlet: Parallel Texts of the First and Second Quartos and the First Folio.* AMS P, 1991.

Blessing, Lee. *Fortinbras.* 1991. *Patient A and Other Plays.* Heinemann, 1995, pp. 99-163.

Braddon, Mary Elizabeth. *Eleanor's Victory.* 1863. Sutton, 1996.

Brode, Douglas. *Sweet Prince: The Passion of Hamlet.* Florida Academic P, 2004.

Bullough, Geoffrey, editor. *Narrative and Dramatic Sources of Shakespeare, Vol. VII: The Major Tragedies.* Routledge and Kegan Paul, 1973.

Clarke, Mary Cowden. "Ophelia: The Rose of Elsinore." *The Girlhood of Shakespeare's Heroines, Vol. II.* 1852. C.S. Francis, 1857, pp. 186-263.

—, "Ophelia: The Rose of Elsinore." *The Girlhood of Shakespeare's Heroines: A New Edition, Condensed by Her Sister, Sabilla Novello.* 1880, pp. 195-225. Edited by Thomas Larque. *Shakespeare and His Critics.* Accessed April 7, 2009.

Concon, Ranulfo. *Joker.* Joanna Cotler, 2006.

Delacroix, Eugène, illustrator. *William Shakespeare: Hamlet, with Sixteen Lithographs by Eugène Delacroix,* edited and introduction by Michael Marqusee, Paddington P, 1976.

Ducis, Jean-François. *Hamlet.* 1769. *Les Oeuvres de J.F. Ducis, Suivi des Oeuvres de Marie-Joseph de Chénier.* Ledentu, 1839.

Fforde, Jasper. *Something Rotten.* Hodder and Stoughton, 2004.

Fiedler, Lisa. *Dating Hamlet.* Holt, 2002.

Fischman, Sheila, translator. *Hamlet's Twin,* by Hubert Aquin, McClelland and Stewart, 1979.

Gélinas, Marc F., translator. *Hamlet, Prince of Quebec,* by Robert Gurik, Playwrights Canada, 1981.

Gilbert, Sir William S. *Rosencrantz and Guildenstern.* 1874. *Original Plays by W.S. Gilbert, Vol. 3.* Chatto and Windus, 1928, pp. 75-89.

Gordon, Alan. *An Antic Disposition.* St. Martin's P, 2004.

Gordon, John. *The Shade of Henry, King of Scotland, to His Son James VI.* 1587. Translated by Geoffrey Bullough. *Narrative and Dramatic Sources of Shakespeare, Vol. VII: The Major Tragedies,* edited by Geoffrey Bullough. Routledge and Kegan Paul, 1973, pp. 125-27.

Gurik, Robert. *Hamlet, Prince du Québec.* Les Éditions de l'Homme, 1968.

Hansen, William F., editor and translator. *Saxo Grammaticus and the Life of Hamlet.* U of Nebraska P, 1983.

Hayter, Alethea. *Horatio's Version.* Faber and Faber, 1972.

Holderness, Graham. *The Prince of Denmark.* U of Hertfordshire P, 2002.

The Hystorie of Hamblet. 1608. *Narrative and Dramatic Sources of Shakespeare, Vol. VII: The Major Tragedies,* edited by Geoffrey Bullough, Routledge and Kegan Paul, 1973, pp. 80-124.

Innes, Michael. *Hamlet, Revenge!* London: Penguin, 1937.

—, *The Hawk and the Handsaw.* 1948. *Three Tales of Hamlet,* by Michael Innes and Rayner Heppenstall, Victor Gollancz, 1950, pp. 11-73.

—, "The Mysterious Affair at Elsinore." 1949. *Three Tales of Hamlet,* by Michael Innes and Rayner Heppenstall, Victor Gollancz, 1950, pp. 75-89.

Innes, Michael, and Rayner Heppenstall. *Three Tales of Hamlet.* Victor Gollancz, 1950.

James, Elias Olan. *Thieves of Mercy.* Eucalyptus P, 1934.

Jonson, Ben. "To the Memory of My Beloved, the Author Mr. William Shakespeare: And What He Hath Left Us." 1623. *The Riverside Shakespeare,* 1st ed., edited by G. Blakemore Evans, Houghton Mifflin, 1974, pp. 65-66.

Klein, Lisa. *Ophelia.* Bloomsbury, 2006.

Kyd, Thomas. *The First Part of Hieronimo, or The Spanish Comedy.* c. 1585. *The First Part of Hieronimo and the Spanish Tragedy,* edited by Andrew S. Cairncross, U of Nebraska P, 1967, pp. 1-58.

—, *The Spanish Tragedy, or Horatio is Mad Again.* c. 1587. *The First Part of Hieronimo and the Spanish Tragedy,* edited by Andrew S. Cairncross, U of Nebraska P, 1967, pp. 59-176.

Lamb, Charles and Mary. *Tales from Shakespeare.* 1807. Nelson Doubleday, 1955.

MacKaye, Percy. *The Mystery of Hamlet, King of Denmark, or What We Will.* Bond Wheelwright, 1950.

Mark, Jan. *Heathrow Nights.* Hodder, 2000.

Mayer, Marcos. *Shakespeare Para Todos.* Planeta, 1997.

Moratín, Leandro Fernández de, translator. *Hamlet: Tragedia de Guillermo Shakespeare.* 1798. Edited by Juan Antonio Ríos Carratalá. *Biblioteca Virtual Miguel de Cervantes.* Accessed July 14, 2009.

Papp, Joseph. *William Shakespeare's "Naked" Hamlet.* Macmillan, 1969.

Perrin, Jean-Baptiste. *Contes Moraux, Amusants et Instructifs, à l'Usage de la Jeunesse, Tirés des Tragédies de Shakespeare.* Law, Robson, Cadell, & Elmsly, 1783.

Poole, John. *Hamlet Travestie.* 1810. *Nineteenth-Century Shakespeare Burlesques, Vol. 1: John Poole and His Imitators.* Edited and introduction by Stanley Wells. Diploma P, 1977, pp. 1-69.

Reisert, Rebecca. *Ophelia's Revenge.* Flame, 2003.

Saxo Grammaticus. *Historiae Danicae,* translated by Oliver Elton. 1894. *Narrative and Dramatic Sources of Shakespeare, Vol. VII: The Major Tragedies,* edited by Geoffrey Bullough, Routledge and Kegan Paul, 1973, pp. 60-79.

Shakespeare, William. *The Riverside Shakespeare,* 1st ed., edited by G. Blakemore Evans, Houghton Mifflin, 1974.

Steele, Hunter. *Lord Hamlet's Castle.* Deutsch, 1987.

Stoppard, Tom. *Rosencrantz and Guildenstern Are Dead.* 1967. Grove P, 1991.

Trafford, Jeremy. *Ophelia.* House of Stratus, 2001.

Turing, John. *My Nephew Hamlet.* Dent, 1967.

Updike, John. *Gertrude and Claudius.* Alfred A. Knopf, 2000.

Vieceli, Emma, illustrator. *Manga Shakespeare: Hamlet,* edited by Richard Appignanesi, Amulet Books, 2007.

Wain, John. *Feng: A Poem.* Macmillan, 1975.

Walker, Lars. *Blood and Judgment.* Baen, 2003.

Williams, Allison. *Hamlette.* Theatrefolk, 2001.

Williams, Marcia. *Tales from Shakespeare.* Candlewick, 1998.

Wyman, Lillie Buffum Chace. *Gertrude of Denmark.* Marshall Jones, 1924.

Secondary Sources

Alter, Jean. "From Text to Performance: Semiotics of Theatrality." *Poetics Today,* vol. 2, no. 3, 1981, pp. 113-39.

Bailey, Helen Phelps. *Hamlet in France: From Voltaire to Laforgue.* Librairie Droz, 1964.

Baker, Herschel. "*Richard II:* Introduction." *The Riverside Shakespeare,* 1st ed., edited by G. Blakemore Evans, Houghton Mifflin, 1974, pp. 800-04.

Bassnett, Susan. "Engendering Anew." *Shakespeare and the Language of Translation,* edited by A.J. Hoenselaars, Arden, 2004, pp. 54-60.

Beare, W. "Plautus, Terence, and Seneca: A Comparison of Aims and Methods." *Classical Drama and Its Influence,* edited by M.J. Anderson, Methuen, 1965, pp. 103-15.

Behind the Name. www.behindthename.com. Accessed June 23, 2009.

Bell, Robert H. *Shakespeare's Great Stage of Fools.* Palgrave Macmillan, 2011.

Beyenburg, Romana. *"Hamlet." Shakespeare in Performance,* edited by Keith Parsons and Pamela Mason, Salamander, 1995, pp. 67-74.

Bonnefoy, Yves. *Shakespeare and the French Poet,* edited by John Naughton, U of Chicago P, 2004.

—, "Transpose or Translate?" *Yale French Studies,* vol. 33, 1964, pp. 120-26.

Brisset, Annie. *Sociocritique de la Traduction: Théâtre et Altérité au Québec.* Le Préambule, 1990.

Büchner, Alexandre. *Hamlet le Danois.* Librairie Hachette, 1878.

Burt, Richard. *Unspeakable ShaXXXpeares: Queer Theory and American Kiddie Culture.* St. Martin's P, 1998.

Campillo Árnaiz, Laura. "Bowdlerizing or Maximizing? Two Strategies to Render Shakespeare's Sexual Puns in Nineteenth-Century Spain." *Revista Ilha do Desterro,* vol. 49, 2005, pp. 25-36.

Chisholm, Roderick M. "Identity Through Possible Worlds: Some Questions." *The Possible and the Actual,* edited by Michael J. Loux, Cornell UP, 1979, pp. 80-87.

Chopoidalo, Cindy, and Khalida Tanvir Syed. "Teaching *Hamlet* in 21st-Century Pakistan and Canada." *English Quarterly,* vol. 43, no. 1-2, 2012, pp. 53-61.

Cohn, Ruby. *Modern Shakespeare Offshoots.* Princeton UP, 1976.

Conejero, Manuel Ángel. *Rhetoric, Theatre, and Translation.* Fundación Shakespeare de España, 1991.

Copeland, B. Jack. "The Genesis of Possible Worlds Semantics." *Journal of Philosophical Logic,* vol. 31, 2002, pp. 99-137.

Coppa, Francesca. "Writing Bodies in Space: Media Fan Fiction as Theatrical Performance." *Fan Fiction and Fan Communities in the Age of the Internet,* edited by Karen Hellekson and Kristina Busse, McFarland, 2006, pp. 225-44.

Crittenden, Charles. *Unreality: The Metaphysics of Fictional Objects.* Cornell UP, 1991.

De Grazia, Margreta. *Hamlet Without Hamlet.* Cambridge UP, 2007.

De Lotbinière-Harwood, Susanne. *Re-Belle et Infidèle/The Body Bilingual.* Les Éditions du Remue-Ménage/Women's P, 1991.

Derrida, Jacques. *De la Grammatologie.* Les Éditions de Minuit, 1967.

Descartes, René. *Principles of Philosophy,* edited and translated by Valentine Rodger Miller and Reese P. Miller, D. Reidel, 1983.

Doležel, Lubomír. *Heterocosmica: Fiction and Possible Worlds.* Johns Hopkins UP, 1998.

—, *Occidental Poetics: Tradition and Progress.* U of Nebraska P, 1990.

Drouin, Jennifer. "Nationalizing Shakespeare in Quebec: Theorizing Post/Neo/Colonial Adaptation." *Borrowers and Lenders,* vol. 3, no. 1, 2007, pp. 1-23.

Erne, Lukas. *Beyond the Spanish Tragedy: A Study of the Works of Thomas Kyd.* Manchester UP, 2001.

Evans, G. Blakemore. "Chronology and Sources." *The Riverside Shakespeare,* 1st ed., edited by G. Blakemore Evans, Houghton Mifflin, 1974, pp. 47-56.

Faucit, Helena. "On Some of Shakespeare's Female Characters: Ophelia." 1880. *Shakespeare and His Critics,* edited by Thomas Larque. Accessed April 7, 2009.

Fischlin, Daniel, and Mark Fortier, editors. *Adaptations of Shakespeare: A Critical Anthology From the Seventeenth Century to the Present.* Routledge, 2000.

Fokkema, Douwe. "The Rise of Cross-Cultural Intertextuality." *Canadian Review of Comparative Literature,* vol. 31, no. 1, 2004, pp. 5-10.

Folkart, Barbara. *Second Finding: A Poetics of Translation.* U of Ottawa P, 2007.

Garber, Marjorie. *Shakespeare and Modern Culture.* Pantheon, 2008.

Gearhart, Stephannie S. "Faint and Imperfect Stamps: The Problem with Adaptations of Shakespeare for Children." *Alif,* vol. 27, 2007, pp. 44-67.

Gianakaris, C.J. "Stoppard's Adaptations of Shakespeare: *Dogg's Hamlet, Cahoot's Macbeth.*" *Comparative Drama,* vol. 18, no. 3, 1984, pp. 222-40.

Girle, Rod. *Possible Worlds.* McGill-Queen's UP, 2003.

Grace, Sherrill E. "Dans le Crystallin de Nos Yeux: *Neige Noire, Caligari,* and the Postmodern Film Frame-Up." *New Comparison,* vol. 5, 1988, pp. 89-103.

Greene, Robert W. "Ever Faithful to Presence: Yves Bonnefoy on Delacroix's Hamlet and on Shakespeare." *French Review,* vol. 74, no. 3, 2001, pp. 506-17.

Hallett, Charles A., and Elaine S. Hallett. *The Revenger's Madness.* U of Nebraska P, 1980.

Hart, Jonathan. "A Comparative Pluralism: The Heterogeneity of Methods and the Case of Fictional Worlds." *Canadian Review of Comparative Literature,* vol. 25, no. 3-4, 1988, pp. 320-45.

Hateley, Erica. *Shakespeare in Children's Literature: Gender and Cultural Capital.* Routledge, 2009.

Hellekson, Karen, and Kristina Busse, editors. *Fan Fiction and Fan Communities in the Age of the Internet.* McFarland, 2006.

Heylen, Romy. *Translation, Poetics, and the Stage: Six French Hamlets.* Routledge, 1993.

Hill, Janet. *Stages and Playgoers: From Guild Plays to Shakespeare.* McGill-Queen's UP, 2002.

Holden, Anthony. *William Shakespeare: The Man Behind the Genius.* Little, Brown, and Co., 1999.

Homel, David, and Sherry Simon, editors. *Mapping Literature: The Art and Politics of Translation.* Véhicule P, 1988.

Howard, Tony. *Women as Hamlet: Performance and Interpretation in Theatre, Film, and Fiction.* Cambridge UP, 2007.

Hulbert, Jennifer. "Adolescence, Thy Name is Ophelia! The Ophelia-ization of the Contemporary Teenage Girl." *Shakespeare and Youth Culture,* edited by Jennifer Hulbert, Kevin J. Wetmore, Jr., and Robert L. York, Palgrave Macmillan, 2006, pp. 199-220.

Hulbert, Jennifer, Kevin J. Wetmore, Jr., and Robert L. York. "This Bard's for You(th), or Get Over Yourself, Ophelia! A Conclusion That Leaves Things Open for a Sequel." *Shakespeare and Youth Culture,* edited by Jennifer Hulbert, Kevin J. Wetmore, Jr., and Robert L. York, Palgrave Macmillan, 2006, pp. 221-30.

Hulse, Clark. *Elizabeth I: Ruler and Legend.* U of Illinois P, 2003.

Hunt, Marvin W. *Looking for Hamlet.* Palgrave Macmillan, 2007.

Hutcheon, Linda. *A Poetics of Postmodernism: History, Theory, Fiction.* Routledge, 1988.

Iqbal, Françoise Maccabée. "Inceste, Onirisme, et Inversion: *Neige Noire* et l'Identité Apocryphe." *Canadian Literature,* vol. 104, 1985, pp. 74-84.

Jameson, Anna. "Ophelia." *Shakespeare's Heroines: Characteristics of Women, Moral, Poetical, and Historical.* George Bell and Sons, 1891, pp. 153-70. *Shakespeare and His Critics,* edited by Thomas Larque. Accessed April 9, 2009.

Jensen, Michael P. "The Comic Book Shakespeare, Part I." *The Shakespeare Newsletter,* vol. 56, no. 3, 2006, pp. 81-82, 97, 104, 113, 118-19.

—, "The Comic Book Shakespeare, Part II." *The Shakespeare Newsletter,* vol. 57, no. 1, 2007, pp. 2, 4, 8, 38-40.

—, "The Comic Book Shakespeare, Part III." *The Shakespeare Newsletter,* vol. 57, no 2, 2007, pp. 42, 62, 66, 68, 78-80.

Joannides, Paul. "Delacroix and Modern Literature." *The Cambridge Companion to Delacroix,* edited by Beth S. Wright. Cambridge UP, 2001, pp. 130-53.

Johnston, William Preston. *The Prototype of Hamlet, and Other Shakespearian Problems.* 1890. Belford, 1972.

Joseph, B.L. "*The Spanish Tragedy* and *Hamlet:* Two Exercises in English Seneca." *Classical Drama and Its Influence,* edited by M.J. Anderson, Methuen, 1965, pp. 119-34.

Jusserand, J.J. *Shakespeare in France Under the Ancien Régime.* 1899. American Scholar Publications, 1966.

Kennedy, Dennis, editor. *Foreign Shakespeare: Contemporary Performance.* Cambridge UP, 1993.

Kripke, Saul. *Naming and Necessity.* 1972. Blackwell, 1980.

—, "Semantical Considerations in Modal Logic." 1963. *Readings in Semantics,* edited by Farhang Zabeeh, E.D. Klemke, and Arthur Jacobson, U of Illinois P, 1974, pp. 801-14.

Langdon, Courtney. "Introduction." *Gertrude of Denmark,* by Lillie Buffum Chace Wyman, Marshall Jones, 1924.

Lanier, Douglas. *Shakespeare and Modern Popular Culture.* Oxford UP, 2002.

Larque, Thomas. *Shakespeare and His Critics.* Accessed April 7, 2009.

Leibniz, Gottfried Wilhelm von. *Philosophical Essays,* edited and translated by Roger Ariew and Daniel Garber, Hackett, 1989.

—, *Theodicy.* 1710, edited by Austin Farrer, translated by E.M. Huggard, Routledge and Kegan Paul, 1951.

Leinwand, Theodore B. "Conservative Fools in James's Court and Shakespeare's Plays." *Shakespeare Studies,* vol. 19, 1987, pp. 219-38.

Lenoff, Leslee. "Life Within Limits: Stoppard on the HMS *Hamlet.*" *Arizona Quarterly,* vol. 38, no. 1, 1982, pp. 45-61.

Lewis, Brenda Ralph, and David Nash Ford. "Narrative History of York." *Britannia.com.* www.britannia.com/history/york/yorkhist4.html. Accessed March 9, 2015.

Lewis, David. "Counterpart Theory and Quantified Modal Logic." *The Possible and the Actual,* edited by Michael J. Loux, Cornell UP, 1979, pp. 110-28.

—, *On the Plurality of Worlds.* Blackwell, 1986.

—, "Possible Worlds." *The Possible and the Actual,* edited by Michael J. Loux, Cornell UP, 1979, pp. 182-89.

Lieblein, Leanore. "Cette Belle Langue." *Shakespeare and the Language of Translation,* edited by A.J. Hoenselaars, Arden, 2004, pp. 255-67.

—, "Pourquoi Shakespeare?" *Shakespeare Made in Canada: Contemporary Canadian Adaptations in Theatre, Pop Media, and Visual Arts,* edited by Daniel Fischlin and Judith Nasby, Macdonald Stewart Art Centre/Guelph UP, 2007, pp. 97-109.

—, "Le Re-making of le Grand Will: Shakespeare in Francophone Quebec." *Shakespeare in Canada: A World Elsewhere?* edited by Diana Brydon and Irena R. Makaryk, U of Toronto P, 2002, pp. 174-91.

Loux, Michael J. "Modality and Metaphysics." *The Possible and the Actual,* edited by Michael J. Loux, Cornell UP, 1979, pp. 15-64.

Maitre, Doreen. *Literature and Possible Worlds.* Pembridge P, 1983.

Malone, Kemp. *The Literary History of Hamlet.* 1923. Haskell House, 1964.

Marriott, J.A.R. *English History in Shakespeare.* E.P. Dutton, 1918.

Mates, B. "Leibniz on Possible Worlds." *Logic, Methodology, and Philosophy of Science III,* edited by B. van Rootselaar and J.F. Staal, North Holland Publishing Co., 1968.

Maus, Katherine Eisaman. "*The Spanish Tragedy,* or The Machiavel's Revenge." *Revenge Tragedy: Contemporary Critical Essays,* edited by Stevie Simkin, Palgrave Macmillan, 2001, pp. 88-106.

Maxwell, Julie. "Counter-Reformation Versions of Saxo: A New Source for *Hamlet?*" *Renaissance Quarterly,* vol. 57, 2004, pp. 518-60.

McClellan, Kenneth. *Whatever Happened to Shakespeare?* Vision P, 1978.

McMahon, Joseph H. "Ducis: Unkindest Cutter?" *Yale French Studies,* vol. 33, 1964, pp. 14-25.

Monaco, Marion. *Shakespeare on the French Stage in the Eighteenth Century.* Didier, 1974.

Murph, Roxane C. *The War of the Roses in Fiction: An Annotated Bibliography, 1440-1994.* Greenwood, 1995.

Murphy, Andrew. *Shakespeare in Print: A History and Chronology of Shakespeare Publishing.* Cambridge UP, 2008.

—, "What Happens in *Hamlet?*" *A Concise Companion to Shakespeare and the Text,* edited by Andrew Murphy, Blackwell, 2007.

Murray, Barbara A. *Restoration Shakespeare: Viewing the Voice.* Fairleigh Dickinson UP, 2001.

Murray, Peter B. *Thomas Kyd.* Twayne, 1969.

Norris, Christopher. "Will the Real Saul Kripke Please Stand Up? Fiction, Philosophy, and Possible Worlds." *Textual Practice,* vol. 17, no. 2, 2003, pp. 225-51.

Orgel, Stephen. "Shakespeare Illustrated." *The Cambridge Companion to Shakespeare and Popular Culture,* edited by Robert Shaughnessy, Cambridge UP, 2008, pp. 67-92.

—, "Shakespeare Imagines a Theatre." *Poetics Today,* vol. 5, no. 3, 1984, pp. 549-61.

Osborne, Laurie. "Narration and Staging in *Hamlet* and Its Afternovels." *The Cambridge Companion to Shakespeare and Popular Culture,* edited by Robert Shaughnessy, Cambridge UP, 2007, pp. 114-33.

O'Toole, Fionn. "Introduction." *Eleanor's Victory,* by Mary Elizabeth Braddon. Alan Sutton, 1996, pp. xi-xiii.

Oxford English Dictionary Online. www.oed.com. Accessed July 3, 2009.

Palmer, Alan. *Fictional Minds.* U of Nebraska P, 2004.

Patterson, Wayne A. *Bertrand Russell's Philosophy of Logical Atomism.* Peter Lang, 1993.

Pavel, Thomas. *Fictional Worlds.* Harvard UP, 1986.

Pemble, John. *Shakespeare Goes to Paris: How the Bard Conquered France.* Hambledon, 2005.

Pignataro, Margie. "Unearthing Hamlet's Fool: A Metatheatrical Excavation of Yorick." *Journal of the Wooden O Symposium,* vol. 6, 2006, pp. 74-89.

Plantinga, Alvin. "Actualism and Possible Worlds." *The Possible and the Actual,* edited by Michael J. Loux, Cornell UP, 1979, pp. 253-73.

Prince, Kathryn. "Illustration, Text, and Performance in Early Shakespeare for Children." *Borrowers and Lenders,* vol. 2, no. 2, 2006, pp. 1-15.

Proudfoot, Diane. "Possible Worlds Semantics and Fiction." *Journal of Philosophical Logic,* vol. 35, 2006, pp. 9-40.

Pujante, Ángel-Luis, and Keith Gregor. "The Four Neoclassical Spanish *Hamlets:* Assimilation and Revision." *Sederi,* vol. 15, 2005, pp. 129-41.

Rescher, Nicholas. *Imagining Irreality: A Study of Unreal Possibilities.* Open Court, 2003.

—, *On Leibniz.* U of Pittsburgh P, 2003.

Richmond, Velma Bourgeois. *Shakespeare as Children's Literature: Edwardian Retellings in Words and Pictures.* McFarland, 2008.

Robinson, Arthur. "*Rosencrantz and Guildenstern:* A Play by W.S. Gilbert." *The Gilbert and Sullivan Archive.* 1993. www.gsarchive.net/gilbert/plays/rosencrantz/index.html. Accessed July 3, 2009.

Ronen, Ruth. *Possible Worlds in Literary Theory.* Cambridge UP, 1994.

Roth, Steve. "How Many Years Had Hamlet the Dane?" *Hamlet: The Undiscovered Country.* 2013. www.princehamlet.com/chapter_1.html

Rothwell, Kenneth S., and Annabelle Henkin Melzer. *Shakespeare on Screen.* Neal-Schuman Publ, 1990.

Rozett, Martha Tuck. *Talking Back to Shakespeare.* U of Delaware P, 1994.

Russell, Bertrand. "On Denoting." 1905. *Readings in Semantics,* edited by Farhang Zabeeh, E.D. Klemke, and Arthur Jacobson, U of Illinois P, 1974, pp. 141-58.

Ryan, Marie-Laure. *Possible Worlds, Artificial Intelligence, and Narrative Theory.* Indiana UP, 1991.

Salaman, Malcolm C. *Shakespeare in Pictorial Art.* Benjamin Blom, 1971.

Sanders, Julie. *Novel Shakespeares: Twentieth-Century Women Novelists and Appropriation.* Manchester UP, 2001.

Shakespeare Illustrated. shakespeare.emory.edu. Accessed March 13, 2008.

Shaughnessy, Robert, editor. *The Cambridge Companion to Shakespeare and Popular Culture.* Cambridge UP, 2008.

Schmitt, Carl. *Hamlet or Hecuba: The Irruption of Time into Play.* 1955. Edited and translated by Simona Draghici, Plutarch P, 2006.

Schoch, Richard. *Not Shakespeare: Bardolatry and Burlesque in the Nineteenth Century.* Cambridge UP, 2002.

Sider, Theodore. "The Ersatz Pluriverse." *Journal of Philosophy,* vol. 49, no. 6, 2002, pp. 279-315.

Simkin, Stevie. "Introduction." *Revenge Tragedy: Contemporary Critical Essays,* edited by Stevie Simkin, Palgrave Macmillan, 2001, pp. 1-23.

Sjögren, Gunnar. *Hamlet the Dane: Ten Essays.* CWK Gleerup, 1983.

Smart, Patricia. "Woman as Object, Women as Subjects, and the Consequences for Narrative: Hubert Aquin's *Neige Noire* and the Impasse of Post-Modernism." *Canadian Literature,* vol. 113-14, 1987, pp. 168-78.

Smith, Helen. "The Publishing Trade in Shakespeare's Time." *A Concise Companion to Shakespeare and the Text,* edited by Andrew Murphy, Blackwell, 2007.

Stabler, A.P. "King Hamlet's Ghost in Belleforest?" *PMLA,* vol. 77, no. 1, 1962, pp. 18-20.

—, "Melancholy, Ambition, and Revenge in Belleforest's *Hamlet.*" *PMLA,* vol. 81, no. 3, 1966, pp. 207-13.

Stallybrass, Peter, and Roger Chartier. "Reading and Authorship: The Circulation of Shakespeare, 1590-1619." *A Concise Companion to Shakespeare and the Text,* edited by Andrew Murphy, Blackwell, 2007.

Taylor, Christopher Charles Whiston. *The Atomists, Leucippus and Democritus: Fragments: A Text and Translation with a Commentary.* U of Toronto P, 1999.

Taylor, Marion A. *A New Look at the Old Sources of Hamlet.* Mouton, 1968.

Tronch-Pérez, Jesús. "The Unavenging Prince: A Nineteenth-Century Mexican Stage Adaptation of *Hamlet.*" *Latin-American Shakespeares,* edited by Bernice W. Kliman and Rick J. Santos, Fairleigh Dickinson UP, 2005, pp. 54-70.

Van Waveren, Erlo. "Commentary: An Interpretation of the *Hamlet* Tetralogy." *The Mystery of Hamlet, King of Denmark, or What We Will,* by Percy MacKaye, Bond Wheelwright, 1950, pp. 659-70.

Vining, Edward Payson. *The Mystery of Hamlet: A New Solution to an Old Problem.* Philadelphia: J.B. Lippincott, 1881. Print.

Warnicke, Retha M. *Mary Queen of Scots.* Routledge, 2006.

Weber, Brenda R. "Confessions of a Kindred Spirit With an Academic Bent."
    Making Avonlea: L.M. Montgomery and Popular Culture, edited by Irene Gammel,
    U of Toronto P, 2002, pp. 43-57.

Wells, Stanley. Introduction. *Nineteenth-Century Shakespeare Burlesques, Vol. 1:
    John Poole and His Imitators,* edited by Stanley Wells, Diploma P, 1977, pp. ix-
    xxvii.

Wetmore, Kevin J., Jr. "The Amazing Adventures of Superbard: Shakespeare in
    Comics and Graphic Novels." *Shakespeare and Youth Culture,* edited by Jennifer
    Hulbert, Kevin J. Wetmore, Jr., and Robert L. York, Palgrave Macmillan, 2006,
    pp. 171-98.

Williams, Ethel Carleton. *Anne of Denmark.* Longman, 1970.

Williams, George Walton. "The Publishing and Editing of Shakespeare's Plays."
    William Shakespeare: His World, His Work, His Influence, Vol. III, edited by John
    F. Andrews, Charles Scribner's Sons, 1985, pp. 589-601.

Williams, Marcia. "Bravo, Mr. William Shakespeare!" *Reimagining Shakespeare for
    Children and Young Adults,* edited by Naomi J. Miller, Routledge, 2003, pp. 29-38.

Winstanley, Lilian. *Hamlet and the Scottish Succession: Being an Examination of the
    Relations of the Play of* Hamlet *to the Scottish Succession and the Essex
    Conspiracy.* Cambridge UP, 1921.

Yagisawa, Takashi. "Beyond Possible Worlds." *Philosophical Studies,* vol. 53, 1988,
    pp. 175-204.

Young, Alan R. *Hamlet and the Visual Arts, 1709-1900.* U of Delaware P, 2002.

INDEX OF NAMES AND TITLES

INDEX OF TOPICS

Achevé d'imprimer en 2018
à Genève (Suisse)